Elections and Democracy in Greater China

Studies on Contemporary China

The Contemporary China Institute at the School of Oriental and African Studies (University of London) has, since its establishment in 1968, been an international centre for research and publications on twentieth-century China. *Studies on Contemporary China*, which is edited at the Institute, seeks to maintain and extend that tradition by making available the best work of scholars and China specialists throughout the world. It embraces a wide variety of subjects relating to Nationalist and Communist China, including social, political, and economic change, intellectual and cultural developments, foreign relations, and national security.

Series Editor

Dr Frank Dikötter, Director of the Contemporary China Institute

Editorial Advisory Board

Elections and Democracy in Greater China

Edited by

LARRY DIAMOND AND RAMON H. MYERS

OXFORD
UNIVERSITY PRESS

OXFORD
UNIVERSITY PRESS

Great Clarendon Street, Oxford OX2 6DP

Oxford University Press is a department of the University of Oxford.
It furthers the University's objective of excellence in research, scholarship,
and education by publishing worldwide in

Oxford New York

Athens Auckland Bangkok Bogotá Buenos Aires Cape Town
Chennai Dar es Salaam Delhi Florence Hong Kong Istanbul Karachi
Kolkata Kuala Lumpur Madrid Melbourne Mexico City Mumbai Nairobi
Paris São Paulo Shanghai Singapore Taipei Tokyo Toronto Warsaw
and associated companies in Berlin Ibadan

Oxford is a registered trade mark of Oxford University Press
in the UK and in certain other countries

Published in the United States
by Oxford University Press Inc., New York

British Library Cataloguing in Publication Data

Data available

Library of Congress Cataloging in Publication Data

Elections and democracy in greater China / edited by Larry Diamond
and Ramon H. Myers.
p. cm.—(Studies on contemporary China)
Includes bibliographical references and index.
1. Elections—Taiwan.   2. Democratization—Taiwan.
3. Taiwan—Politics and government—1945–   4. Elections—China.
5. Democratization—China.   6. China—Politics and government—1976–
7. Elections—China—Hong Kong.   8. Democratization—China—Hong Kong.
9. Hong Kong (China)—Politics and government—1997–
I. Diamond, Larry. II. Myers, Ramon Hawley, 1929–   III. Series.
JQ1538 .E437 2001   324.951'05—dc21   2001021137
ISBN 0-19-924417-0

1 3 5 7 9 10 8 6 4 2

Printed in Great Britain by
Biddles Ltd., Guildford and King's Lynn

Contents

Notes on Contributors

RICHARD BAUM is Professor of Political Science and Director of the Center for Chinese Studies at UCLA.

LINDA CHAO is a novelist and short story writer as well as Research Fellow of the Hoover Institution, Stanford University. She specializes in political developments in Taiwan and China.

LARRY DIAMOND is Senior Research Fellow at the Hoover Institution and co-editor of the *Journal of Democracy*, as well as co-director of the International Forum for Democratic Studies of the National Endowment for Democracy. He is the author of *Developing Democracy: Toward Consolidation*, and his recent edited books include *Democracy in East Asia* (with Marc F. Plattner) and *The Self-Restraining State: Power and Accountability in New Democracies* (with Andreas Schedler and Marc F. Plattner).

LIANJIANG LI is Assistant Professor in the Department of Government and International Studies at Hong Kong Baptist University. His current research is focused on the impact of village elections on the political attitudes of Chinese peasants.

RAMON H. MYERS is Curator–Scholar of the East Asian Collection and Senior Fellow of the Hoover Institution. He specializes in the political economy of Taiwan and China.

KEVIN J. O'BRIEN is Associate Professor of Political Science at Ohio State University. He is the author of *Reform without Liberalization* and his current research focuses on popular politics in the Chinese countryside.

JEAN C. OI is Associate Professor of Political Science and Director of the Center for East Asian Studies at Stanford University. She is author of *State and Peasant in Contemporary China: The Political Economy of Village Government* (1989), of *Rural China Takes Off: Institutional Foundations of Economic Reform* (1999) and co-editor, with Andrew Walder, of *Property Rights and Economic Reform in China* (1999). Her current research is about the relationship between rural economic development and political institutions.

ROBERT A. PASTOR has been Professor of Political Science at Emory University since 1985 and was a Fellow at The Carter Center (1985–98) and Founding Director of the Democracy Program and the China Election Project until September 1998. He recently edited *A Century's Journey: How the Great Powers Shape the World* (Basic Books, 1999).

SUZANNE PEPPER is a Hong Kong-based writer. She is the author, among other things, of *Civil War in China: The Political Struggle, 1945–1949* (1978 and 1999, second edition).

SCOTT ROZELLE is an associate professor in the Department of Agricultural and Resource Economics, University of California, Davis and member of the Gianinni Foundation. Scott's research agenda has covered a wide number of topics in rural China (focusing in recent years on China's food supply, demand, marketing, and trade policy; the assessment of poverty program investments; and the impact of the reforms on rural institutions). Scott is the chair of the international advisory board of China's Center for Agricultural Policy (CCAP).

TIANJIAN SHI is assistant professor of Political Science at Duke University and the author of *Political Participation in Beijing* (Harvard University Press, 1997). His current research focuses on political culture and political participation in mainland China, Taiwan, and Hong Kong.

QUINGSHAN TAN is an associate professor of political science at Cleveland State University and was a member of the Carter Center delegations in observing Chinese village elections.

Introduction: Elections and Democracy in Greater China

Larry Diamond and Ramon H. Myers

No global political trend in the last quarter of the 20th century has been more far-reaching and profound than the growth of democracy. During what Samuel P. Huntington has called the "third wave" of democratization, the percentage of states in the world that are democratic has grown from 27 (when the third wave began in 1974) to 61 per cent.[1] The trend was particularly powerful during the first half of the 1990s, when the number of democracies increased from 76 to 117, where it has essentially remained the subsequent four years.[2]

One of the paramount questions in global affairs today concerns the future of this world-wide tide of democracy. Will it continue its remarkable advance through non-Western civilizations, to become the predominant form of governance throughout the world, or will it retrogress and struggle to survive alongside other types of political regimes? And what will determine whether democracy spreads beyond its current boundaries to the remaining authoritarian states of the world?

These questions formed the backdrop for a conference hosted by the Hoover Institution (Stanford University) in March 1999, which considered whether an electoral democracy might evolve any time soon throughout Greater China. As defined by the scope of the essays, Greater China includes the territories of mainland China (the People's Republic of China, or PRC), Hong Kong and related territories (the Special Administrative Region, or SAR), and Taiwan and its offshore islands (the Republic of China, or ROC). We have neglected the case of Macau although it presents a considerable variation of the Hong Kong case. The questions addressed in this volume are the following. How and why did electoral democracy emerge in Taiwan between 1950 and 1987, when the ROC government had imposed martial law? What implications might that pattern of political development have for the prospects of electoral democracy to evolve in the next decade or so in the PRC and the Hong Kong SAR? Finally, what are the prospects that the limited elections that are now taking place in the PRC and the Hong Kong SAR might lead to their eventual democratization?

To begin to address these questions, the first section analyses the concept of democracy (and of democratic elections) through reference to four ideal types of political regimes, and then these categories are used to take a closer

---

1. Larry Diamond, *Developing Democracy: Toward Consolidation* (Baltimore: Johns Hopkins University Press, 1999), p. 25, Table 2.1. For the original formulation and the trends through 1990, see Samuel P. Hungtington, *The Third Wave: Democratization in the Late Twentieth Century* (Norman: University of Oklahoma Press, 1991).

2. For the most recent data, and reflections on the trends in recent years, see Larry Diamond, "The End of the Third Wave and the Beginning of the Fourth," in João Espada and Marc F. Plattner, (eds.), *The Democratic Invention* (Baltimore: Johns Hopkins University Press, forthcoming).

look at global trends of regime change. In the context of this global political regime, this chapter reflects on the possible avenue for democratic political change in the PRC and the Hong Kong SAR by making comparisons with Taiwan's democratization under martial law. Our analytical framework to make this comparison and provide answers for the above questions is a typology of how the political centre relates to society. Using this theoretical approach and concepts such as the ideological, economic, political and organizational marketplaces, etc., we describe how the chapters of this book answer the questions that have guided our research.

Democracy and Democratic Elections

For the past decade and a half, the study of democratic transitions has comprised one of the main sub-fields of comparative politics. Yet despite the profusion of theoretical and empirical work to elucidate models and conditions for transition from authoritarian to democratic rule, important gaps in understanding remain. One gap derives from the limited scope of theory and conceptualizing. Transitions *to* democracy (or *from* authoritarian rule) are mainly analysed as political games or struggles within a fairly limited and well-defined period of time.[3] Processes of democratic evolution that occur more incrementally over an extended historical period are poorly treated. Incremental democratization involves in part evolution in the competitiveness, transparency and meaningfulness of elections. Yet little scholarly attention has been devoted to "limited elections" as a political phenomenon, and to the conditions under which limited elections eventually lead to a genuine democracy.

Electoral democracy is (following on the minimalist conception of Joseph Schumpeter) "a civilian, constitutional system in which the legislative and chief executive offices are filled through regular, competitive, multiparty elections with universal suffrage."[4] But to be democratic, elections must not only be regular, competitive and meaningful (in the sense of filling, directly or indirectly, the major roles that exercise political power), they must also be free and fair. Elections are "free" when the legal barriers to entry into the political arena are low, when there is substantial freedom for candidates and partisans of different political parties to campaign and solicit votes, and when voters experience little or no coercion in exercising their electoral choices. The latter condition requires a secret ballot. Elections may be free enough to qualify, more or less, as democratic, even in countries where there are serious human rights violations. But freedom to campaign requires some considerable freedom of speech, movement, assembly and association in electoral politics, if not in the ongoing life of civil society. Even if some types of parties are barred from contesting, a regime may still qualify as democratic if elections are sufficiently open and competitive for opposing parties to contest and win elections.

---

3. For the seminal formulation, see Guillermo O'Donnell and Philippe C. Schmitter, *Transitions from Authoritarian Rule: Tentative Conclusions about Uncertain Democracies* (Baltimore: Johns Hopkins University Press, 1986).
    4. *Ibid.* p. 10.

Elections are "fair" when they are administered by a neutral authority not controlled by the ruling party; when that neutral authority is also sufficiently organized, resourceful and competent to take various precautions to prevent fraud in the voting and vote counting; when the police, the military and the courts treat competing candidates and parties impartially during the campaign, the vote counting and the resolution of any post-election disputes; when competing parties and candidates all have access to publicly controlled (or state-influenced) mass media; when electoral districts and rules do not put opposition parties at a systematic disadvantage; when party and independent monitors may monitor the voting and vote-counting at all locations; when the secrecy of the ballot is protected; when the procedures for organizing and counting the votes are transparent and known to all; and when there are transparent and impartial procedures for resolving election complaints and disputes.[5] In addition, an election can only be democratic if essentially all adults have the right to vote.

Elections may be democratic, by and large, even if the larger political system suffers many democratic defects. If we take a broader, developmental view, democracy is not an either/or phenomenon but rather a continuum. Even systems that are above the threshold of democracy in the conduct of elections may suffer regular and extensive violations of human rights, suppression of minority group rights, flagrant abuses of state power, hidden domination by the military or other centres of power not accountable to the public, and serious constraints on the ability of various interests to organize and be heard. It is therefore necessary to identify a point on the continuum beyond which a distinctly higher quality of democracy exists.

In addition to the elements of electoral democracy, liberal democracy provides for the horizontal accountability of officeholders to one another, constraining executive power and upholding constitutional rule; extensive individual and group freedoms, which make possible vigorous pluralism in economic, political, organizational and intellectual life (called the "four marketplaces"); a strong rule of law, based on an independent and professional judiciary, to protect freedom and constitutionalism; and civilian control of the military.[6] Increasingly, liberal democracy connotes the ideal form of democratic governance that many elites and ordinary people in the world strive to achieve. Countries that approximate the characteristics of liberal democracy also score high according to the Freedom House ranking of political rights and civil liberties. This includes not only the industrialized, advanced democracies but also such recent third-wave democracies as Taiwan, South Korea, Chile, Poland, Hungary and the Czech Republic.

More than 30 states in the world today regularly hold competitive, and relatively free, fair and meaningful elections but afford their citizens considerably less freedom than in liberal democracies, or have levels of executive domination, judicial inefficacy, military interference or other problems that place them in the category of (non-liberal) electoral democracy. Such states as Turkey, Pakistan, Russia, Ukraine and Brazil fall into this category.

5. This draws from Jorgen Elklit and Palle Svensson, "What Makes Elections Free and Fair?" *Journal of Democracy*, Vol. 8, No. 3 (1997), pp. 32-46.
6. Diamond, *Developing Democracy*, pp. 10–12.

A third category or ideal type is comprised of regimes which "are less than minimally democratic but still distinct from purely authoritarian regimes." These can be called pseudodemocracies, for while they have formal democratic political institutions, including regular multiparty elections, in reality a single ruling party or authority dominates the political system to a degree that precludes free and fair competition for power.[7] Contemporary Hong Kong is a pseudodemocracy because the PRC has imposed strict political rules constraining the Hong Kong SAR's electoral process while using the Basic Law to give the chief executive great power and ensure there are no political checks and balances upon his authority. Although Hong Kong still has a relatively wide scope of individual freedom and considerable rule of law, self-censorship is pervasive, political parties are weak and the political opposition has no chance to form a government. At the time of writing the new Macau SAR looks set to follow a similar path. Other examples of pseudodemocracies include Mexico (at least until 1997), Kenya and Singapore.

What distinguishes pseudodemocracies from other nondemocracies is that they tolerate the existence of at least some opposition parties that constitute a degree of real and independent opposition to the ruling party. Typically, this also is accompanied by more space for organizational pluralism and dissident activity in civil society than is tolerated in the most repressive authoritarian regimes. These distinctions among non-democratic regimes matter. The presence of legal opposition parties that may compete for power and win some seats in parliament, and of the greater space for civil society that tends to prevail in such systems, constitute important foundations for future democratic development

By contrast, the fourth ideal type, which can be simply termed the authoritarian regime, rules out formal political opposition of any kind. This type encompasses both the remaining communist states, the People's Republic of China (PRC), North Korea, Vietnam, Laos and Cuba, as well as many other regimes that not only repress individual rights but forbid real opposition parties from operating legally or contesting elections. Burma, Bhutan, Afghanistan, Libya and Saudi Arabia also fall into this category.

One of the peculiar features of the latter period of the "third wave" of democratization has been the growing distinction between liberal and electoral democracy. While the percentage of states that are democratic has more than doubled since 1974, the percentage of *liberal* democracies in the world has increased much more modestly (from about 27 to 42 per cent). A number of states have oscillated across an empirical boundary between liberal and electoral democracy, and the percentage of all the world's democracies that are liberal has shrunk significantly.[8] Most of the third-wave democracies have made at best only uneven progress towards consolidation, in part because of the problems of democratic functioning charac-

---

7. *Ibid*. p. 15.
8. *Ibid*. p. 28, Table 2-4. Following Diamond's categorization, we take here as the empirical indicator of liberal democracy a rating of a state as "free" by Freedom House in its annual survey. The number of liberal democracies in the world did increase during 1998, but a substantial gap between liberal and electoral democracy persists. See Diamond, "The End of the Third Wave."

terized by their non-liberal or only very tenuously liberal status. Yet despite this failure to garner the broad and deep legitimacy at all levels of society that makes a regime truly secure, most of these new democracies have not broken down and retrogressed to the authoritarian type. The military establishments in these countries have been reluctant to seize power; their voters are not eager for a return to authoritarian rule; and finally, there has been no anti-democratic ideology to challenge the ideas and principles of democracy and to persuade enough elites and citizens to embrace authoritarian rule.[9]

One reason why many countries so far have failed to consolidate a liberal democratic regime is because their political leaders have been reluctant to devolve power from the political centre to local authorities and groups in society. Another reason is that their elite and popular cultures have not become compatible with the values and beliefs necessary to affirm democratic practices. A third is that their political parties and civil societies have not developed sufficient strength to represent and aggregate the interests of citizens, champion important social issues and try to improve the political system.

Limited Elections and Democratic Change

One of the more interesting questions for political development concerns the dynamics of pseudodemocracies (or what in some cases can be called semidemocracies). Such regimes stand out from their purer authoritarian counterparts in that they do allow limited electoral competition. How and when do such limited elections contribute to the emergence of democracy, rather than to the consolidation of one or another form of pseudo-democracy?

There are various different ways in which elections may be limited, or less than democratic. They may be limited in the franchise to participation by a modest or even very small proportion of the electorate. This, Robert Dahl notes, was historically the developmental path most likely to produce a smooth emergence of democracy because it was most likely to generate a system of "mutual security" between government and opposition.[10] However, the classic historical path of slow expansion of the franchise is no longer open to late democratic developers because the expectation of political equality of citizens inherent in the universal franchise is now so widespread and is being deepened by the globalization of democratic values and norms.

Is there some way of mimicking this historical sequence by which mutual security gradually developed? In particular, if there is no option to institute electoral competition while expanding participation gradually, can a country achieve a system of mutual security by instituting mass electoral

---

9. See Diamond, *Developing Democracy*, ch. 2 (pp. 62–63) for why many third wave democracies have retrogressed but not yet become authoritarian regimes. The next paragraph is also based on Diamond's account.

10. Robert A. Dahl, *Polyarchy: Participation and Opposition* (New Haven: Yale University Press, 1971), pp. 33–37.

participation and expanding competition gradually? This is essentially what the ruling Kuomintang (KMT) did in Taiwan over four decades, beginning in 1950 and ending with the emergence of a fully democratic system of electoral competition in the 1990s. Much can be learned from the Taiwan case about how the accumulation of experience with electoral competition, the growing self-confidence on the part of the ruling party, and the maturity, skill and resourcefulness on the part of the opposition can enable limited elections to evolve into electoral democracy.

If elections are not limited in the inclusiveness of voter participation, they may be limited in their freedom, their fairness or their meaningfulness. Elections may be open and competitive, but they may be rigged to ensure the victory of the ruling party. Or they may construct a highly constrained arena of competition, perhaps outlawing all opposition parties, but provide for relatively fair and neutral procedures of electoral administration and vote counting, within that constrained arena. Or elections may be both free and fair (relatively speaking) but confer only very limited power on those elected. It may be speculated that the least harmful limitation for future democratic evolution is on the meaningfulness of elections, where the only obstacle is the lack of effective power for those elected, while the most harmful limitation is when an electoral process is degraded by the absence of fairness, through fraud and partisan, opaque, corrupt administration. Again, the Taiwan case appears to support this proposition, but at this point we can only affirm its plausibility. It remains to be seen whether free and technically fair but structurally rigged and less than meaningful elections in the Hong Kong SAR will help to generate pressures for full democratization, or whether they will instead eventually produce political alienation and withdrawal in response to the rising frustration and polarization that Richard Baum observes in his contribution to this volume.

The Political Centre and Its Relationship to Society

Two of the most profound questions for the future of political development in the world are these. First, can the 50-plus states that have an unconsolidated and in many cases distinctly illiberal democracy move forward to deepen and consolidate their democratic systems? Secondly, can the remaining 74 nondemocratic states (whether pseudodemocracies or blatant dictatorships) negotiate transitions to democracy, and if so, how? It is the latter question that this special issue is concerned with, and there is no more important country to which it applies than the People's Republic of China.

Suppose that the PRC and the Hong Kong SAR, which now include more than 1.2 billion people (and two of the most dynamic economic centres of Asia), initiate political reforms and gradually develop the competitive and pluralistic structures of democracy (and eventually even liberal democracy)? This remarkable achievement would surely influence political developments in other parts of Asia and the world. In fact, it would probably transform global politics at every level: political, ideological, normative and strategic. Not only for China studies, then, but for comparative and international politics, there is no more important question than whether Greater China might some day become a democracy, and if so, whether this transition would follow the evolutionary path and respond to the same structural and cultural pressures experienced by the only Chinese democracy so far in the world, Taiwan. To answer these questions, one must first consider the concept of the political centre, defined to mean the "legally most powerful roles and collectivities in a society, along with their subordinate and centripetal elites."[11] Thomas A. Metzger has used this concept to delineate three distinctive systemic relationships between the political centre and the rest of society.

One such relationship uses relatively free elections and free public media to subordinate the political centre to the demands of the rest of society. Metzger refers to this type of political centre, which may correspond to different models and degrees of democracy (from electoral to liberal), as the subordinated political centre. Such a systemic relationship emerged in Taiwan following the lifting of martial law on 15 July 1987.

At the other extreme, the political centre may possess enormous, unrestrained power over society because of the centre's autocratic core, made up of a ruling party, government structure, and the ruling party's auxiliary organs and its domination of ideology. This political centre dominates through normative, remunerative and coercive sanctions. It also has the power to mobilize the population and the skills to maintain leadership stability by recruitment and replacement. Metzger calls this systemic relationship the uninhibited political centre because society passively complies with the centre's ideology, policies and sanctions. This type includes totalitarian and other extreme authoritarian-mobilizational regimes. Between 1950 and 1978 the PRC's Communist Party and state organs behaved like an uninhibited political centre.

The final relationship between the political centre and society is one in which the "center does not control many of society's resources, and it gives much leeway to other loci of decision making, such as 'self-propelled adults' using their own judgment rather than following state commands to decide where to reside, how to pursue education, what intellectual and moral choices to make, and what political causes to support."[12] Although inhibited in varying degrees by socio-economic forces and even political associations, this political centre projects great power; its powerholders efficaciously use their power to crush any challengers or criticism of their authority. The inner tensions shared by this centre's leaders and elites originate from their accepting the moral-intellectual dissonance of the three marketplaces (ideological, economic and political) which are incompatible with certain mainstream orientations in 20th-century Chinese thinking which called for an ideologically unified, morally harmonious societal order. These tensions, in turn, influenced the Chinese to eliminate or try to control the three marketplaces or view them as free of such dissonance. Metzger calls this systemic

11. Thomas A. Metzger used the concept *political centre* to describe his three systemic relationships between the political centre and society in Ramon H. Myers, (ed.), *Two Societies in Opposition: The Republic of China and the People's Republic of China after Forty Years* (Stanford, Calif.: Hoover Institution Press, 1991), pp. xvii–xviii. Metzger's ideal types were also used by Linda Chao and Ramon H. Myers, *The First Chinese Democracy: Political Life in the Republic of China on Taiwan* (Baltimore: Johns Hopkins University Press, 1998), pp. 7–9.

12. Myers, (ed.), *Two Societies in Opposition*, pp. xvii–xviii.

relationship the inhibited political centre, which includes pseudo-democratic as well as many (today, probably most) authoritarian regimes. The inhibited political centre has characterized the PRC's reform era from 1978 to the present, Taiwan under martial law, and Hong Kong under colonial rule and its current SAR status.

The implication of this framework is that a society is much more likely to achieve a subordinated centre, or an electoral democracy, if it is evolving from an inhibited rather than an uninhibited political centre. In particular, democracy is more likely if there is first a period of limited democracy, in which an inhibited political centre (or what Robert Scalapino terms an "authoritarian-pluralist" system) permits some (growing) scope for genuine electoral competition in the selection of representatives and leaders of government at the local or sub-central levels.[13] From this perspective, it may be regarded as significant that the PRC has been shifting from an "uninhibited political centre with transformative policies toward an inhibited centre with accommodative policies," or in other words, from a totalitarian to a more conventional authoritarian (if not authoritarian-pluralist) system.[14]

Types of Inhibited Political Centres and Paths of Regime Change

The inhibited political centre and society can interact through four arenas or "marketplaces" – economic, political, ideological and organizational. The first is the market for factors of production, goods and services. The second is the arena of contestation for power. The third and fourth involve the play of competing ideas (including norms, values and ideologies) and of social organizations, movements and interest groups; it is in these two marketplaces that civil society is located. We now speculate, with reference to historical evidence, on which of these patterns of interaction is more likely to alter the political centre's thinking about whether to give society more freedom to gradually subordinate the centre to its demands.[15]

13. The concept of the "inhibited political centre" bears some important similarities with Robert Scalapino's model of "authoritarian pluralism." This "can be defined as a system wherein political life remains under the unchallenged control of a dominant-party or single-party regime; strict limits are placed on liberty (albeit with some circumstantial variations possible); and military or national security organs keep a close eye on things." At the same time, however, there exists a civil society with some autonomy from the state and some capacity to express diverse interests, as well as a mixed or increasingly market-oriented economy. Both South Korea and Taiwan experienced long periods of authoritarian pluralism, in Scalapino's view, on the way to democracy. Robert A. Scalapino, "Will China Democratize? Current Trends and Future Prospects," *Journal of Democracy*, Vol. 9, No. 1 (1998), pp. 38–39.

14. Thomas A. Metzger, "Will China Democratize? Sources of Resistance," *Journal of Democracy*, Vol. 9, No. 1 (1998), p. 20. During the 1949–78 period, China's political development displayed all the attributes of an "uninhibited" political centre's total control over society. Therefore, the systemic switch in political centre policies after 1978 was a momentous event for China, reversing the development path taken by Mao Zedong, which radically diverged from that taken by Taiwan's Chiang Kai-shek's very inhibited political centre of the 1950s. For a comparison of these divergent development paths and expressions of different political centres' power, see Myers, ed., *Two Societies in Opposition*.

15. We acknowledge Thomas A. Metzger for his conceptualization of the first three marketplaces. See note 3 in the essay in this volume by Linda Chao and Ramon H. Myers for reference to the works in which those concepts are developed. We have added here the notion of an organizational marketplace as well. Civil society consists of independent organizations, networks, and media of communication and expression acting in the public sphere. For further discussion, see Diamond, *Developing Democracy*, ch. 6.

An inhibited political centre may leave much of society free to function in private and family life, but it can still tightly control society through its ruling party, state organs and collective organizations. Under this more rigid model of centre–society relations, the inhibited centre grants little autonomy to groups and organizations and permits very little activity by civil society, because the state quickly co-opts or shuts down any significant non-governmental organizations.[16] The centre permits no comprehensively competitive electoral process; it limits the discussion and exchange of ideas (forbidding, in particular, advocacy of opposing political doctrines); and it restricts private enterprise. These conditions resembled the PRC during the 1980s and 1990s.

A more relaxed relationship between an inhibited political centre and society is characterized by the limited elections held in Taiwan under martial law and in Hong Kong after the early 1980s. Although direct elections for village committees evolved in the PRC during the 1980s and 1990s, the following characteristics of the three marketplaces and civil society do not exist there as they did in Taiwan under martial law and in Hong Kong of the 1980s and early 1990s. In Taiwan and Hong Kong, the ideas and ideals of Western liberal democracy were discussed and debated, even advocated as a doctrine for the political centre to consider and adopt.[17] Local elites and ordinary people competed in elections and learned democratic practices in the embryonic political marketplace. Although political parties were illegal in Taiwan's martial law era, they are still allowed in Hong Kong after 1997, albeit with severe restrictions on how many party candidates can be directly elected to the Legislative Council. In both systems, a market economy evolved and generated enough wealth to finance political candidates and party activities, and new groups in civil society formed and struggled for the rights of voters and the interests of their various constituencies.

Finally, there may be a very loose relationship between an inhibited political centre and society. In such circumstances, the centre allows opposition parties, permits some expansion of direct elections for national government leaders and representatives, tolerates discussion and debate of opposing political doctrines, allows private financing of opposing political parties and candidates, and puts up with a rejuvenated civil society that monitors and evaluates the behaviour of the political centre. These new patterns of political behaviour are associated with powerful impulses for reform that arise in both the political centre and civil society to expand the electoral process and build a genuine democracy. Almost all these conditions existed in Taiwan by the early 1980s (an opposition party formed only in September 1986) and signified that pressures were growing on the inhibited political centre to initiate a democratic breakthrough, but these conditions do not exist in either the Hong Kong SAR or the PRC.

16. For recent fieldwork confirming these activities by the PRC's inhibited political centre, see Gordon White, Jude Howell and Shang Xiaoyuan, *In Search of Civil Society: Market Reform and Social Change in Contemporary China* (Oxford: Clarendon Press, 1996).

17. For the example of Taiwan, see Thomas A. Metzger, "The Chinese Reconciliation of Moral-Sacred Values with Modern Pluralism: Political Discourse in the ROC, 1949–1989," pp. 3–56 in Myers, (ed.), *Two Societies in Opposition*. For Hong Kong, see the essay in this volume by Suzanne Pepper.

An examination of these diverse patterns of centre–society relationships, ranging from very little to quite considerable autonomy for society, reveals that historically two breakthrough phases seem necessary to alter the systemic relationships between the centre and society. The first comes when the inhibited political centre's leaders and elites first grant some autonomy to independent groups and actors in the four marketplaces.[18] These reforms represent a momentous step for an authoritarian regime and an important achievement for society, but they are usually not recognized as significant by contemporary observers.[19] The essays in this volume illustrate that such an initial political breakthrough began as early as 1950 in Taiwan, when the ruling party, the KMT, allowed limited elections, permitted the discussion of Western liberal democracy and took actions to develop a capitalist market economy. All these reforms occurred under martial law and oppressive military and police rule. Similarly, in Hong Kong of the early 1980s, a political breakthrough occurred when British authorities permitted limited elections, a reform decision made because England and the PRC had agreed on the return of Hong Kong to China. Finally, in the 1980s and 1990s PRC leaders permitted (indeed, promoted) direct, contested elections for village committee members and chairmen. Whether this reform represents (or will mature into) a similar political breakthrough that will widen the electoral process, liberalize society and institutionalize the four marketplaces remains to be seen.

The second breakthrough brings a transition at least to electoral democracy. In this instance, the inhibited political centre's leaders and elites have decided that the electoral process must be expanded, and they initiate reforms to establish new, more democratic rules and principles for political competition and for the other three marketplaces. In this transition from the inhibited to subordinated political centre, society's political developmental process is uncertain and can be reversed or subjected to zigs and zags.[20]

The different centre–society developmental patterns described in these essays confirm the significance of these two political breakthroughs for expanding the limited electoral process and altering the systemic relationships between society and the inhibited political centre. Three developmental patterns may facilitate the leadership decisions that initiate these political breakthroughs: cultural change, intellectual elites mobilizing society to expand the electoral process, and economic development, or what Seymour

18. See the essay in this volume by Linda Chao and Ramon H. Myers as well as their *The First Chinese Democracy*, chs. 2–4. See also Ramon H. Myers, "A New Chinese Civilization: The Evolution of the Republic of China on Taiwan," *China Quarterly*, No. 148 (December 1996), pp. 1072–90. We acknowledge Thomas A. Metzger for describing how different systemic relationships between the inhibited political centre and society (the four marketplaces) can evolve and change.

19. In the 1950s and 1960s, Professor David Nelson Rowe of Yale University's Department of Political Science was one of the few academics who argued that local elections in the ROC on Taiwan were significant and meaningful for the evolution of democracy. We thank Lucien Pye for this information.

20. For classic treatments of the process of transition from authoritarian to democratic rule, see Guillermo O'Donnell and Philippe Schmitter, *Transitions from Authoritarian Rule: Tentative Conclusions about Uncertain Democracies* (Baltimore: Johns Hopkins University Press, 1978); and Samuel P. Huntington, *The Third Wave*, pp. 121–163.

Martin Lipset termed "social requisites."[21] These patterns are distinct but may overlap and influence one another.

Alex Inkeles notes that throughout the Pacific-Asian region in recent decades there has been "a remarkable reorientation and transformation of values and lifestyles that, in its depth, scope, speed, and intensity closely matches the extraordinary economic development that over the last decades has been enjoyed by those same populations."[22] Although some traditional beliefs, including ancestor worship and traditional ways of elite thinking, persist, especially in mainland China,[23] value change has involved a "massive abandonment of tradition" regarding family ties, marriage and kinship.[24] Stimulated by increasing incomes, education, information and global connectedness, more and more people affirm their individualism and value leisure time. The young prefer popular culture from the West. As more people redirect their energy and time towards new occupational and leisure pursuits to satisfy these new personal goals, they insist that their government be more efficient and honest as well as respectful and attentive to their community and personal demands. They also are more likely to demand the right to choose their leaders and promote their interests through democratic elections. These changes in beliefs and values correspond to others that have occurred around the world as increasing education, income and other aspects of modernization have made individuals politically more knowledgeable and concerned, more self-confident and assertive, and more active and participatory.[25]

This new individualism and citizen awareness that government could become just, responsive and efficient, and provide more and better services has received a powerful stimulus from the writings and activities of the intellectual elites who have argued that political authority should not be vested in the powerful, privileged few, but in the name of the people. Moreover, their justification of the democratic ideal has made sense to many and resembles the historical process described by Reinhard Bendix in Western Europe during the 15th and 16th centuries before the age of democratic revolution and reform commenced. According to Bendix, a remarkable group of intellectual elites in those centuries produced the Reformation and

21. These ideas and the analysis that follows owe much to our discussions with Thomas A. Metzger.

22. Alex Inkeles, "Continuity and Change in Popular Values on the Pacific Rim," *Hoover Essays* (Stanford, Calif.: Hoover Institution Press, 1997), p. 7.

23. *Ibid.* pp. 8–12. Referring to Thomas A. Metzger's research findings and writings, Inkeles points out these key attributes of traditional Chinese elite thought: *utopianism* as a way of defining the goal of human life, *epistemological optimism* "holding that a total, objective, systematic understanding of human life can be obtained to guide action," *history perceived as a teleological process* moving inexorably toward the ultimate goal of humankind, and *agency of a socially prominent group*, usually seen as the intellectuals, who can grasp the right theoretical system (*tixi*) and use it to influence the course of development of China and perhaps the whole world (p. 12).

24. *Ibid.* p. 13.

25. Gabriel A. Almond and Sidney Verba, *The Civic Culture: Political Attitudes and Democracy in Five Nations* (Princeton: Princeton University Press 1963); Alex Inkeles and David Smith, *Becoming Modern: Individual Change in Six Developing Nations* (Cambridge, MA: Harvard University Press, 1974); and Alex Inkeles, "Participant Citizenship in Six Developing Countries," *American Political Science Review*, Vol. 63, No. 4, pp. 1120–41.

humanism, invented printing and developed modern science.[26] These new ideas rapidly spread across Western Europe, undermined the authority of kings and weakened the support they received from the clergy and aristocracy, who enjoyed enormous privilege and high social status. More intellectual elites and ordinary people began to believe that government in the name of the people was far superior to government by kings. They demanded that the authoritarian political centre be restructured, either by revolution or reform, and an electoral process established.

Once the ideal of democracy is taken seriously by the inhibited political centre's leaders and supporting elites, it must then be legitimated in the four marketplaces, and direct elections must be established and expanded. To achieve that legitimation, Lipset has argued, crucial "social requisites" must have crystallized in society.[27] First, society's political culture must have become compatible with the spirit and principles of democracy (a point also stressed by Almond and Verba, Inkeles, Dahl, and many others). For the electoral process to facilitate democracy, political leaders and representatives must affirm the spirit of political compromise and accommodation, the willingness to agree to disagree, and most of all a readiness to accept defeat, without resorting to undemocratic and unconstitutional behaviour.[28] Secondly, society's religious traditions must not condone or support formal organizations that obstruct the government's political reforms to expand elections and promote democracy. Finally, as already suggested above, society must experience sufficient economic development to ameliorate severe income inequality and eliminate widespread poverty. These "social requisites" enable the four marketplaces to become more efficient and viable; in particular, they help to legitimate and sustain democracy in the marketplace of electoral politics. As the four marketplaces interact and become robust, society's demands and power grow, compelling political elites to adopt reforms that deepen the formal structures of electoral democracy and transform the inhibited political centre into a liberal democracy.

Our conceptual framework enables us to understand why in Greater China during the latter half of the 20th century only Taiwan experienced the two strategic political breakthroughs that transformed the political centre first into an inhibited centre, then into a subordinated one and gradually a liberal democracy. The essays in this volume to explain, first, why only Taiwan has become a liberal democracy; secondly, why the Hong Kong SAR is unlikely to become a liberal democracy any time soon (especially not before 2007); and thirdly, why in the near future the direct election process in mainland China will be confined below, at most, the country administration level and merely supplement the existing indirect electoral process of China's leaders and representatives.

26. Reinhard Bendix, *Kings or People: Power and the Mandate to Rule* (Berkeley: University of California Press, 1978), introduction and ch. 8.

27. Seymour Martin Lipset, "The Social Requisites of Democracy Revisited," *American Sociological Review*, Vol. 59, No. 1 (February 1994), pp. 1–22.

28. For a review of the literature on these cultural correlates of democracy, see Diamond, *Developing Democracy*, pp. 165–174.

The Contributions to this Volume

Chao and Myers have elsewhere described Taiwan's first political break-through as occurring in 1950–51.[29] Defeated and humiliated by the KMT's defeat on the mainland, Chiang Kai-shek resolved to build a different Chinese society on Taiwan. He restructured the KMT, established local elections (an embryonic political marketplace), permitted Western ideas of liberal democracy to challenge the state's ideology based on the ideas of Sun Yat-sen (an embryonic intellectual marketplace), allowed a capitalist market economy to develop, and did not abolish religious and private associations unless they threatened party-state rule.

In this volume Chao and Myers describe how the KMT-state–controlled political centre established local elections but used its enormous power to manipulate them and guarantee that KMT candidates won at least 80 per cent of the representative and leadership seats in local government. By establishing a single, non-transferable voting system among multiple candidates and by using local factions, dirty tricks, and the iron votes of military and government party members and their relatives, the KMT restricted the number of opposition candidates competing and modulated election outcomes in its favour. But from the early 1950s until around 1977, some intellectual elites within and outside the "inhibited" political centre repeatedly criticized the KMT's principle of "democratic revolution" as too slow and phony. Meanwhile, throughout Taiwan society there was the relentless advancement of the development-related "social requisites" as a consequence of elite mobilization and socio-economic change, and the electoral process was repeatedly challenged by an opposition that changed its tactics in the 1970s.

As Taiwan's four marketplaces evolved, young educated and innovative politicians inside and outside the KMT argued for a reconfiguring of the political landscape. As Chao and Myers point out, many of these intellectual elites, who began calling themselves *dangwai* (nonparty), were former KMT members, well educated and ambitious. They not only believed in democracy but used the democratic ideal to differentiate their political agenda from that of the KMT. They were also supported by liberals in the KMT as they perfected new campaign methods and appealed to the voters as underdogs worthy of being elected because they championed the reforms that voters wanted.

In Taiwan's pre-1977 elections, the KMT had won the overwhelming majority of seats in the Taiwan Provincial Assembly, the Taipei and Kaohsiung city councils, and for county magistrates and city mayors. But after 1977 that pattern changed as the political opposition began capturing more votes in local elections and even in the expanded national quota elections for the parliament that had begun in 1969 (see Figures 1 and 2). The arrest of many *dangwai* leaders after the 10 December 1979 disturbance in Kaohsiung city briefly reversed their victories, as indicated by some *dangwai* defeats in the 1981 and 1985 elections. But the *dangwai* recovered, and in late

29. For a description and analysis of the crises confronted and overcome by this young democracy, see Chao and Myers, *The First Chinese Democracy*, chs. 2–4.

September 1986 a group of them illegally formed the Democratic Progressive Party (DPP). The KMT's chairman, Chiang Ching-kuo, took no action to suppress the new party, and in the 1989 election voters increased their support for DPP candidates.

By the late 1970s the opposition politicians, voters and ruling party leaders had learned from their election experiences and changed their political behaviour. Opposition politicians learned how to get elected and to comply with the rules of their elected office. They also learned how to use elections to educate voters about political participation and how to demand political reform. Local elections also taught opposition politicians how to translate public grievances into votes to win elections so they could build their political careers by championing the public policies that voters supported.

Citizens learned that they possessed the power to change laws and policies if they effectively used the voting ballot to express their demands. They realized too that their votes made a difference when they elected vigorous, honest and creative leaders and representatives to make government more efficient and responsive to their demands. By sometimes voting for the opposition, voters also signalled to the ruling party their displeasure that it had not worked hard enough on their behalf.

The ruling party also learned that election defeats did not mean the end of their candidates' political careers. Voters invariably supported the KMT candidates in new elections if they believed them to be sincere talented, and honest. The ruling party steadily regained confidence from some election victories as it learned that good performance in government was the only way to stay in power.

The government, meanwhile, had been working since November 1973 to produce a new election law, and in May 1980 that new law was passed, making elections more open, fair, free and democratic. Liberals within the ruling party were also urging the leadership to speed up democratic reform. The political opposition demanded similar reforms. Even citizens were becoming restless for change. Pressures were mounting for a second political breakthrough. That moment came in late March 1986 when ruling party chairman and ROC president Chiang Ching-kuo announced the KMT's intention to launch political reforms to democratize Taiwan. In mid-July of the next year, the government lifted martial law. Democratization rapidly followed: in 1988–89 dozens of political parties immediately formed and a free press began to flourish; constitutional reform took place in early 1992, and the electoral process began to expand; finally, in March 1996 the first national election for president and vice-president took place, making Taiwan the first Chinese democracy. The top-down guided democracy initiated by the KMT leadership in the early 1950s and the bottom-up democratic process that gradually evolved, driven by opposition politicians and voters, meshed to expand direct elections, culminating in a political breakthrough in 1986 and leading to Taiwan's democratization in the 1990s.

Hong Kong's political history was very different. Far smaller in population and geographical size than Taiwan, part of this Chinese territory had not been free of British colonial rule since 5 April 1843, when Queen Victoria proclaimed Hong Kong a crown colony and made Pottinger its governor. As the Hong Kong territory expanded under new treaties between England and imperial China, a definitive pattern of colonial rule evolved. British authorities brooked no political opposition and permitted no electoral process, but they gave Chinese inhabitants the freedom to live their lives and manage their family and lineage affairs.

Even after the Second World War, the British refused to introduce an electoral process for creating a legislative body to propose and approve laws and monitor the colony's budget. According to Suzanne Pepper's essay, British authorities considered the Hong Kong Chinese to be "politically apathetic" and feared that mainland Chinese communist politics would penetrate the colony's political life and sow dissension and troubles. Colonial officials and friendly business elites continued to favour minimal government intervention in society. Meanwhile, the authorities allowed the population's anti-communist majority to quietly go about their daily lives to raise their families and improve their livelihood. This low political profile strategy operated until 1978, when the British government decided to discuss Hong Kong's future with Beijing's communist leadership.

In 1979 British and PRC leaders met, talked and decided that Hong Kong's status must change. The very next year, British colonial officials planned political reforms for Hong Kong that represented the first political breakthrough for the colony's inhibited political centre. In January 1981 the authorities published a white paper setting out a limited electoral process that was held between March and September 1982. In September 1982 Margaret Thatcher visited Beijing and confirmed that on 1 July 1997 Hong Kong would be returned to China. Thereafter, the Hong Kong authorities promoted a limited electoral process as set forth in various Hong Kong government papers published in 1984. Powerful business elites soon opposed these political reforms, but an articulate Chinese minority of intellectuals, professionals and middle class people supported them.

Events after 1984 produced a slightly expanded electoral process and the drafting of a constitution, the Basic Law, for governing the SAR after 1 July 1997. When Hong Kong's new governor, Chris Patten, arrived in mid-1992, he immediately tried to expand the electoral process. His plan called for more direct elections of Legislative Council (LegCo) members, creating more directly elected seats than the 30 designated by functional constituencies as outlined in Beijing's new Basic Law. Patten's electoral reforms gave democrats a majority voice in the new LegCo.

Beijing's leaders denounced Patten and began working with pro-Beijing groups in Hong Kong to roll back his electoral reform and limit the electoral process. Richard Baum's essay describes how that new electoral process has worked since retrocession to SAR status. The Basic Law stipulated that two-thirds of the LegCo's 60 seats would be indirectly elected in functional constituencies or chosen by members of a small, designated election committee drawn from functional constituencies. Only one-third would be directly elected in geographical constituencies. The Basic Law said nothing about political parties.

On 24 May 1998, the voter turnout for the three electoral constituencies exceeded previous elections (at 53.3 per cent of registered voters). Because three democratic parties fielded candidates, and because the Beijing authorities shrewdly switched the electoral system from single-member-district to proportional representation in multi-member districts, none of the democratic parties received a majority of the directly elected seats despite winning 60 per cent of the votes. For the first time, a pro-Beijing party won five directly elected LegCo seats, and these, combined with the two-thirds of seats that were indirectly elected, left pro-Beijing parties firmly in control of the LegCo. Since that election, the pro-democracy legislators have criticized Chief Executive Tung Chee-hwa's poor management of Hong Kong, temporarily uniting most of the opposition against the executive chief.

However, as Baum shows, the directly elected democrats are not only in the minority, they lack a unified vision of how to democratize Hong Kong. Moreover, they are also increasingly divided on how to deal with Hong Kong's deepening economic and social challenges. Baum sees a new line of cleavage (loosely, pro-welfare versus pro-business) to be cutting across and displacing the old cleavage between democrats and pro-Beijing forces. The new politics of voting based on class and socio-economic interests is not only eroding the dominance of the traditional government–business coalition, Baum argues, it is challenging the identity and coherence of democratic parties, particularly the Democratic Party (by far the largest).

Meanwhile, intellectual elites are quiescent, and the LegCo is so constitutionally weak that even as some pro-Beijing legislators have joined in criticizing the Chief Executive, the result has been political polarization and paralysis, not the invigoration of democratic forces. Voters, oddly enough, have a strong sense of the democratic ideal because the 4 June 1989 Tiananmen incident enhanced citizen awareness that only the rule of law can guarantee their human rights and personal freedoms. Equally important, Hong Kong citizens want efficient, fair and honest government. If they do not believe the Executive Branch can deliver those services under the Basic Law, they could demand that Hong Kong's Chief Executive expand direct elections for leaders and representatives who could make government work better.

Hong Kong's future prospects for democracy will depend on political developments in the next seven years. The Basic Law's timetable for seats calls for increasing the proportion of directly elected LegCo seats to one-half in the third-term election in 2003. By the subsequent election in 2007, the SAR government promises to hold a plebiscite to solicit views about creating a Legislative Council that is entirely democratically elected. If the political centre's leaders and supporting elites manage the SAR poorly, a bottom-up, party-driven political process could intensify and demand expansion of the electoral process. Hong Kong citizens, most of whom are middle class, have beliefs and values that facilitate democracy. The missing element is vigorous intellectual elite mobilization to build strong political parties, produce capable leaders and create a new vision of Hong Kong's democracy that will inspire a majority to struggle on behalf of the ideal of democracy.

Whether the bottom-up political process will force the political centre to promote a political breakthrough is problematic for two reasons. Beijing's authorities can always intervene in Hong Kong's political life as they did in July 1999, when the National People's Congress overturned Hong Kong's High Court ruling ordering that citizenship be given to children with at least one Hong Kong parent. Furthermore, Hong Kong's patriotic groups and conservatives strongly support the Beijing government, and they are currently trying to establish a new ruling party that can dominate the electoral process in the future.[30] This new political force would challenge any bottom-up opposition process for accelerating Hong Kong's democratization.

Turning to mainland China, its inhibited political centre still tightly controls society after 20 years of gradual reforms. These reforms have not been robust enough to produce even the first political breakthrough in which the inhibited political centre grants greater autonomy to the four marketplaces, as in Taiwan in the early 1950s and Hong Kong in the early 1980s. The reasons for this are the following.

The PRC leaders have never endorsed even limited direct elections to build a genuine democracy. They have repeatedly stressed their determination to avoid adopting any Western political models and instead design a Chinese-style polity, governed by a single ruling party that combines socialism and democracy with Chinese customs and thought.[31] In a practical sense, they endorse the Communist Party's selection of candidates for indirect elections of representatives to serve in city and provincial congresses and the National People's Congress. Functional constituencies, supervised by the Communist Party, elect representatives to township, city, and county congresses. These bodies, as well as the recently (1996) created commissions in the Chinese Communist Party, primarily monitor, review and recommend their findings to leading Party and state authorities.[32] Nor have Party leaders been willing to give the four marketplaces (particularly the noneconomic ones) the degree of limited autonomy that Taiwan's society enjoyed under martial law and that Hong Kong had before assuming SAR status. But they have permitted direct, contested elections for village committee and chair, a development that has been unfolding since 1988. Are the village elections truly democratic, and are they likely to be expanded to higher administrative levels? Can this limited electoral process promote the

30. A pro-government bloc of Legislative Council politicians formed in summer 1999, with the blessing of Chief Executive Tung Chee-hwa. If this informed, pro-government bloc can deliver future votes and become a ruling party, the democratic parties will be severely challenged. For recent developments of this bloc, see Bruce Gilley, "United We Stand," *Far Eastern Economic Review*, Vol. 162, No. 29 (22 July 1999), p. 26.

31. For a recent example of Chinese Communist Party instructions to party *ganbu* to avoid Western-style "peaceful evolution" and properly follow the party line to build a Chinese-style socialism, see Zhongguo zhungyang dangxiao (Chinese Communist Central Party School), *Dangchien dangzheng ganbu guanzhu ti shencengci sixiang lilun wenti (The Profound Ideological and Theoretical Issues That Our Present Party Cadres Should Pay Close Attention To)* (Beijing: Dangjian duwu chubanshe, 1998).

32. For a brief description of these Communist Party committees and their functions since 1996, see Zhongguo guoqing yanjiuhui (Chinese Association for Research on National Conditions), *Zhongguo guoqing baogao (Report on National Conditions in China)* (Beijing: Zhongguo tongji chubanshe, 1998), pp. 3–7. But an interesting new development occurred in Guangdong in fall 1999: for the first time, a provincial People's Congress allowed members of the public to express their opinions and criticism of proposed legislative changes. See Frank Ching, "China: Seeds of Change," *Far Eastern Economic Review*, 30 September 1999, p. 22.

changes in political culture, in intellectual elite mobilization and in socio-economic development that will open up the four marketplaces and thereby generate greater demands from below for political reforms?

According to O'Brien and Li, village elections originated as early as 1931–34 in the Jiangxi Soviet, continued in the Yan'an base area during the Sino-Japanese war (1937–45), ended in 1949, but resumed in 1981–82 in two villages of Guangxi province. When news of that event reached the National People's Congress chairman, Peng Zhen, he encouraged other provinces to experiment in electing village councils because he believed that self-governance might revitalize communist cadres' behaviour in the country-side. This experiment set off a debate in the Party and state bureaucracy, especially at the township level, about the costs and benefits of directly elect-ing village councils. Some feared the elected village council members would listen only to villagers and not to township leaders. Others argued these elec-tion would reduce village corruption and resentment towards the Communist Party.

In 1987 the Ministry of Civil Affairs submitted a law to the National People's Congress for villages to elect their council representatives. This law, too, sparked debate, with those opposed worrying that village self-gover-nance would allow villages to "lurch out of control" of the Communist Party. As the debate intensified, Peng Zhen urged the National People's Congress to approve the ministry's draft law. Even after the Congress's approval, the state did not implement the law until Bo Yibo, a Communist Party elder, other supporters, and the Party Central Committee's endorse-ment compelled the Ministry of Civil Affairs to do so. Since 1988, villages across mainland China have been observing the law. Assessments vary as to how many villages so far have adopted self governance. By 1996, perhaps one-quarter to one-third of villages had participated in elections that com-plied with the ministry's legal guidelines.

Are village elections truly democratic? Robert A. Pastor and Qingshan Tan have observed many such elections and offer some observations. Party village secretaries usually served on (or chaired) the village election com-mittee that supervised village elections, thus giving them considerable influence over election outcomes. Villages used different voting procedures, but the Ministry of Civil Affairs has tried to standardize them. Fair tallying of ballots has steadily improved, and there appears to be growing use of the secret ballot. Numerous problems remain, including widespread use of proxy votes and roving ballot boxes that do not assure a secret, individual vote. However, as Pastor and Tan note, democracy involves a process of incremental improvement, and village elections continue to evolve. Probably no more than half of mainland villages elect council representa-tives and chairs competitively, according to the law. But the experience shows that even poor, uneducated farmers can master the procedures of democratic elections, and the data reviewed by Pastor and Tan indicate that a significant portion of incumbent chairs are defeated in some provinces. Because of China's huge size, it will take several years before most or all vil-lages implement the law, and this will require a significant improvement in technical capacity at various levels.

Will the village Communist Party secretary always serve on the village council and exert considerable influence on council activities, thus revitalizing the Communist Party's leadership at the grass roots, as the deceased Peng Zhen hoped? Or are direct village elections creating real democracy so that genuine competition between candidates prevails and villagers have real choice to select their council representatives? Where are the real loci of village power?

Jean Oi and Scott Rozelle address these important questions. Their survey findings reveal that both the broadly inclusive village assemblies and the partially elected village representative assemblies meet only infrequently. Moreover, there is a bias in the operation of the latter favouring non-elected members belonging to the CCP, and many elected representatives do not participate because they are too busy trying to become rich. As for the smaller village committees (typically five to seven members), for which the 1987 Organic Law mandates direct elections, there appears to be wide variation in their actual power. In some villages, the elected committee is the seat of decision-making, while in others the village branch Party secretary "keeps tight control of power, in spite of elections." Through analysis of their own survey data on village economic and political life, Oi and Rozelle trace this variation in power relations to the structure of the village economy. Where villagers have a clear stake in village decision-making – in agricultural villages with little or no income from outside the village – the elected village committee is more likely to have real power, and participation in village assembly meetings is greater. Where villagers' interests heavily lie elsewhere, as a result of extensive engagement in economic activity outside the village, and where the Party elite have a strong incentive to exert control, in villages with collectively owned industrial enterprises, political interest and participation are lower, contested elections are less common, and village Party elites do exercise more control (especially over the real power centre, village enterprises). There are some twists to this pattern, however (more participation and more frequent contested elections in villages with large revenues), and the authors treat their own results as only preliminary and suggestive. Most intriguing, perhaps, is their speculation that the advance of industrialization and spread of wider market relations may, as they raise incomes, paradoxically diminish interest and participation in the political life of the village. Yet the impact on political interest and demands at higher level of authority could be quite different.

The Oi and Rozelle findings suggest that when villages become wealthy, their entrepreneurial leaders play a formidable role in that accomplishment. If the village Party secretary is such an entrepreneurial leader, the elected village committee is likely to be less important in the life of villagers. But we cannot rule out the prospect that households will confront new problems and demand that their village committee representatives resolve them. In that case, villagers' yearning for democracy might grow. Popular demand for democracy will also be influenced by the values, beliefs and behavioural patterns that constitute the political culture of elites and ordinary people (many of whom participate in village elections). Fortunately, with the emergence of public opinion surveys based on nation-wide representative

samples for all of mainland China, it is possible to move beyond the realm
of speculation to carefully examine whether popular attitudes and sentiments are likely to support or inhibit democratic behaviour. This is what
Tianjian Shi does in the final contribution to this volume.

Tianjian Shi's survey findings lead him to conclude that over one-fifth of
the Chinese people have a strong interest in political and governmental
affairs, a level that seems to be around the minimum necessary to sustain
democracy (as suggested by the comparative findings from Almond and
Verba's survey of several Western democracies, conducted around 1960).
The level of individual political competence (efficacy) is low, but on one
measure it is equal to Italy in 1960. Orientations towards power and authority are still mainly traditional, deferring to authority and shying away from
conflict. However, a majority of Chinese supports both political and economic reform, and the younger and more educated the individual, the
greater the interest in reform and elections. In fact, Shi's multivariate analysis lends strong support to the modernization theories of Inkeles and Lipset
that education increases interest and participation in politics, promotes
political efficacy and support for political reform, and fosters such other
democratic tendencies as a non-hierarchical orientation towards power and
authority. In striking affirmation of Inkeles' many studies, Shi's data shows
that no other variable has such a powerful and robust effect on different
aspects of democratic culture as education. While the experience of voting
in contested village elections appears (as yet) to have little independent
impact on political values and orientations, it does increase interest in politics. On balance, Shi believes that mass political culture in China now has the
minimum level of democratic orientation necessary to sustain democracy.
Although he has no evidence that elite orientations are adequate for democratic change, his findings suggest that if elites opt to move China towards a
democratic breakthrough like that in Taiwan, popular attitudes and sentiments are not likely to pose a major obstacle and could even generate strong
support for reform.

Both mainland China and Taiwan's ruling parties dominated their limited electoral processes long after direct voting commenced. Citizens in both
regimes also acquired voting experience, and voting turnout in both societies was high, usually 80 to 90 per cent. Their direct voting experience also
encouraged the demand to expand direct election to higher levels of governance. But great differences in these two limited electoral experiences still
exist. We know little about Taiwan's direct elections between 1945 and 1980,
whereas much is already known about mainland China's village elections of
the 1990s. Taiwan adopted Japan's system of the single, non-transferable
vote in multi-member districts, but mainland China uses "past the post
methods plus requiring a majority vote."[33] In this way Taiwan's voting system allowed opposition candidates to be elected but without achieving control, whereas the mainland's system "marginalizes those who might oppose

33. James A. Robinson, "China's Local Elections Contrast with Taiwan's," *American Asia
Review*, Vol. 18, No. 3 (fall 2000), p. 196. Our remarks are drawn from this important essay by
a veteran Taiwan election-watcher.

the ruling party."[34] Moreover, Taiwan's limited-election democracy embraced local to county affairs, but mainland China has so far held only one direct election for township chief, in Buyun township of Sichuan Province, and other townships have been dissuaded from doing the same because it is unconstitutional.

It is possible that at some point in the coming decade China's Communist Party elites will see their own interest to be served by negotiating the first breakthrough to a looser and more pluralistic relationship between the political centre and society, what Scalapino calls "authoritarian pluralism." This might lead to competitive elections at higher levels of authority, such as the township or even county. If such higher-level elections were to be implemented nation-wide, it would represent a genuine political breakthrough, but the process would take a considerable time. Yet there is little sign that this generation of Communist Party elites has any willingness to allow the much greater – and riskier – pluralism of permitting opposition parties to organize openly and contest the ruling party. In this crucial respect, China seems many years away even from a semidemocracy, not to mention the genuine electoral democracy that would place the Communist Party's control of the national state at stake. It will be some time before the political centre's leaders and elites dare to redesign their relationships with society in such a far-reaching way, and in the near term pressures for democratization are more likely to come from below than above. After all, nearly 40 years had to pass before significant momentum for democracy occurred in Taiwan, and conditions in Taiwan were very different from those of mainland China and Hong Kong.

Elite support for Western-style democracy with direct elections is weak in mainland China and the Hong Kong SAR. Most elites prefer a polity governed by a strong ruling party that relies on indirectly elected council representatives and leaders to monitor, review and recommend decisions. Yet the advent of limited elections, even at the village level, as in mainland China, is of considerable importance and deserves continued study and evaluation. Limited elections can be co-opted and contained by the political centre, at least for some time. But there are signs that limited elections, interacting with other patterns of economic, social and cultural change, may be generating pressures, expectations and capacities that could foster the emergence of democracy in mainland China, the Hong Kong SAR, and eventually the Macau SAR. Unless the PRC state rapidly implodes in a fashion similar to the Soviet Union, democratic change will likely follow the gradual pace of Taiwan, and clues to its possibilities must be gleaned from the character and evolution of limited elections.

34. *Ibid.*

How Elections Promoted Democracy in Taiwan under Martial Law

Linda Chao and Ramon H. Myers

In October 1952, while addressing the Seventh Congress of the Kuomintang (KMT), the party chairman and president of the Republic of China (ROC) on Taiwan, Chiang Kai-shek, reminded his audience that "Sun Yat-sen's highest goal was to build a political system in which sovereignty resided with the people [*zuchuan zaimin*]."[1] Chiang then said that "in order to oppose communism and recover our nation, the primary task of our party is to carry out local elections, build our nation's political system, and establish the solid foundations for our people to practise democracy."[2]

Until his death on 5 April 1975, Chiang never mentioned when an opposition political party could participate in elections, nor had Chiang Ching-kuo, who succeeded to the presidency on 25 March 1978, ever publicly declared when democratic elections for the central government and parliament should be held. Was the KMT serious about creating an electoral system entrusting sovereignty to the people, or did it hope to continue to manipulate the election process only to preserve its hold on political power? For the next three decades, the historical record suggests that the answer to both questions was "yes ... but!"

As early as July 1950 the majority of Taiwan's people still resented their new rulers, and many did not speak Mandarin Chinese as the regime's lingua franca. Moreover, most Taiwanese elites deeply resented the regime and could not forgive its harsh suppression of the 28 February 1947 protests against ROC governance over the island only 16 months after Japan had transferred Taiwan to Nationalist China on 25 October 1945.

From the outset, the KMT leadership, its party members and central government officials wanted Taiwan to become a bastion for the future recovery of mainland China, should the communist regime ever lose popular support and collapse, to restore ROC governance over the mainland. The new government's immediate concern was to prevent communist subversion and Taiwanese nationalism from undermining ROC governance over Taiwan province, Chin-men (Quemoy) and Ma-tsu. To achieve those ends, the ROC government and ruling KMT suppressed any activities that might weaken their authority. They did this as early as 19 May 1949, when Taiwan's governor, Chen Cheng, imposed martial law and began establishing the legal and bureaucratic machinery to determine when public assembly, political criticism or threat to public

---

1. Jiang Zhong-zheng, *Jiang zongtong yanlun xuanji fangong fuguo de lilun yu shijian* (*A Collection of Chiang Kai-shek's Speeches and Essays: The Theory and Implementation of Opposing Communism and Recovering Our Country*) (Taipei: Zhongyang wenwu gongyingshe, 1977), p. 73.
   2. *Ibid.*

order became seditious enough to charge individuals under the law and adjudicate them by a military court, and if found guilty either imprison or execute them.

But the new government also did something else. It tried to win popular support for its efforts to build a new Taiwan society to show the world that its moral virtues, material prosperity and democratic practices were superior to those of the communist regime on the China mainland. To that end, the regime allowed households considerable freedom of choice in the economic marketplace and society to act in accordance with their interests, thus greatly expanding what Ralf Dahrendorf has referred to as individual "life chances." It did this by incremental reforms, which by the late 1960s had created what Thomas A. Metzger has called the "three marketplaces" (the economic, ideological and political market-places) that in embryonic or, later, in advanced form began transforming Taiwan.[3]

A land reform, completed by 1956, produced more equitably dis-tributed rural property rights. By 1960, a reformed foreign exchange rate system encouraged enterprises to increase their production for export and promoted domestic and international market integration. The govern-ment's commitment to promoting primary education for all households expanded the number and quality of middle and high schools, vocational colleges and universities, which by 1960 were producing a large, edu-cated and skilled workforce eager for employment. But it was the local elections, beginning in·1950–51, that drew the people into a new process for selecting their representatives and leaders to govern their political life.

In 1969 the ROC government expanded the limited electoral process by introducing a supplementary quota of elected representatives to serve in the National Assembly, the Legislative Yuan or Parliament, and the Control Yuan of the central government. By 1980 the electoral process had improved to the extent that the government now passed a new law that imposed fairness, openness and rule-abiding behaviour for conduct-ing elections, reflecting a more tolerant attitude towards the political opposition by the KMT. Then, in late March 1986, President Chiang Ching-kuo announced that the KMT would launch major political

3. Thomas A. Metzger has discussed these three marketplaces in his various publications in the past decade. For the economic marketplace see his "Confucian culture and economic modernization: an historical approach," in *Conference on Confucianism and Economic Development in East Asia* (Taipei: Chung-hua Institution for Economic Research), Conference Series, No. 13 (1989), pp. 141–195. Reprinted in Tzong-shian Yu and Joseph S. Lee (eds.), *Confucianism and Economic Development* (Taipei: Chung-hua Institution for Economic Research, 1995), pp. 97–148. For a discussion of the evolving ideological marketplace in Taiwan see "Introduction: two diverging societies," written by Thomas A. Metzger, in Ramon H. Myers (ed.), *Two Societies in Opposition* (Stanford: Hoover Institution Press, 1991), pp. xiii–xlv; and the essay by Thomas A. Metzger entitled "The Chinese reconciliation of moral-sacred values with modern pluralism: political discourse in the ROC, 1949–1989," in *ibid*. pp. 3–56. For his commentary on a political marketplace in China see Thomas A. Metzger, "Will China democratize? Sources of resistance," *Journal of Democracy*, Vol. 9, No.1 (January 1998), pp. 18–26; and "Friendly U.S. relations with an undemocratic China? Weighing contemporary Chinese objections to capitalism and democracy," in *Hoover Essays* (1999).

reforms to democratize the polity. That was followed in late September 1986 by a group of opposition politicians illegally forming the Democratic Progressive Party (*Minzhu jinbu dang*, or DPP), an act that Chiang Ching-kuo took no action to suppress. Finally, on 15 July 1987, the government lifted martial law, and local and national elections quickly became more democratic, leading to the great democratic breakthrough of the 1990s. How, then, did limited elections promote Taiwan's democratization in the era of martial law, when the KMT-led inhibited political centre tightly controlled society?

Establishing Limited Elections and Their Outcomes

Between 1935 and 1945, Japan's colonial rulers in Taiwan had allowed only males over 25 years old and able to pay a five yen poll tax to vote for half of the seats of the colony's township, city and prefectural councils. After Taiwan came under ROC government rule on 25 October 1945, Taiwan's provincial governor, Chen Yi, decreed that island-wide elections be held in April 1946. All citizens over the age of 20 could vote, without paying a poll tax, for village warden, township councillor, township head, and county and city council members. The county and city councils then elected the delegates for the Taiwan Provincial Assembly. The momentum for holding local elections ended after the 28 February 1947 tragedy but resumed in 1949 when Taiwan's governor, Chen Cheng, appointed a commission of 29 legal and academic experts, chaired by Zhang Lisheng, to create new administrative and electoral districts based on Taiwan's population density patterns at that time.[4]

Based on these new administrative districts and electoral zones, government work teams in early 1950 trained personnel to operate the voting stations in the electoral districts, and appointed officials to instruct voters and candidates to register, while preparing to conduct and monitor local elections. By 1951 elections were in full swing for the Taiwan Provincial Assembly as well as for village, township, city and county councils and for the chiefs or leaders of villages, townships and Taiwan's 21 counties and major cities. Although the central government appointed the Taiwan provincial governor to head the Taiwan Provincial Assembly, in effect local elections had become a reality.

Taiwan's elites welcomed these elections and urged the people to use their voting power to advance their interests by electing capable leaders and representatives to build a democracy. Writing in March 1952 in the *Free China Fortnightly* (*Ziyou Zhongguo*), Chen Kewen said, "we can definitely say that holding local elections is the road to freedom and democracy."[5] In February 1953 the scholar and liberal thinker, Dr Hu

---

4. Zhang Lisheng, *Taiwan sheng difang zizhi yanjiu zhuankan* (*A Special Report on the Study of Taiwan's Self-Governance*) (n.p.: n.p., 20 December 1949). Hoover's East Asian Collection has the original 173-page report commissioned by Governor Chen Cheng on 15 August 1949.
5. Chen Kewen, "Difang zizhi yu minzhu zhengzhi" ("Local elections and democratic politics"), *Ziyou Zhongguo* (*Free China Fortnightly*), Vol. 6, No. 16 (16 March 1952), p. 12.

Shi, stated that Taiwan had already become part of that great tidal wave sweeping the world called "democracy and freedom." "In this great movement," he said, "we have not chosen the wrong road."[6]

Between 1950 and 1987, five types of local elections were held at least once every three years: village, city, county, municipal city and province. Voting participation ranged between the high 50s to 70 per cent of the eligible voters, without declining. By the late 1980s more than twice the number of people voted as in the early 1950s. More candidates competed for the different council seats than for the county and major city leadership positions. The county and city councils and Taiwan Provincial Assembly representatives elected had the power to recommend, review and approve legislation; they also interpellated officials as well as reviewed, discussed and approved budgets.[7] The elected leaders of villages, townships, counties and main cities acquired the power of their offices and governed according to the formal regulations of those offices.

In 1969 the KMT expanded this electoral process. As early as March 1966, the National Assembly had proposed that the president, by the authority granted to him according to the Temporary Articles of the 1948 Constitution, recommend that additional central government representatives be routinely elected.[8] The National Assembly reasoned that in the area of Free China (Taiwan and its offshore islands) enough population expansion had occurred to justify the people electing additional central government representatives to carry out the duties of the National Assembly, the Legislative Yuan and the Control Yuan. That is what the official record reveals.

The non-official record is another matter. By 1966 the KMT worried that the central government representatives elected in 1948 were rapidly declining because of death, illness and retirement.[9] To ensure that enough national government representatives served to legitimate the ROC government in the pursuit of its goals, the KMT reasoned that new laws were needed to begin electing from Taiwan central government representatives to replace those who no longer served. The ROC president

---

footnote continued

Dai Duheng argued at the same time that local elections helped promote the parliamentary system and enabled different political parties to elect parliamentary representatives; see Dai Duheng, "Cong jianjie minzhu dao zhijie minzhu" ("From indirect democracy to direct democracy"), *Ziyou Zhongguo*, Vol. 6, No. 12 (16 June 1952), pp. 5–8, and Vol. 7, No. 1 (1 July 1952), pp. 17–20.

6. Hu Shi, "Sanbai nianlai shijie wenhua de qushi yu Zhongguo ying caiqu di fangxiang" ("The world cultural trend of the past 300 years and the direction that China should take"), *Ziyou Zhongguo*, Vol. 8, No. 3 (1 February 1953), p. 4.

7. For a recent study of how Taiwan provincial assembly representatives learned democracy, see Ramon H. Myers, "The devolution of power, democracy, and economic development in Taiwan: the Taiwan Provincial Assembly, 1949–65," in Gustav Ranis, Sheng-cheng Hu and Yun-peng Chu (eds.), *The Political Economy of Taiwan's Development into the Twenty-first Century: Essays in Memory of John C.H. Fei*, Vol. 2 (Northampton, MA: Edward Elgar, 199X], pp. 311–334.

8. Dong Xiangfei (ed.), *Zhonghua minguo xuanju gaikuang* (*The General Conditions Regarding Elections in the Republic of China*) (Taipei: Zhongyang xuanju weiyuanhui, 1984), Vol. 1, p. 156.

9. Based on interviews of former top KMT officials conducted by the authors in Taipei.

instructed the Executive Yuan (cabinet) to take appropriate action. On 1 July 1966 the cabinet established a committee to study the issue.[10] This committee finally recommended that the existing number of central government representatives be increased by holding supplementary quota elections every three years. The cabinet then introduced a new law, approved by the Legislative Yuan, to elect a supplementary quota of national representatives on 20 December 1969 for the National Assembly and Legislative Yuan, and another on 29 December 1969 for the Control Yuan.

These elections were managed in complex ways to ensure that as few non-KMT representatives as possible were elected. The quota of representatives for the National Assembly were allocated on the basis of votes by county and Taipei city population size, by aboriginal voters living in two separate districts, by occupation (workers and farmers), and by female gender. Representatives for parliament were also elected according to county and Taipei city population size, including Chin-men and Lien-chiang counties. Finally, the Taiwan Provincial Assembly and the Taipei and Kaohsiung city councils, dominated by the KMT, elected a small quota of representatives for the Control Yuan.

Although the quota of elected national representatives increased in every election, non-KMT candidates still found it difficult to win a place on the ballot, let alone to compete with KMT candidates and expect to win. By 1980, voters still elected only 76 National Assembly representatives, just 6 per cent of the National Assembly in 1983. Voters also elected only 70 new legislators out of a total of 373 seats, just 14 per cent, and only a few were non-KMT members.

National Assembly representatives served six years, and Legislative and Control Yuan representatives served only three years. The elections enabled some non-KMT candidates to be elected to the Legislative Yuan. Their numbers were too few to initiate legislation, but they interpellated government leaders and expressed their political views with great skill and passion.

By the late 1970s, then, more than six million people voted in routine, orderly local and national elections. Voters and candidates had learned how to use the election process to advance their interests. The leaders and representatives elected to village, county, city and provincial offices participated in a political dialogue with the ruling party and national and provincial government officials. They learned the art of compromise in order to agree on new legislation and the annual budget.[11]

As early as 1969 and 1970, new politicians critical of the KMT began differentiating themselves from KMT candidates. They called themselves the *dangwai*, literally "outside the ruling party," and gradually mobilized more popular support for their candidates in local and national elections. By 1980, they skilfully campaigned to win voters' support.

---

10. See Dong Xiangfei, *The General Conditions*, pp. 157–169.
11. *Ibid.*; Myers, "The devolution of power, democracy, and economic development," pp. 327–29.

Figure 1: **The Votes for KMT and Opposition (non-KMT) in the Legislative Yuan Elections, 1972–92**

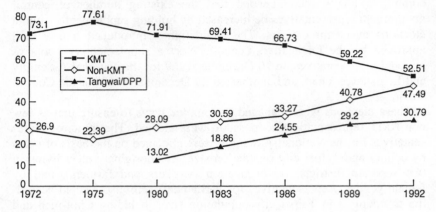

Source:
  Hung-Mao Tien (ed.), *Taiwan's Electoral Politics and Democratic Transition: Riding the Third Wave* (Armonk, NY: M. E. Sharpe, 1996), p. 16.

These developments, along with other complex changes in society, produced a major watershed for Taiwan's elections between 1977 and 1980. Before 1977 the percentage of votes cast for the KMT and non-KMT candidates had been very stable: 60–70 per cent for the former as opposed to 25–34 per cent for the latter for the magistrate-mayor races, provincial assemblypersons and city councillors. After the watershed period the percentage of non-KMT votes cast in county and city elections for magistrates and mayors rose to 44 per cent in 1981, fell to 39 per cent in 1985, and then continued to rise after martial law was lifted in 1987 (see Figure 2). As for the national election quota for the Legislative Yuan, the pattern after 1980 was also an upward trend for non-KMT votes (see Figure 1). As more registered voters after 1977 supported *dangwai* candidates, democracy deepened, culminating in the passing of the May 1980 election law and the forming of an opposition party in September 1986. These contrasting election patterns before and after 1977 indicate that democratic practices were gradually crystallizing in Taiwan's society.

How Democratic Were Taiwan's Early Elections?

From the outset, ROC officials designed a local election system permitting many candidates to complete in an electoral district but granting each voter only one vote. The KMT used this single, nontransferable voting and multiple-candidate electoral system to discourage opposition candidates from competing while diverting votes from rival

Figure 2: **The Votes for KMT and Opposition (non-KMT) in the County Magistrate and City Mayoral Elections, 1954–63**

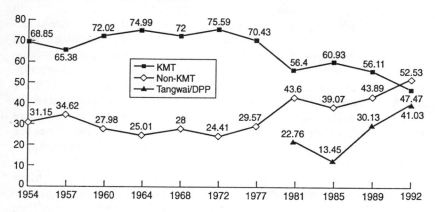

Source:
Hung-Mao Tien, *Taiwan's Electoral Politics*, p. 17.

candidates to its nominees.[12] The ruling party only nominated the candidates of its choice, while trying to block other KMT members from competing against its preferred choices.

Another ruling party strategy called for nominating as few candidates as possible to give local factions or friendly candidates a chance to run and even win. In this way, the KMT not only avoided creating enemies who might collude to form a political party or local faction committed to defeating KMT candidates, but preserved friendly ties with the local factions.[13]

Yet another tactic the KMT used, especially for concurrently electing county and city leaders, was to target key voting areas to avoid excessive competition that might split votes between the KMT and non-KMT candidates. The party assigned task forces to "responsibility zones" to help its candidates. Within each zone the party task force helped distribute campaign literature, converse with voters, and mobilize people familiar with voting patterns to distribute gifts and money and host banquets to introduce the KMT nominee.[14] These task forces became so experienced that they usually delivered the required votes from their "responsibility zones" to ensure that their candidates were always elected. The ruling party also mobilized military personnel and their families, government and provincial employees and their families, and school teachers and their relatives to support KMT-nominated candidates. By

---

12. This observation is advanced by Chia-lung Lin, "Paths to democracy: Taiwan in comparative perspective," Ph.D. dissertation, Department of Political Science, Yale University, May 1998, pp. 165–67.

13. *Ibid.* pp. 168 and 171.

14. *Ibid.* pp. 172–73.

relying on these methods, KMT cadres delivered large blocks of votes –
iron votes (*tie piao*) – to guarantee their candidate's victory.

The ruling party not only had formal networks in every community but
had developed irregular networks to gather political intelligence information which proved useful for preventing non-KMT candidates from
winning.[15] The party also had enough funds to conduct public opinion
surveys so it could nominate the appropriate candidate while discouraging non-KMT candidates from competing, or failing that, discredit the
non-KMT candidate in the eyes of the voters. In these different ways, the
ruling party intervened in local elections to guarantee that its candidates
not only won a high percentage of the local election races but controlled
the local councils, the Taiwan Provincial Assembly, and county magistrates and city mayors.

After the second-term county council election (1952–53), many
politicians and elites complained that the Taiwan provincial government's rules restricted the places where candidates could express their
views to voters and the length of time they could speak.[16] They also
complained that candidates could only use one car during the short
campaign period, and that their speeches could not exceed 300 Chinese
characters. Others pointed out that overstaffed administrative offices in
many areas enabled officials to interfere in their campaigning.[17] The
editors of *Ziyou Zhongguo* concluded that "all of these hindrances were
only the KMT's way of restricting the election process."[18]

By 1956, six years after local elections commenced, the most frequent
criticism was that few non-KMT candidates dared to compete to challenge the ruling party. In autumn 1956, a member of the China Youth
Party (*Qingnian dang*) in Nantou district, one of two political parties long
tolerated by the KMT on the mainland because of its friendly stance
toward the KMT, stated that the local police had warned him not to
compete in the election for Nantou county magistrate. When he had tried
to register, the Nantou election committee imposed so many obstacles
that he finally decided not to run.[19]

On 21 April 1957, when the Taiwan Provincial Assembly and 21
county magistrate elections took place, some 4.2 million voters turned out
to give the KMT a huge victory. In only one county was a non-KMT
candidate, Ye Tinggui of Tainan county, elected. Of the 66 Taiwan
Provincial Assembly seats, the KMT won 44. The ruling party had made

---

15. *Ibid.* pp. 173–76.
16. "Jingxuan huodong ying kan zuo zhengzhi jiaoyu" ("Regard competing election activity
as political education") (editorial), *Ziyou Zhongguo*, Vol. 8, No. 2 (16 January 1953), p. 3.
17. Yuan Yichen, "Taiwan sheng shishi difang zizhi di jiantao" ("An examination and
evaluation of Taiwan province's implementation of local government"), *Ziyou Zhongguo*,
Vol. 8, No. 11 (1 June 1953), p. 10.
18. See n. 16, in which the editorial members of *Ziyou Zhongguo* complained that KMT
district chiefs visited each district, city and town to confer with election committees as to how
election rules should be tightened to limit the use of microphones and the length of time each
candidate could speak (only 15 minutes).
19. Wang Fengzeng, "Lun Taiwan sheng de xuanju" ("A discussion of Taiwan provincial
elections"), *Ziyou Zhongguo*, Vol. 16, No. 7 (1 April 1957), pp. 9–10.

every endeavour to smother the opposition by discouraging opposition candidates from competing and drawing heavily upon its iron votes from the military and government voting groups. The KMT candidate, Huang Qirui, obtained nearly 40 thousand military votes to defeat the popular opposition candidate, Gao Yushu. Rumours had circulated that if the government and military personnel did not vote for Huang they would be punished. Many government and provincial officials and their families had also received free train tickets to return to their home towns to cast their votes.[20] One woman reported that when she started to write Gao Yushu's name on her ballot, a voting poll official seized it and instead wrote the name of Huang Qirui.[21] Although she vigorously protested, causing a fight to ensue, this illegal behaviour was not reported nor was the election official punished.

A politician named Yang Jichen bitterly complained that the main reason for his defeat in the December 1957 election was that local officials had harassed him and limited his time to campaign, treatment not experienced by his KMT opponent.[22] He also insisted that the KMT had circulated vicious rumours to discredit his character,[23] and as he received little financial support he had no time to rebut these lies. The local police had even harassed his friends. Therefore, the KMT candidate had won the election by a huge landslide because his party had used unfair means.

By the end of the 1950s, the small chorus criticizing Taiwan's local election process agreed that the KMT "lacked any real sincerity to hold honest local elections" and "lacked the genuine belief that party politics was desirable and should be promoted." They also claimed that the KMT "had no wish to conduct fair elections and abide by the law."[24] These critics concluded that the ruling party's slogans of "democratic revolution" and "to develop a legal system and democracy" were empty words. Moreover, the KMT possessed neither the proper psychology nor the right spirit to build democracy on Taiwan, because its power remained concentrated in the hands of the wrong people.[25]

Even so, some elites were optimistic that the ruling party might still allow the election of a Taiwan provincial governor because "the Taiwan people were now prepared and had the necessary political, economic and cultural understanding to support democracy. For that reason, the central government did not have to worry about such an election."[26] They gave the KMT high marks for its economic reforms, but pointed out that the

20. Fu Zheng, "Dui benjie difang xuanju de jiantao" ("An examination and review of this term's local elections"), *Ziyou Zhongguo*, Vol. 16, No. 9 (1 May 1957), p. 14.
21. *Ibid*. p. 15.
22. Yang Jizhen, "Wo cong jingxuan shibai zhong dedao de zhishi" ("The knowledge that I gained from the failure of my election campaign"), *Ziyou Zhongguo*, Vol. 17, No. 22 (16 December 1957), p. 9.
23. *Ibid*. pp. 10–11.
24. Zhu Wanbo, "Zhizhengdang kongzhi Taiwan difang xuanju de xinli fenxi" ("A psychological analysis of the ruling party's control of Taiwan's local elections"), *Ziyou Zhongguo*, Vol. 18, No. 1 (5 January 1958), p. 20.
25. *Ibid*. p. 21.
26. Guo Yuxin, "Min xuan shengzhang ci qishiyi" ("This is the time to have the provincial governor elected by the people"), *Ziyou Zhongguo*, Vol. 22, No. 1 (5 January 1960), p. 11.

majority of people still did not approve of KMT-managed elections, saying that "many people liked Gao Yushu, but they were not able to elect him because the KMT did not want him to run."[27]

In the 1960 election for the Taiwan Provincial Assembly and 21 county magistrates, some critics suggested that "to have really fair, legal elections, the election supervisory officials should be selected by the China Youth Party and the China Social-Democratic Party (*Minshe dang*) as well as by non-party individuals – a minimal requirement if elections were to be called democratic."[28] Some elites now argued that a new political party must challenge the KMT to make local elections truly democratic.

After the 1960 election results were published, critics of the ruling party bitterly concluded that the "KMT ignores the popular will" and "democracy can never be promoted if there is only one party, no checks and balances, and no voice of a political opposition."[29] They noted that in nine of the 21 county magistrate elections held in 1960, the KMT nominees ran unopposed, and in Keelung city, where two candidates were supposed to compete for the mayor's race, only one KMT nominee ran.[30]

On 18 May 1960, desperate and resentful, some 30 non-KMT elites who had just competed in local elections assembled in Taipei for a discussion meeting (*zuotanhui*) to exchange views about how to promote democracy. The group included such politicians and journalists as Wu Sanlian, Gao Yushu, Li Wanju, Guo Yuxin, Guo Guoji, Lei Zhen and Shen Yunlong, with Li Wanju presiding and Gao Yushu in the chair.[31] For the first time, Taiwanese and mainland politicians, as well as elites, assembled in public to evaluate Taiwan's local elections and map a blueprint for democratic political action. They expressed general dismay that an unfair and undemocratic electoral process still existed. Some opined that the China Youth Party and the Chinese Social Democratic Party might be revitalized to force the ruling party to make elections truly democratic.

Many described their personal experiences, pointing out how some near victories had been snatched from them at the last moment by the

27. Cao Dawo, "Guomindang xing-shuai zhi guanjian zai xuanju" ("The key to the success or failure of the KMT depends on elections"), *Ziyou Zhongguo*, Vol. 22, No. 4 (20 February 1960), pp. 10–12. Cao and other critics of the KMT believed that "the KMT should rapidly cultivate an equally powerful opposition party, which would demonstrate that the KMT was creating a true democracy" (p. 11).

28. "Duiyu difang xuanju liang dian qima yaoqiu" ("There are two minimum requirements for having local elections") (editorial), *Ziyou Zhongguo*, Vol. 22, No. 6 (20 March 1960), p. 1. For a similar argument see Wang Fengzeng, "You difang xüanju kan minzhu zhengzhi de qiantu" ("The future of a democratic polity as seen from local elections"), *Ziyou Zhongguo*, Vol. 22, No. 7 (5 April 1960), pp. 11–13.

29. "Qing tou zai yedang he wudang wupai houxuanren yi piao" ("Please cast one vote for the nonruling party and nonfaction candidates") (editorial), *Ziyou Zhongguo*, Vol. 22, No. 8 (20 April 1960), pp. 3–4.

30. Lei Zhen, "Women weishenme poqie xuyao yi ge qiangyouli de fanduidang" ("Why do we urgently need a strong, powerful opposition party?"), *Ziyou Zhongguo*, Vol. 22, No. 10 (20 May 1960), p. 10.

31. This meeting was discussed in *Ziyou Zhongguo*, Vol. 22, No. 11 (5 June 1960), pp. 20–24.

KMT mobilizing its "iron votes" and using "dirty tricks" to elect its nominees. The meeting ended by underscoring the point that if the KMT had not cheated in so many elections, many other candidates would not have been defeated. Gao Yushu, elected as Taipei mayor in 1954, revealed that when he told his American friends about how the KMT manipulated the election process, they had replied, "but how did you win?" Gao retorted, "I was elected because the KMT believed I could not be elected. And if the KMT thought I might be elected, they would never have let me run."[32]

Several months later, Lei Zhen, the chief editor of *Ziyou Zhongguo*, and several others tried to form a political party; the authorities quickly arrested Lei and three others, and a military court found them guilty of engaging in subversive activities and imprisoned them. During the next decade, critical voices evaluating local elections were rarely heard. The KMT continued to manipulate the electoral process as in the past, even passing a special law in 1967 abolishing mayoral elections for Taipei and Kaohsiung cities and not resuming those elections until 1994. By 1969, however, a new generation had begun to emerge. As the 1970s unfolded, Taiwan society prospered as cities boomed and the countryside flourished; more non-KMT politicians spoke out, and some even won their elections.

How Elections Became More Democratic Under Martial Law

From 1960 to 1970, Taiwan experienced unprecedented rapid economic growth and structural change. Real GNP grew at the annual rate of 9.6 per cent.[33] In 1970, for the first time since the pre-war period, Taiwan's exports began to exceed imports. Gross savings as a share of GNP, already quite high in 1952 (15.3 per cent), increased to 25.6 per cent, and the distribution of income was becoming more equal because of land reform and rapid economic growth, which increased consumption and expanded the number of small and medium-sized, family-run enterprises. Real income per capita more than doubled, though it was still very low, just short of US$4,000 per year. But manufacturing in both rural areas and cities had surged in the 1960s, so that in 1970 only 36 per cent of the labour force worked in farming, fishing and so on, compared to 50 per cent in 1960. The share of manpower in manufacturing also exceeded that working in the primary sector, revealing for the first time that a large labour force had shifted from farming to mining, manufacturing, construction and utilities. Taiwan's huge pool of underemployed labour in the 1950s, residing mostly in villages and towns, was now moving to the cities to work. Because urban demand for labour rose rapidly as the supply of rural labour declined, real wages increased more quickly after 1970.

32. *Ibid.* p. 24.
33. The economic information presented hereafter is derived from Council of Economic Planning and Development, *Taiwan Statistical Data Book, 1995* (Taipei: CEPD, 1995).

As the expanding domestic market economy rapidly integrated with the international economy, not only did Taiwan's market economy grow in scale but its participants became wealthy. Numerous *nouveaux riches* businessmen, as well as corporate executives, became prosperous enough to support charities, community projects and their favourite political candidates. Business prosperity also made it possible for Taiwanese elites to find enough financial support to publish their journals, some with a political content. These developments made possible what Thomas A. Metzger has conceptualized as an evolving ideological marketplace, where new ideas materialized, competed for acceptance, and produced new ways of thinking and acting.[34] New journals flourished and advanced new ideas. The authorities responded by banning those regarded as subversive and undermining social order.

In September 1960 the authorities banned the publication of *Ziyou Zhongguo*; in 1961–65 *Wenxing zazhi* (*Literary Stars*) appeared; in 1968–73, *Daxue zazhi* (*The Intellectual*) briefly circulated, only to be banned; in 1975 *Taiwan zhenglun* (*Taiwan Political Review*) briefly appeared and was banned; and in 1978–79 *Meilidao* (*Beautiful Formosa*) was a big hit but was then banned. These political magazines rallied a growing number of Taiwanese and mainlander elites to promote the cause of democracy, representing that intellectual elite mobilization mentioned by Reinhard Bendix.[35] The journals critically evaluated the current state of Taiwan democracy, especially the electoral process, and concluded that it was underdeveloped. Articles argued that single-party KMT rule was the main obstacle for democracy's development. By the early 1970s these ideological journals had not only exerted a profound influence on elite thinking but had transformed the beliefs and values of ordinary people, as observed by Alex Inkeles. Many individuals believed that politics was a vocation worthy of personal sacrifices in order to build a real democracy.

Meanwhile, another important development converged with the above two trends. The top KMT leaders had realized as early as the mid-1960s, if not earlier, that the ROC government would not soon recover mainland China, perhaps not even in their lifetime. Faced with the reality of government and party ranks thinning and the fact that mainland Chinese constituted less than 15 per cent of the island's population, the ruling party began making greater efforts in the early 1970s to recruit young Taiwanese and promote them to high positions in the ruling party and government. At the same time, the KMT worked harder to win the support of the Taiwanese people. Its leaders realized that they could stay in power only if elections became fair and democratic.

Meanwhile, critics debunked the ruling party's acclaimed "democratic revolution" cliché as ignoring the will of the people. KMT leaders and propagandists did not offer a credible defence of their party's ban of

---

34. See Metzger, "The Chinese reconciliation of moral-sacred values with modern pluralism." See also the discussion of Taiwan intellectual elites in Linda Chao and Ramon H. Myers, *The First Chinese Democracy: Political Life in the Republic of China on Taiwan* (Baltimore: Johns Hopkins University Press, 1998), pp. 90–100.
35. See introduction by Larry Diamond and Ramon H. Myers to this volume.

opposition parties except to argue that because Communist China still threatened Taiwan, martial law could not be lifted or opposition parties allowed to exist. This argument lost credibility. For many voters, the old opposition label of "nonparty" (*wudang*) candidates meant the KMT did not regard them as worthy to represent the party in local election races. Many voters thought "nonparty" candidates supported the same platform as the KMT and therefore did not perceive them as having a political message any different from the KMT candidates. Consequently, few *wudang* candidates won elections, and their total votes were only 10 to 15 per cent of all those cast.

Meanwhile, the ruling party continued to use the same campaign tactics that had always guaranteed their dominance of the electoral process. But in the 15 November 1969 election for Taipei council members, citizens elected a college graduate named Kang Ningxiang, who had once worked at a gasoline station. In 1998 Kang recalled, "I felt the time had come! That is why I plunged into political activity."[36] On 20, December, five weeks later, the people voted Huang Xinjie to the Legislative Yuan.[37] What made these two election victories unusual was that Kang and Huang had broken with the tradition of calling themselves *wudang* and instead had campaigned under the label of being "outside the ruling party" (*dangwai*). In this way, they presented a different kind of candidate to the voter: their political label symbolized a challenge to the ruling party, and their campaign message demanded that true democracy be practised and represent the people's will.

A year before, in 1968, several Taiwanese had published a magazine called *Daxue zazhi* (*The Intellectual*), which discussed Taiwan's political life. In 1970, the voters elected to the Taiwan Provincial Assembly two *dangwai* candidates, Zhang Junhong and Xu Xinliang, who had campaigned by arguing how their political message differed from that of the KMT. In 1973 the voters elected Kang and Huang to the Legislative Yuan. Then in 1977 voters elected four *dangwai* to be country magistrates, another 21 to the Taiwan Provincial Assembly, and six to Taipei's city council. For the first time since local elections began, the opposition politicians championed a platform very different from that of the KMT, challenging the ruling party to start practising real and full democracy.[38] The 1977 election of so many *dangwai* politicians sent shockwaves throughout the KMT and Taiwan's embryonic political marketplace.

The Taiwanese and mainlander elites and intellectuals were now mobilizing academics and educated youth to question the authority of the KMT and to explain why the people should acquire that authority to govern. In October 1971, the editors of *Daxue zazhi* offered the following explanation for convening a conference to study Taiwan elections and

36. An interview with Kang Ningxiang, as recalled in Lian He and Tai Shi (eds.), *Xuanju xuanju* (*Elections and Elections*) (Taipei: Changqiao chubanshe, 1978), p. 83.

37. Li Xiaofeng, *Taiwan minzhu yundong sishi nian* (*Forty Years of the Taiwan Democratic Movement*) (Taipei: Zili wanbao wenhua chubanshe, 1987), p. 112.

38. *Ibid.* pp. 238–241.

governance: "While making the unification of China our great goal, we must urgently think about how to make Taiwan better. We must effectively manage this small locality before we can manage an area 300 times our size."[39] Conference members agreed their goal could only be achieved through a fair, open, free, democratic electoral process in which the people freely elected their representatives and leaders to carry out the will of the people.

On 8 July 1972 the same journal sponsored another "discussion meeting" to prepare candidates for the next year's elections. The participants included mainlander liberals like Wang Xingqing, Shuo Nanfang, Wang Xiaobo, Wu Fengshan, Hu Fu and Gao Yuren, and Taiwanese politicians who had campaigned in local and supplementary quota national elections. In their exchange of views about how elections could be made more democratic, Kang Ningxiang pointed out that so many members of the ROC National Assembly had aged that only 400 of the 2,000 could be regarded as active and competent to perform.[40] He argued that elections for that body should be greatly expanded.

As for campaigning, Kang complained that the election rules limited candidates to speak for only ten minutes at a rally. If a candidate participated in the eight rallies legally allowed, that meant only a grand total of 80 minutes to speak to the voters. Assuming that around 500 people attended a political rally, Kang argued that eight rallies only enabled a political candidate to address 4,000 people. But a candidate needed at least 5,900 votes to be elected to Taipei's city council. The rules governing political rallies had to be changed if elections were to be fair, free and open. Kang's second point was that competing candidates and their families and friends should be protected from being harassed.

Finally, too many ruling party candidates had the unfair advantage of having too much money to buy votes. Other conference speakers echoed Kang's complaints. Shu Zikuan pointed out that "if candidates from an organization like the KMT can use its resources to host banquets and hold political rallies, they have no difficulty winning enough votes to be elected."[41] In the end, the conference condemned the unfair election practices perpetrated by the KMT just as *Ziyou Zhongguo* had done two decades before.

As this intellectual elite mobilization campaign stimulated the public to think deeply about promoting democracy, the regime suppressed their printing and distribution of journals and pamphlets. Meanwhile, *dangwai* politicians provoked great excitement during the elections. Could their movement continue to grow? Would the ruling party tolerate more *dangwai* to convene meetings, publish journals and expand their number? And if voters did take the *dangwai* seriously, would the ruling party still promote elections? Taiwan's electoral process had now entered a critical

39. "Guoshi zhengyan" ("Some suggestions regarding national affairs"), *Daxue zazhi*, No. 46 (October 1971), p. 6.

40. "Zhongyang ji difang xuanju wenti" ("The problem of central government and local elections"), *Daxue zazhi*, Vol. 10, No. 56 (15 August 1972), pp. 35–37.

41. *Ibid.* p. 38.

phase. The KMT dared not suppress the *dangwai* because they had not broken any laws and that would delegitimize the KMT's advocacy of "democratic revolution". The *dangwai* did not have sufficient skills to win enough votes to defeat the majority of KMT candidates and win power. For democracy to mature under martial law, the voters, *dangwai* and KMT needed to legitimate the embryonic political marketplace.

In that maturation phase, elections could become democratic if candidates had more opportunity to address the voters.[42] The *dangwai* then might compete with the powerful, entrenched ruling party and persuade more voters to demand democratic reforms. But *dangwai* leaders had to restrain their extremists and nominate better candidates if they expected to win more elections. If the KMT perfected its message to promote democracy, it had a chance of retaining voters' support. A maturing electoral process also mitigated a government crackdown and arrest of dozens of *dangwai* politicians after a riot in Kaohsiung city on 9 December 1979, when crowds assembled to celebrate Human Rights Day and police clashed with demonstrators.

From 1977 until the government lifted martial law on 15 July 1987, Taiwan's elections peacefully evolved and became more democratic. In this maturation phase, the Legislative Yuan approved a new election law, which the Executive Yuan promulgated on 14 May 1980. Meanwhile, voters became more sophisticated and mature; *dangwai* candidates learned to campaign effectively; and the KMT tolerated an opposition and changed its tactics to win elections.

The Maturing of Limited Elections under Martial Law

The year 1977 marked the beginning of a new era in Taiwan's electoral process. For the first time the pattern of a low, flat trend of votes cast for opposition candidates changed to one of increasing voter support.[43] This owed much to citizens' eagerness to support candidates opposing the KMT and their demand for democratic reforms. Secondly, *dangwai* politicians learned to attract voters' support, and, finally, the KMT displayed its willingness to establish democratic elections.

As the public awaited the late 1978 supplementary national government elections (they were suspended and postponed to 1980 because the United States broke diplomatic relations with the ROC government), the *dangwai* politician Xu Xinliang observed that "the overall voters' pas-

42. We are indebted to Kang Ningxiang's assistance and our two-hour interview with him on 10 December 1998 for clarifying many issues regarding the critical decade (1977–86) when Taiwan's embryonic marketplace matured and "limited democracy" took a great leap forward.

43. For a detailed discussion of these changes in Taiwan's political life, see Chao and Myers, *The First Chinese Democracy*. See also Hung-mao Tien, "Elections in Taiwan's democratic development," in Hung-mao Tien (ed.), *Taiwan's Electoral Politics and Democratic Transition: Riding the Third Wave* (Armonk, NY: M. E. Sharpe, 1996), pp. 16–17. The data used by Hung-mao Tien come from the excellent study by Huang Defu, *Minzhu jinbu dang yu Taiwan diqu zhengzhi minzhuhua* (*The Democratic Progressive Party and the Democratization of Taiwan's Local Politics*) (Taipei: Shiying chubanshe, 1993), ch. 5.

sions are greater, and they are more concerned about the forthcoming elections."[44] Voter thinking had indeed changed. By the late 1970s voters were younger and more educated. Many had travelled abroad and lived in Japan and the West. Open-minded, receptive to reform and prosperous, they contributed funds to the *dangwai*, read their journals and voted for *dangwai* candidates. The ideal of democracy appealed to voters under 40, and a growing majority of citizens now wanted the government to be accountable to them.

In the 19 November 1977 elections for county magistrates and city mayors, a newspaper editorial described the orderly, dignified way that voters went to the polls and voted:

Five government elections were held throughout Taiwan yesterday on a fair, clear day with the weather beautiful and warm. The ordinary citizens were equipped with their newly acquired knowledge about democratic politics and local elections. They took pride in their right to vote and were very eager about doing so. This was the most unique event since local elections were held in the province twenty-seven years ago ... People lined up to vote as early as 7.00 a.m. in most places. At 8.00 a.m. most shops in Taipei had closed for the day. Many workers went to cast their votes before going to work, while the elderly were helped to vote by their grandchildren. Housewives carried their grocery baskets to the voting booths ... Everyone went to vote. So by noon yesterday, already half of the people had cast their ballots.[45]

The press, like the authorities, was surprised by the large number of votes cast for nonparty and *dangwai* candidates. A journalist for *Lianhebao* (*United Daily*) admitted that "until now we still did not understand why the nonparty candidates won so many votes." After alluding to the recent conflation of negative circumstances – America's diplomatic break with the ROC government, rural income failing to keep pace with industrial wages and a spate of natural disasters – this writer concluded as follows: "One thing we can be certain about is that those who voted for the outside-the-party candidates were attracted by their ideal of reform and their critical spirit of demanding reform. This election marked a turning point in Taiwan's political climate."[46] The voters' enthusiasm demonstrated in the 1977 election continued to be expressed in high voting participation rates and increasing support for opposition politicians in elections throughout the 1980s.

At the same time, the *dangwai* were adopting new tactics to win voter support for their goal of promoting democracy.[47] For example, they cultivated those social networks all Chinese favoured, personal and kinship ties (*renqing guanxi*) along with community factions, and they tried to reach out to male voters, knowing their wives voted as their husbands did. They targeted voters under 40 years of age, especially

44. An interview with Xu Xinliang as recorded in Lian He and Tai Shi, *Elections and Elections*, p. 83.

45. Quoted from Chao and Myers, *The First Chinese Democracy*, p. 97.

46. See the articles by the special features columnist for *Lianhebao*, Huang Nian, *Taiwan zhengzhi fashao* (*Taiwan's Political Fever*) (Taipei: Siji chuban shiye yuxian gongsi, 1980), p. 410.

47. For these examples see Lian He and Tai Shi, *Elections and Elections*, pp. 103–111.

of Taiwanese ethnicity. The more educated and older the voter, the greater the tendency to vote for the KMT, so the *dangwai* carefully studied voters' habits and tried to appeal to those who felt powerless to influence their local officials, operated small businesses, taught the young, laboured, farmed or fished. More importantly, the *dangwai* learned how to play to the voters' compassion for the underdog.

In 1972 the *dangwai* Zeng Wenpo used that approach to win a seat on the Taichung city council, and in 1977 he became Taichung city's mayor.[48] After becoming city councillor, Zeng wrote a book expressing his dismay about Taichung's failure to realize its developmental potential.[49] His book caught the public's attention, and when Zeng mysteriously disappeared during the Taichung mayor's race, rumours circulated that the authorities had imprisoned him. An outpouring of sympathy swelled for Zeng, and then he suddenly appeared before election day, walking the streets and modestly saying to everyone who stopped to listen to him, "I belong to everybody (*dajia de Wenpo*)." By playing on voters' sympathy, keeping the public in suspense and mystifying the opposition, Zeng managed to win the Taichung mayorship against a powerfully backed KMT opponent named Chen Duantang.

Another way the *dangwai* appealed to voters' sense of compassion was to ask family members of imprisoned *dangwai* to stand in for their husbands in future elections.[50] In the 1980 supplementary national government election for the Legislative Yuan and National Assembly, Xu Rongshu, wife of Zhang Junhong, ran and won; Zhou Qingyu, wife of Yao Jiawen, competed and won; and the younger brother of Xu Xinliang and the older brother of Lü Xiulian competed on behalf of Xu and won. Even the lawyers who defended the *Meilidao* publishers and the *dangwai* arrested after the Kaohsiung Incident, like You Qing, Chen Shuibian, Xie Changting and Su Zhenchang, ran in the 1981 Taipei city council and Taiwan Provincial Assembly elections and won.[51]

Still another tactic was that employed by the Pingtung county lawyer and *dangwai* politician Qiu Lianhui. He cultivated the image of being a fair-minded lawyer who struggled to release allegedly innocent convicts (*baoqingtian*). When Qiu ran in the 1981 Pingtung county race, enough voters supported him to become the first non-KMT district chief in Pingtung's history.[52]

---

48. For this example of Zeng Wenpo, see Zhang Yongcheng, *Xuanzhan zaoshi: zaoshi shi xuanzhan chenggong de bu'er-famen* (*The Strategic Campaign to Win the Election War: The Only Way for Winning the Election War Is to Wage a Strategic Campaign*) (Taiwan: Yuanliu chugan gongshe, 1992).
49. *Ibid.* pp. 153–56. Xu Xinliang had also written a book that made him very popular in Taoyuan district, called *Fengyu zhisheng* (*The Wind and the Rain*). His book, based on his tenure as a Taiwan Provincial Assemblyman, evaluated the conduct and performance of various assemblypersons in the Taiwan Provincial Assembly.
50. *Ibid.* p. 185.
51. *Ibid.* p. 188.
52. *Ibid.* p. 180. Consider, too, the strategy used by Kang Ningxiang, who relied on slogans like "Cut the defence budget" and "From today on, let us not ask what government can do for us but what we really need" (see p. 178).

Xu Xinliang's victory in the 1977 race to become the first non-KMT chief of Taoyuan county owed much to his popularity among the voters. When Xu left the KMT, he expressed his resignation as "having deep regrets that the high hopes I held for the KMT had not borne fruit as I had expected (*hen tie bu cheng gang*).[53] While campaigning, Xu adorned his headquarters with flags and pictures of KMT leaders and martyrs, signalling to the public that he did not hate the KMT, still respected it, but wanted voters to elect him so that he could press it to perform better. Xu was careful to criticize his opponent in a fair, concrete way; he stressed to voters which laws were unfair and criticized officials dispensing "special privileges"; he identified the corruption that voters knew could be eliminated; and he strived to achieve a consensus with voters about what problems could be resolved if they elected him to office.[54] In this way Xu won a race that no one expected him to win.

The above tactics helped many *dangwai* to defeat better-funded KMT candidates. Throughout the 1980s the *dangwai* sharpened their political message and called for greater democracy. When campaigning for the supplementary national government elections, they appealed to voters to elect them to replace the ageing, decrepit national representatives elected on the mainland in 1947, arguing they would work harder on the public's behalf. Some *dangwai* won enough votes to participate in those national bodies. These *dangwai*, as well as the nonparty candidates, continued their criticism of the ruling party's reluctance to lift martial law and permit political parties to compete in fair elections so that Taiwan could show the free world and Communist China it practised real democracy.

But many *dangwai* conceded that the ruling party and government had begun to treat them with courtesy, fairness and respect, improvements that owed much to the party's top leaders like Chiang Ching-kuo, who wanted to make the electoral process more democratic. After Xu Xinliang was elected as the Taoyuan county magistrate, he told a reporter in 1978 the following:

The KMT allowed the non-KMT candidates to campaign freely. This was a real breakthrough. The KMT also allowed more non-KMT candidates to campaign on their own. Thus, we had to nominate our candidates very carefully so we would not be likely to lose that race. Further, from the top to the bottom, there was the shared view among officials that the nomination of candidates had to be done fairly and according to the law.[55]

Xu still contended that election rules in the late 1970s were restrictive, but he admitted that "it is not accurate to say that the ruling party did not have the will or intent to improve elections. I only believe there still existed a gap between what the ruling party wanted to do and what it was actually doing."[56]

53. See Huang Nian, *Taiwan's Political Fever*, p. 413.
54. *Ibid.* p. 414.
55. Zhang Yongcheng, *The Strategic Campaign*, p. 80.
56. *Ibid.* p. 83.

After the 1977 election the *dangwai* Lin Zhengjie stated that "the major development I witnessed in that election was the ruling party tolerating the opposition politicians' views and opinions. They did not consider our elected candidates to be hostile or their enemy."[57] This perception of government officials treating all candidates alike was shared by other *dangwai*. Monitoring elections was also of serious concern for the ruling party and government, as reflected in the time and energy the government expended in the 1970s studying, reviewing and reforming election laws.

As early as 1972, many election officials had proposed that the 1950 law and its subsequent revisions governing local elections, as well as those of 1969 regulating the election of supplementary national government representatives, should be combined into one law to reduce expenditures and rationalize the election process.[58] Beginning on 27 November 1973, a group of scholars, officials and political representatives met 32 times over a 15-month period to draw up the "Election and Recall Law for Officials during the Period of Rebellion." This law, with nine chapters and 98 articles, was submitted to the Executive Yuan on 25 March 1975, and after review that organ approved it. But because the December 1978 election was postponed until 1980, the law did not become operational as expected.

Meanwhile, the Ministry of Interior decided to review the law once more. It invited specialists and officials from the national security sector, cabinet, judiciary, and the provincial and municipal governments to many study and review meetings.[59] Between 30 March and 5 September 1979, this group of some 100 specialists met 20 times and made further revisions according to two guidelines: the new law must promote democracy and must be implemented; further, the law must satisfy the concerns that had justified martial law, namely, to prevent subversion of the ROC government, uphold the constitution, and maintain law, order and peace.

On 8 January 1980 the Ministry of Interior finally submitted the amended election law to the cabinet, which approved and forwarded it to the Legislative Yuan, where further study and review took place.[60] Between 14 January and 14 April, various committees studied the law and frequently summoned the ministers of interior and justice for interpellations. After more meetings, the Legislative Yuan approved the law on 6 May. On 9 May it submitted the draft to the president, who promulgated it as law on 14 May 1980.

A detailed study of this law's evolution and impact is beyond the scope

---

57. *Ibid.* pp. 92–93.
58. Dong Xiangfei, *The General Conditions*, p. 393.
59. *Ibid.* p. 395.
60. For a good discussion of how the Legislative Yuan reviewed and amended the law, see Bashi niandai chubanshe (The Eighties Publishing Company), *Xuanju lifa shi-moji* (*A Record of the Passage of the Election Law from the Beginning to the End*) (Taipei: Bashi niandai chubanshe, 1 November 1980). This book describes the role played by *dangwai* politicians like Yao Jiawen and Kang Ningxiang to pass the new election law. Both Yao and Kang believed this law would promote open, fair and democratic elections.

of this article. But this much can be said. The law was a milestone in Taiwan's election process because it set out when all elections were to begin and end, made all candidates register and campaign under the same rules, and standardized voting procedures, counting of votes and reporting of votes.

As for monitoring candidates' activities, the law limited the time that candidates could hold political rallies paid from private resources and decreed that the government had to pay candidates for a designated number of days for political rallies.[61] Article 49, for example, stated that the government had to pay for seven of the 15 days of political rallies for the supplementary quota election for National Assembly and Legislative Yuan (candidates paid for the remaining eight days).[62] Under the old law, candidates had to pay for all 15 days. As for the Taiwan provincial assembly, county magistrate and city mayor elections, the government had to pay candidates' expenses for five of the ten days they were allowed to hold political rallies (under the old law candidates paid for all ten days).

Under the old election rules, candidates first held their own rallies, to be followed by government-organized political rallies, a procedure opposition candidates wanted reversed to give them the opportunity to generate added excitement and focus on their message as the campaign period ended. The new law reversed the old sequence to comply with opposition candidates' wishes. The old law's rules severely limited the means by which candidates communicated their message, the number of cars to be used, the length of the candidates' speech, the number of rallies to be held and their length of time. The new law allowed all available means of communication to be used, expanded the allotted length of the candidates' speech, increased the number of rallies to be held per day and their duration, and increased the number of cars that candidates could use. In brief, the new law gave election organizers greater freedom to plan their campaigns and more opportunity for candidates to present their message to the voters.[63]

This law pleased opposition politicians and excited voters. The less-advantaged, privately supported candidates were guaranteed a limited number of days to hold political rallies and persuade voters to support them. Non-KMT candidates now had greater opportunity than before to compete with KMT candidates on an equal basis.

61. See the commentary on the election law by Xie Ruizhi, *Minzhu zhengzhi yu xuanju bamian fa* (*Political Democracy and the Election and Recall Law*) (Taipei: Liming wenhua shiye gongsi, 1989), pp. 142–43. For a comparison of these laws see Zhongyang xuanju weiyuanhui (Central Election Commission), *Gongzhi renyuan xuanjü fagui yibian* (*A Compilation of the Election Law for Officials*) (Taipei: printed by the Central Election Commission, August 1980), p. 70, and pp. 22–23 for old law.
62. *Ibid.* p. 153.
63. See Bashi niandai chubanshe, *The Passage of the Election Law*, pp. 38–39 and 337–38.

The Second Political Breakthrough

As early as 1950, the party-state-controlled political centre in Taiwan had allowed households considerable freedom to act. People freely established business enterprises, voted in local elections, read and discussed political doctrines like Western liberal democracy (but not Marxism and Leninism), and formed their associations as long as they did not establish a competing political party and engage in activities the regime regarded as threatening and delegitimizing of its rule. This first political breakthrough, enacted in the early 1950s by the KMT, put in place an electoral process that the KMT dominated and manipulated to guarantee that at least 80 per cent of its candidates were elected as representatives and leaders of local government.

Society, therefore, had significant freedoms and even some power to inhibit the powerful political centre in the four marketplaces (including a civil society). In the economic marketplace, private enterprise competed and gradually reduced the economic power of the state sector's ownership and control, so that by 1987 only 16 per cent of industrial production was state-owned, compared to 60 per cent in 1952. In the ideological marketplace, Western liberal democracy was freely discussed as a doctrine and competed with the ruling party's official doctrine of Sun Yat-sen's thought. Thomas A. Metzger has also emphasized the "amateur view" shared by ordinary people, which praised the prosperity brought by the KMT, admired the activities of extremist intellectuals and students who challenged the KMT and supported the KMT without idealizing it. This same viewpoint also praised democracy and urged political reform to expand democracy.[64]

The party-state-controlled centre also permitted a limited electoral process as described above in which nonparty candidates could compete, although under great adversity, to create an embryonic political marketplace. Finally, the centre allowed religious and private associations to organize and conduct their affairs as long as they did not challenge the political centre's authority, thus allowing for a private organizational marketplace. Therefore, this first political breakthrough was of momentous importance because the ruling authorities gave society some significant freedoms to act compared to the restrictions imposed on society in the period under Japanese colonial rule (1895–1945).

Until the lifting of martial law, Taiwan's electoral process became more open, fair, competitive and free – that is to say, democratic – culminating in the important election law of 1980, which made it much easier for the opposition to compete in the political marketplace. By 1986, the last election under martial law, most of the political opposition's top leaders were in prison on charges stemming from the 10 December 1979 Kaohsiung Incident. Even under these difficult circumstances, the opposition still won the same number of seats in the Taipei and Kaohsiung municipal councils as in the 1981 election; it also won the

64. See Chao and Myers, *The First Chinese Democracy*, pp. 96–97.

same number of county magistrate and city mayor seats as in the previous two elections (1977 and 1981), but lost four seats for the Taiwan provincial assembly compared to 1977 and 1981. Yet in the 1986 election for the Legislative Yuan, the opposition had formed a political party and won 33 per cent of the votes, compared to 30 per cent in the 1983 election and 28 per cent in the 1980 election. In other words, just before the lifting of martial law, the political opposition had become a formidable force the KMT could no longer treat as in the past.

Moreover, Taiwan had been radically transformed from a poor, pre-dominantly rural and uneducated society in the early 1950s to something very different by the mid-1980s. The economy, an efficient and powerful engine of growth, bosted a per capita income of US$4,839 in 1981. The modernization values emphasized by Alex Inkeles had taken root in Taiwan society.[65] The "social requisites" described by Seymour Martin Lipset were in place.[66] Intellectual elite mobilization had been taking place for more than two decades. All these developments institutionalized the four marketplaces (including civil society).[67]

As early as 1982, liberals in the KMT like Tao Baichuan, an adviser to Chiang Ching-kuo, had urged the president to democratize Taiwan soon. Tao feared that the many difficulties confronting the KMT "would only increase the misuse of party power; public resources would be used by selfish officials; new political energy could not be generated; the polity would be moving against the world tide; bad political habits would be cultivated; and there could not be any progress."[68] A few years later, President Chiang Ching-kuo decided to initiate reform. At the 29–31 March 1986 Third Plenum of the KMT, he announced the establishment of a 12-person committee that would be responsible for creating six subcommittees to study how political reform could be introduced.

On 28 September of the same year, 130 *dangwai* politicians met and agreed to form a political party. That evening, two spokespersons, You Qing and Xie Changting, announced that "our party is an open-style democratic party."[69] Chiang Ching-kuo took no action to crush this party. Instead, he repeated his instructions to party leaders to accelerate political reform.[70] Taiwan's second democratic breakthrough had begun and peacefully evolved over the next decade into the 21st century.

65. Alex Inkeles, "Continuity and change in popular values on the Pacific Rim," *Hoover Essays* (Standford: Hoover Institution on War, Revolution, and Peace, 1997), pp. 1–28.
66. Seymour Martin Lipset, "The social requisites of democracy revisited," *American Sociological Review*, Vol. 59, No. 1 (February 1997), pp. 1–22.
67. A sociological, ideological-political process first described in Reinhard Bendix, *Kings or People: Power and the Mandate to Rule* (Berkeley: University of California Press, 1978), p. 10.
68. Cited in Chao and Myers, *The First Chinese Democracy*, p. 123.
69. *Ibid.* p. 132.
70. For the story of how Chiang Ching-kuo initiated Taiwan's democratic breakthrough, see Chao and Myers, *The First Chinese Democracy*, ch. 5.

Conclusion

Limited elections promoted Taiwan's democracy under martial law in several ways. First, the inhibited political centre's ruling party and paramount leader, Chiang Kai-shek, had publicly declared that, after establishing local elections, they would continue to promote a "democratic revolution." That action committed the inhibited political centre to Taiwan's eventual democratization. By making this commitment, the KMT now ran the risk of delegitimizing itself if it reneged on its promise. But as Taiwan enjoyed peace and steady progress, the KMT found it difficult to explain why its "democratic revolution" progressed so slowly and why martial law was still justified.

Secondly, as voters became educated and informed and as a political opposition formed in the 1970s to challenge the KMT, many favourable developments in the four marketplaces had converged to persuade voters, opposition candidates and the KMT to make elections the means for improving government performance and solving society's many problems. The opposition continually reminded the ruling party of its failures to achieve a "democratic revolution" if it did not expand the electoral process and democratize the polity. Meanwhile, elites within the ruling party urged its leaders to promote democracy by expanding elections.

Finally, as voters gradually supported more opposition candidates who were winning elections, the KMT realized that to stay in power, it had to win votes. But to do that, the government had to conduct fair, open, free and competitive elections to persuade voters and the opposition alike that it took democracy as seriously as they did. Thus, voters, the ruling party and the opposition gradually realized that democratization provided positive benefits for each that could be realized only by expanding the electoral process and making the polity truly democratic.

Elections, Political Change and Basic Law Government: The Hong Kong System in Search of a Political Form*

Suzanne Pepper

During the two decades preceding its 1997 reunification with China, imaginations in Hong Kong ran the gamut from fear to euphoria. Preparations for transfer from British to Chinese rule continued accordingly and Hong Kong's political development has been shaped by the conflicting imperatives responsible for those extremes. Most simply put, the imperatives grew from Hong Kong's fear of Chinese communism and China's fear of an anti-communist Hong Kong. Anxieties were greatest in the colony during 1982 and 1983, when Chinese leaders made known their determination to resume full sovereignty after the 1997 expiration of Britain's leasehold on 90 per cent of Hong Kong's territory. Apprehensions peaked again in 1989, following the military suppression of Beijing's student protest movement in Tiananmen Square. Yet fear also alternated with expressions of great bravado, when the dangers of latter-day Chinese communism seemed to pale before the prospect of China's inevitable "Hong Kong-ization." Between these two extremes, confidence levels waxed and waned as Chinese and British leaders responded, first by negotiating safeguards and then by writing them into law.

Reinforcing the effect of safeguards and constitutional guarantees, and helping to bolster confidence throughout, was the economic relationship which bound colonial capitalist Hong Kong to the communist Chinese mainland. Conventional ties still predominated in the early 1980s, via a two-way exchange that guaranteed food and water for Hong Kong while providing China with the bulk of its foreign exchange earnings. By 1997, those ties had been completely transformed as economic integration raced ahead of political reunification, with the bulk of Hong Kong's industrial capacity relocating inland. When it began in the early 1980s, this economic restructuring had nothing to do with 1997, being rather the natural consequence of China's own post-Mao reforms together with Hong Kong's need to reduce production costs. Subsequently, the 1997 factor created further impetus leading Hong Kong and China to become, with some qualifications, each other's largest investor and trading partner.

With Hong Kong's free-wheeling capitalist ways putting down roots in mainland Chinese soil, political integration on Hong Kong's terms did not seem totally beyond the bounds of reason. Yet Hong Kong could not be certain how a political system "on its own terms" might actually function. A general outline had emerged from the 1982–84 negotiations

* Conference participants contributed to this essay in many different ways. I would like to thank especially discussants Ming Chan and Lynn White for their comments and criticism, as well as Ramon Myers, Larry Diamond, Shelly Rigger and Kevin O'Brien for their questions and comparative perspectives.

between Beijing and London. The "Sino-British Joint Declaration on the Question of Hong Kong" then became the basis for a fuller elaboration intended to serve as Hong Kong's post-1997 constitution. The latter, or "Basic Law of the Hong Kong Special Administrative Region," was promulgated in 1990. The promise of local autonomy for Hong Kong written into these two foundation documents was popularized by the Chinese as "one country, two systems," and reaffirmed with a new twist when Beijing leaders added an old Chinese saying to their repertoire of trenchant phrases. "Well water and river water should not mix" (*jingshui bu fan heshui*) thus reflected not Hong Kong's apprehensions but those of Beijing after Tiananmen confirmed everyone's worst fears about the dangers of dictatorship and democracy. That upheaval gave added impetus to an argument championed by some Hong Kong activists throughout the 1980s, namely that real protection lay not in negotiated promises but in the political transformation of China itself. Meanwhile, Tiananmen-style popular protest movements swept across the communist world, precipitating its collapse. This new unfolding drama renewed determination, both in Hong Kong and Beijing, to keep protective lines of separation firmly drawn between them.

Inevitably, however, the new Basic Law constitution was also replete with grey areas that could only be clarified as implementation proceeded. Hence it was not until the first year under Chinese sovereignty had passed that a clear picture of Hong Kong's new political system emerged from the dust of transitional battles into full public view. That system can best be described as an unprecedented mix of political forms – combining liberal pluralism, corporatism and democratic-centralism – designed to provide protection for all concerned. By Hong Kong's second year under Chinese rule, of course, the strains of trying to govern with so awkward a design were already evident. That peculiar "three-in-one" combination of checks and balances nevertheless defines the parameters within which Hong Kong's political evolution must now proceed. Accordingly, the combination also represents several themes necessary for exploring Hong Kong's place in the larger question, "whither Chinese democracy?" Those themes concern specifically: origins, political legacies, reception within the local community, design and constraints, including those deriving from sources both local and national.

Origins: The Colonial Legacy

In terms of its chronology, Hong Kong's political development is usually characterized as minimal to non-existent until the early 1980s. Only at that point, roughly about the time British officials learned of China's intention to resume sovereignty, was Hong Kong allowed to take its first tentative steps toward genuine political reform. Incremental progress in laying the foundations of elected representative government then interacted with the Sino-British negotiations over Hong Kong's post-1997 future. Ultimately, the British and Hong Kong governments did not demonstrate much energy in promoting political reform until the very end of the colonial era. This story is also typically enlivened by two questions, namely, why London waited so long; and why it then suddenly sprang to life during the 1992–97 tenure of Hong Kong's last British governor, Christopher Patten.

Unfortunately, the documents necessary to provide definitive answers for these questions have yet to enter the public domain. A general understanding can nevertheless be gleaned from records that are available and should suffice here. As to why Britain procrastinated along the path to political reform, official statements provide an interrelated combination of reasons and excuses. Chief among them by the latter half of the 20th century were lack of pressing local demand and various manifestations of what is referred to in Hong Kong today as the "China factor." On closer inspection, however, these considerations, which all date from the decades following communism's 1949 victory in China, follow in a logical progression from arguments as old as Hong Kong itself.

The foundations. Having been acquired in 1842 to serve as a free port and commercial centre for the purpose of promoting trade with China, Hong Kong was always somewhat different from other colonies, or "more unique than any other."[1] Its political life developed as a reflection of that difference, dominated always by London's determination to preserve its sovereignty and control within a prevailing Chinese environment. Hong Kong's fast-growing population was from the start overwhelmingly Chinese and primarily transient. By the mid-1890s, this population numbered close to a quarter of a million and was 95 per cent Chinese, a proportion that would remain basically unchanged thereafter. Thus, as Britain's commercial "Gibraltar of the East," Hong Kong did not follow the typical evolution from direct colonial rule, to local appointed representative government, to partially elected self-government, fully-elected self-government, and on to eventual independence, whether within the empire and the commonwealth or outside it.

British colonies were typically led by all-powerful governors sent out from London, who appointed the members of their Executive and Legislative Councils. The latter advised the governor on the promulgation of laws and the former served at his pleasure to advise and assist generally. The local administration they provided was subject in different ways to direct control by the Colonial Office in London and that office was subject in turn to the authority of the British Parliament.[2] Hong Kong's governing arrangements did not remain entirely static, however, and its snail's pace progression reflected the prevailing arguments for and against reform. The ongoing incremental changes also reflected centuries of British experience in devising legislative refinements that combined

1. Sir Charles Jeffries, *The Colonial Office* (London: George Allen and Unwin, 1956), p. 87.

2. D.B. Swinfen, *Imperial Control of Colonial Legislation, 1813–1865* (Oxford: Clarendon Press, 1970); Charles Jeffries, *The Colonial Empire and Its Civil Service* (Cambridge: Cambridge University Press, 1938).

varying degrees of limited local representation with the realities of British interest and centralized decision-making in London.[3]

Accordingly, Hong Kong's Legislative and Executive Councils soon began to grow and differentiate from the original handful of founding members.[4] The standard colonial practice of appointing "unofficial" members – or representatives of the local citizenry exclusive of government and military personnel – was introduced in 1850. Thirty years later, Singapore-born lawyer Ng Choy (Wu Tingfang) simultaneously broke two barriers when he became the first Chinese member of the Legislative Council and its first non-commercial unofficial representative. Thereafter, the principle of including at least one Chinese member was maintained, although the requirement that they be British subjects limited the pool of qualified contenders since most of those who established residence in Hong Kong retained their Chinese nationality. The first Chinese member of the Executive Council was not appointed until the 1920s. In 1884, an elective principle of sorts was introduced when the Chamber of Commerce and Justices of the Peace were granted formal right to nominate two unofficial legislators. By that time, the Legislative Council had a total of 11 members, not including the governor, with six officials and five unofficials. British commercial and banking interests dominated both the new constituencies (which had a combined membership of less than 100) and unofficial members were drawn overwhelmingly from these occupational categories throughout the pre-Second World War years.[5]

In fact, from the start of its existence, substantive proposals inspired by contemporary trends in colonial government reform were raised and considered by Hong Kong's governors and its British residents. All such proposals inevitably came to little or nothing, however, reflecting those same contemporary trends which inspired in Hong Kong's colonial rulers a need to maintain liberal appearances and a simultaneous fear of liberal consequences. London thus remained fearful of entrusting its strategic East Asian trading and military post either to Hong Kong's Chinese majority or to its small British mercantile elite, regarding the former alternative to be unsafe and the latter unsound. Enlightened leadership from London was always deemed preferable to any of the local alternatives.[6]

Post-First World War demands for reform were distinguished by growing Chinese interest. This evidently inspired Hong Kong's governor to advise in 1922 against introducing European-only elections since the Chinese might then demand equal rights which would give them a

3. E.g. Martin Wight, *The Development of the Legislative Council, 1606–1945* (London: Faber and Faber, 1946).
4. George Pottinger, *Sir Henry Pottinger: First Governor of Hong Kong* (New York: St Martin's Press, 1997).
5. G. B. Endacott, *Government and People in Hong Kong, 1841–1962* (Hong Kong: Hong Kong University Press, 1964), Appendix B and Appendix D.
6. For a survey of the electoral reform proposals in Hong Kong's past going back to the beginning, see Endacott, *Government and People, passim.*

majority and mark the end of British rule.[7] Little therefore came of the continuing weak pressures for change as London's 19th-century excuses were gradually reinforced by more familiar 20th-century concerns. In this way, colonial conservatism survived the first upsurge of Chinese national-ism in the 1920s, economic depression during the 1930s, the 1941–45 Japanese occupation, and then the next attempt at political reform as well, adapting with relative ease to Hong Kong's changing post-war environ-ment. This last offered a new rationale in the form of Chinese commu-nism and an excuse to update the old 19th-century logic which had distrusted both Hong Kong's British businessmen-adventurers and its Chinese majority. In post-war Hong Kong, London finally found elite representatives of both who could be trusted to govern "responsibly" and all united against the Chinese majority or, more accurately, against certain "dangers" posed by an active minority developing in its midst.

Reaffirming the political legacy, 1945–52. The new formulation emerged during a painstaking exercise which continued between 1945 and 1952, when the arguments against political reform again emerged triumphant. As had happened several times before in Hong Kong, de-mands for change were initiated from above, in this case by a Hong Kong governor, Mark Young, and the Colonial Office itself. London's aim was to give Hong Kong residents a "more responsible share in the manage-ment of their own affairs" and thereby win public support for Britain's continued sovereignty over it, against the rising anti-colonial claims of China's national Kuomintang-led government. Opponents included Young's successor, Alexander Grantham, and all the Legislative Coun-cil's unofficial members representing Hong Kong's most powerful British and Chinese business interests.[8] Although the exercise came to nothing, it was important for the precedents it set. Just as earlier reform proposals had always provided opportunities to reaffirm the logic of conservative colonial rule, so the 1945–52 experience did the same, reformulating an antiquated political philosophy that Hong Kong would carry back to China 50 years later, and on into the 21st century. That legacy is best illustrated in the arguments mustered against the reform proposals which elaborated two main themes: appropriate forms of governance and the dangers of political disruption.

Underscoring elite concerns, however, were some popular voices that took up the cause of reform with unanticipated vigour. This new constitu-ency included British professionals and other expatriates, but members were most numerous among an intermediate "middling" group of Chinese merchants, manufacturers, professionals, trade unionists and others. Their interests were channelled through a host of local organizations, chambers

7. N. J. Miners, "Plans for constitutional reform in Hong Kong, 1946–52," *The China Quarterly*, No. 107 (September 1986), p. 464.
8. On this period, see especially, Steve Yui-Sang Tsang, *Democracy Shelved: Great Britain, China, and Attempts at Constitutional Reform in Hong Kong, 1945–1952* (Hong Kong: Oxford University Press, 1988); also Miners, "Plans for constitutional reform," pp. 463–482.

of commerce, residents associations, political reform clubs and the like. Reacting to the Legislative Council's June 1949 unanimous vote against Young's plan, representatives of 142 such organizations, with a combined membership of 141,800 people, signed a petition in July calling for that plan and much more. They not only liked Young's new city council idea but wanted Legislative Council reforms as well, proposing a majority of unofficial members, most of whom would be Chinese irrespective of nationality, with all unofficials elected under an unrestricted franchise.[9]

Hong Kong's ruling elite nevertheless won the day, albeit with arguments that evolved somewhat between 1949 and 1952, as the mainland victory of Chinese communism provided new excuses to reinforce old assumptions. The most forthright statements opposing reform, "before and after" that victory, were those of unofficial Legislative Council member Sir Man Kam Lo and Governor Grantham. In his speech preceding the 22 June 1949 vote, which vetoed Young's plan while proposing an intermediate alternative, Lo said that Hong Kong's government was responsible for the community as a whole and unofficial Legislative Council members represented its interests without racial or sectoral bias. He belaboured the difficulties of devising constituencies that would fairly reflect Hong Kong's ethnic and national diversities, but was especially emphatic in denying that elected representatives could do a better job of representing the community than appointees.[10]

Governor Grantham himself then devised another scheme, which he proposed as the most appropriate of all, based solely on the nomination or indirect election of unofficial legislators by corporate and occupational bodies. Eventually, in 1952, the unofficials requested that all reforms be dropped and London concurred. Only much later did Grantham spell out fully why he had agreed with the opponents of democratic reform. First, as a result of its unique historical circumstances, Hong Kong could never proceed like other colonies towards independence but must remain a colony or revert to China. Secondly, Hong Kong could not proceed towards self-government because it was a Chinese city and the Chinese were "generally speaking, politically apathetic" preferring "to leave the business of government to the professionals." Thirdly, most Hong Kong Chinese did not regard themselves as permanent citizens and so felt little loyalty to the colony. As for immediate practical concerns, Grantham and the unofficials finally understood in 1952 the potential "difficulties and dangers" of the course they instinctively opposed. They worried specifically about the ease with which Chinese politics could infiltrate an elected Hong Kong legislature and the probable disruptive effect of such an occurrence.[11]

9. Endacott, *Government and People*, pp. 194–195; Tsang, *Democracy Shelved*, pp. 143–150.

10. *Hong Kong Hansard: Reports of the Meetings of the Legislative Council of Hong Kong*, Session 1949, 22 June 1949, pp. 188–205.

11. Alexander Grantham, *Via Ports: From Hong Kong to Hong Kong* (Hong Kong University Press, 1965), pp. 111–12, 195. Grantham was governor of Hong Kong from 1947

These reasons or variations thereof constituted the basis for all replies to questions about political change in Hong Kong for the next 30 years. Usually, official British and Hong Kong sources would assert simply that there was no local demand or at least no consensus, and as time progressed the "dangers" were elaborated by suggesting that China itself would not tolerate any alterations in Hong Kong's form of government.[12] By 1949, in any event, it was somewhat disingenuous to suggest that Chinese were politically apathetic. Nationally, they had just spent the preceding 30 years engaged in a partisan political conflict so intense that it culminated in all-out civil war. Closer to home, an articulate Chinese minority in Hong Kong was demonstrating considerable enthusiasm for electoral reform. The reality in 1949, then, was not too little Chinese interest in politics but too much, forcing Grantham and his successors to seek refuge in conservative Chinese arguments about the 20th century's disruptive impact on traditional forms of "professional" governance. British and Chinese Hong Kong leaders thereafter joined as one in proclaiming that all Chinese in their hearts preferred the "benevolent autocracy" of an idealized Chinese past and stable colonial present, to the dangerous uncertainties of elected government.[13]

Reunification and Democratic Reform: 1982–1997

From the perspective of those who made it, the 1952 decision to abandon democratic reform seemed to be vindicated by all that followed. The colony survived as an island of calm in the developing cold war confrontation with communism and became the refuge of choice for those fleeing the excesses of China's revolution. Hong Kongers also prospered economically with incomes and living standards many times better than those of their mainland compatriots. In these ways, common bonds of economic interest and ideological commitment were established between Hong Kong's elites and the general public that often mystified outsiders.

The political price of Hong Kong's colonial idyll finally came due exactly 30 years after the 1952 bargain was struck, however, when China announced its intention to resume sovereignty as of 1997. The price was

---

footnote continued

to 1957. His above-cited views, published in 1965, were identical to those he articulated internally in 1950 (see Tsang, *Democracy Shelved*, esp. pp. 122–23).

12. With the most sensitive government files still closed, despite Britain's 30-year access rule, all the arguments remain tentative for want of authoritative documentation. For an updated review of relevant documents available, see Peter Wesley-Smith, *Unequal Treaty, 1898–1997: China, Great Britain, and Hong Kong's New Territories* (Hong Kong: Oxford University Press, rev. ed., 1998), pp. 237–270; Steve Tsang, "Strategy for survival: the Cold War and Hong Kong's policy towards Kuomintang and Chinese Communist activities in the 1950s," *Journal of Imperial and Commonwealth History*, Vol. 25, No. 2 (May 1997), pp. 294–317; and, David Clayton, *Imperialism Revisited: Political and Economic Relations Between Britain and China, 1950–54* (New York: St Martin's Press, 1997), ch. five (pp. 96–122).

13. The term "benevolent autocracy" was used by Grantham and later by Patten critic Percy Cradock, to characterize Hong Kong's form of colonial government. See Tsang, *Democracy Shelved*, p. 64; and Percy Cradock, *Experiences of China* (London: John Murray, 1994) p. 226.

substantial both in terms of political positives lost during those three decades and the negatives gained. Concerning the losses, a city of five million people had no experience with self-government either in principle or practice, whether as a subject of study in the classroom or an arena for direct participation, and concepts about political power deriving from the people governed were non-existent.[14] This blank space seemed all the more anomalous in that Hong Kong advertised itself as an open society with all the basic rights and freedoms. Hong Kong did in fact enjoy all such benefits – except as applied to public participation in government and politics.

As for negative acquisitions, Hong Kong's political philosophy of "benevolent autocracy" had taken on some hard edges while defending the colony's interests, and its people were not necessarily the undifferentiated mass of happy subjects suggested by their common interests and commitments. First, the basic rationale had been allowed to calcify. Decision-makers evidently came to accept as unbending truth that democratic reform must be equated with representative government, which in turn meant self-government and independence, which China would never tolerate. Thus, there is no evidence that less drastic intermediate alternatives were ever even raised with Chinese leaders much less rejected by them. There are many indications, however, that Chinese leaders also came to accept the Grantham-ite logic which equated political reform by definition with independence.

Secondly, the ways and means of governing had also been allowed to calcify. From Grantham's day onwards, the Hong Kong government's greatest immediate fear was always said to be the disruptive potential of Chinese civil war politics. Curbs on home-grown as well as imported political activity were strictly enforced to prevent that potential for conflict between Chinese communist supporters and opponents from ever being realized. All kinds of potentially destabilizing public activism were therefore nipped in the bud. Besides the selective deportation of ringleaders and outside agitators, a range of other more and less subtle means of getting the message across became accepted modes for countering even the most innocuous expressions of dissent, and these means continued in use until the early 1980s.

Since most conventional forms of political activity were also disallowed, there remains no way of knowing what the public's preferences actually were, which points to a third negative consequence. Eventually it became apparent that an intense unarticulated polarization had taken root. In 1949, when political reform became a subject of some community interest, China's civil war politics did not loom very large.

14. A fairly extensive critical literature now exists on civic education past and present in Hong Kong. See, for example, Paul Morris, "Preparing pupils as citizens of the Special Administrative Region of Hong Kong: an analysis of curriculum change and control during the transition period," in Gerard A. Postiglione (ed.), *Education and Society in Hong Kong* (Armonk, NY: M. E. Sharpe, 1992), pp. 117–145; Thomas Kwan-choi Tse, *The Poverty of Political Education in Hong Kong Secondary Schools*, Hong Kong Institute of Asia-Pacific Studies, Chinese University of Hong Kong, Occasional Paper no. 69 (November 1997), esp. the reference list which includes both Chinese and English sources.

Representatives, both official and otherwise, of the warring Communist and Nationalist Parties had long been based in Hong Kong and both sides could claim supporters locally. But the public as a whole seems not to have been particularly partisan. Wider polarization only set in gradually, as the newly victorious communist revolution progressed through its ever more radical phases, sending repeated waves of disaffected émigrés across the border into Hong Kong.

After a mass one-million exodus during the Japanese occupation, Hong Kong's population had returned to its pre-war level of about 1.6 million by late 1946. Then in 1949, the next influx from China began. The population reached 2.25 million in 1952, 3 million in 1960 and 5 million in 1980. The 1981 census suggested that Hong Kong was beginning to acquire a more "settled" aspect since 57 per cent of its people were found to be locally born. Yet it still would not have been an exaggeration to claim that a majority of Hong Kong's residents were either themselves migrants from post-1949 China or related to someone who was.[15]

Whatever people's individual histories, at some point their experiences coalesced just enough to transform Hong Kong into an anti-communist town. Hence by the early 1980s, it also would not have been an exaggeration to say that a majority of Hong Kong people at both popular and elite levels, the latter including both British and Chinese, were essentially united in their negative views about Chinese communism. This basic orientation was moderated but not substantially altered by the leftward drift of student activists in the early 1970s, and the growing economic ties between Hong Kong and China in the 1980s. Indeed, so strong was the anti-communist mainstream that an equally committed "opposition" remained all but invisible. This was Hong Kong's own pro-China pro-communist minority (which preferred to be called *aiguo* or patriotic before 1997 but now sometimes distinguishes itself as *chuantong zuopai* or traditional left). Unacknowledged lines were drawn around this minority excluding its members from all the colony's social, intellectual and governing establishments. A kind of unspoken agreement thus evolved whereby Hong Kong's pro-China partisans kept to themselves, ran their own schools, read their own newspapers and worked in China-oriented organizations. Largest and most long-standing among these was the Federation of Trade Unions with an affiliated membership of nearly 200,000 in the 1980s. The multi-purpose local branch of the New China News Agency (NCNA or Xinhua) served as a news service, as well as China's *de facto* embassy in the territory, headquarters for its patriotic community and cover for Hong Kong's "underground" or unacknowledged Chinese Communist Party (CCP) branch.

15. *Hong Kong Annual Report, 1952* (Hong Kong Government Printer), p. 27; *Hong Kong: Report for the Year 1961* (Hong Kong Government Press, 1962), p. 24; *Hong Kong 1982* (Hong Kong Government Printer, 1982), pp. 227–28; John P. Burns, "Immigration from China and the future of Hong Kong," *Asian Survey*, June 1987, pp. 661–682.

Confronting the Hong Kong conundrum. The terms of engagement then changed dramatically, once reunification loomed as an inescapable reality. Unlike virtually all Britain's possessions before it, Hong Kong remained unschooled in the civilian arts of formal political self-defence, and the transition back to Chinese rule would take place in full view of a world for which colonialism had long since been discredited. Meanwhile, China itself had just embarked on a new path of national reform suggesting that the political skills Hong Kong should have learned under British tutelage might actually be put to good use. Hence as soon as Britain had to begin contemplating precedents, legacies and historical verdicts, the old conundrum was almost instantly transformed. In the past, concern about the Chinese and China had always blocked constitutional change. Suddenly the dilemma was turned on its head: fear of China made reform essential.

The precise timing of London's reversal is not yet clear in relation to China's 1982 decision on resuming sovereignty, since what the British knew and when they knew it remains undocumented. Hong Kong's governor, Murray MacLehose, visited Beijing in 1979 and asked for some word on Hong Kong's future, but Chinese leader Deng Xiaoping refused to give a definite answer except for his enigmatic advisory about telling investors to put their hearts at ease. According to one authoritative Chinese source, Deng said specifically that China might resume sovereignty but no decision had yet been made. Informal exchanges then occurred between 1979 and 1981, during which the Chinese tried in vain to win British approval for a "Macau solution." Following Portugal's 1974 revolution and consequent offer to return Macau immediately, Lisbon conceded sovereignty but agreed to maintain the status quo indefinitely under Portuguese rule, albeit at China's discretion.[16]

Thus from 1979, British leaders at least knew what the public did not, namely that some change in Hong Kong's status might well occur. Decisions were then evidently made in deference to the changing context, since within a year after the governor's March 1979 visit to Beijing political reform was under way in Hong Kong. The historic nature of the policy shift was obscured by its seeming insignificance, having been announced only in the form of a government green paper, or official proposal, entitled "A Pattern of District Administration in Hong Kong." Issued in June 1980, it suggested the addition of an "elected element" in the diverse local advisory boards and committees that had grown up during the 1970s. Elections would be direct, by universal suffrage, for a

16. Huang Wenfang, *Zhongguo dui Xianggang huifu xingshi zhuquan de juece licheng yu zhixing (China's Resumption of Sovereignty Over Hong Kong: Decision-Making and Implemention)* (Hong Kong: Institute for East-West Studies, Baptist University, 1997), ch. 1 (pp. 1–24). As a senior NCNA official in Hong Kong, Huang had considerable first-hand knowledge of the events described. Evidently, Britain's Labour government had actually been considering some such Macau-type solution, but the idea was dropped by its Conservative successor, which won the general election in early 1979. See Robert Cottrell, *The End of Hong Kong: The Secret Diplomacy of Imperial Retreat* (London: John Murray, 1993), pp. 49–50. After the die was cast, Britain did try in 1982–83, without success, to barter sovereignty for a continuing British administrative presence.

portion of members only, and Urban Council elections should also be conducted in the same manner. The Urban Council was responsible for recreation, public sanitation and a few other such basic chores.

The policy was formalized in a January 1981 white paper on "District Administration in Hong Kong." Reforms then unfolded swiftly, considering the century and more spent contemplating their dangers. Local bodies were rationalized territory-wide into District Boards. Boundaries were drawn, constituencies formed and the proportion of elected to appointed seats fixed. The former numbered roughly one-third of the new District Board membership or about 130 people in all. A Regional Council was also created to oversee, for suburban areas, the same tasks long performed by the Urban Council in town. The more important aim was to create a uniform territory-wide second tier of representative public offices to serve, along with the District Boards, as grassroots training grounds for both voters and budding politicians. Hong Kong's first ever direct election under universal suffrage, for the District Board seats, occurred in a phased sequence beginning in March and completed in September 1982, the same month Margaret Thatcher went to Beijing and confirmed Hong Kong's 1997 date with China.

In the hue and cry that ensued, Hong Kong's governance was initially the least of everyone's concerns. Once it became clear there could be no post-1997 British presence, however, their negotiators set about writing as many safeguards as possible into the reunification agreements. Thereafter the idea took hold, with official encouragement, that Hong Kong must provide its own last line of defence and that this was best done through institutions of local self-government. The 1984 Joint Declaration formally conceding sovereignty contained China's 12-point guarantee as well, promising autonomy and continuity of social and economic systems, but saying nothing about democratic reform. British negotiators took credit for plugging the loophole with an elaboration in the accompanying annex. The legislature, it declared, "shall be constituted by elections" and executive authorities "shall be accountable to the legislature," which would imply a substantial change over the existing colonial system.

The September 1984 Joint Declaration was also bracketed by another pair of Hong Kong government green and white papers in July and November respectively. Entitled, "The Further Development of Representative Government in Hong Kong," they extended political reform to the Legislative Council (LegCo). The aim was now forthrightly stated: to develop a system of government, "firmly rooted" in Hong Kong and "more directly accountable" to its people. Interestingly, Hong Kong now seemed to pick up where it had signed off on electoral reforms in the late 1940s, when people had in turn seemed to pick up where they left off in the 1920s. Initiatives were taken by Hong Kong's British leaders, for whatever reason, but an articulate Chinese "middling" minority soon took up the cause of political reform, while the government's erstwhile elite Chinese allies began building the case against it. The Hong Kong government, for its part, seemed to be reaching back to Grantham's 1950 counter-reform plan for indirect Legislative Council elections by corporate or professional bodies only.

Grantham's proposal actually derived from long-standing Hong Kong custom which had evolved from its earliest days and then lived on in the practice, taken up more systematically by Governor MacLehose than his predecessors, of appointing unofficial legislators from a growing cross-section of community leaders. By the 1980s, these were still being drawn primarily from business and banking, but included also representation from industry, the professions and trade unions. The 1984 changes formalized this practice by creating nine "functional constituencies" and giving them the right to elect 12 unofficial legislators. An additional 12 would be chosen by an electoral college composed of all members (including both elected and appointed) of the District Boards, plus those of the Urban and Regional Councils. A "safe" majority of appointed official and unofficial members (10 and 22 respectively) was retained in LegCo's 56-seat chamber, exclusive of the governor who served concurrently as council president. A review, scheduled for 1987, would consider the possibility of progression towards direct elections. Hong Kong's inaugural Legislative Council poll under the new functional constituency system was held in September 1985.

Relevant Chinese reactions indicated the mix of local pressures for continuity and change. Conservative views dominated among the pillars of Hong Kong's various establishments and, like their predecessors in the 1940s, these community leaders continued to be well represented in the Legislative Council. When it debated the July 1984 green paper, they were also still worrying about everything. Stability was foremost in their minds as the main prerequisite for maintaining investor confidence and prosperity. Hong Kong's colonial government was based on principles of consultation and consensus, in keeping with the conventional Chinese preference for public harmony. Electoral reform anticipated just the opposite, admonished the councillors, and would therefore be anathema within the local community. They claimed that the "avalanche" of public demands for democracy and elections represented only a "thin slice" of public opinion, while the majority in fact ranged from "total indifference to complete ignorance." Councillors therefore argued that direct elections were premature. Meanwhile, appointments, indirect election and the functional constituencies would "permit the elite of our community" to continue in service to its people.[17]

Advocates of political change, by contrast, were mostly young, outspoken and uninhibited in their enthusiasm for Western concepts of popular authority and accountable government. Virtually everyone nevertheless confined their activism within the boundaries defined by the government's limited initiative, albeit mindful of its promise to consider direct elections. Public consultations were held on the July 1984 green paper and "for the first time in Hong Kong's history," the proposed

17. Councillors' commentaries are from the Legislative Council debate on the 1984 green paper, in *Hong Kong Hansard*, 2 August 1984, pp. 1352–1412.

reforms brought together 89 separate interest groups for a mass rally in September. A thousand people from varied backgrounds – teachers, social workers, journalists, students and trade unionists among others – joined in demanding democratic self-administration.[18]

If this emerging liberal-conservative divide evoked memories of the past, however, 1997 produced the main new impetus for change. Lawyer Martin Lee's surprise victory over a favoured opponent contesting the legal constituency seat in the 1985 Legislative Council election signalled the force of the new element. His victory gave the council its most articulate advocate for a faster pace of democratization, on the grounds that popularly elected government would provide the best safeguard against the possible future excesses of Chinese rule.[19] The business community disparaged this perspective as well, arguing that Hong Kong's survival depended not on antagonizing China but on contributing to its economic development. Lee and like-minded partisans were nevertheless undaunted, and Hong Kong's political spectrum emerged from the debates over this question, with China's suspicions encouraging both elite reservations and popular enthusiasm for more democratic reform rather than less.

China's Basic Law solution. Bound by the conflicting imperatives of Hong Kong's transition, Britain had to balance awkwardly between its new liberal and old conservative roles. China, for its part, inherited all the departing sovereign's fears about democracy and especially about the endemic dangers of 20th-century Chinese politics which lived on beneath Hong Kong's placid political surface. While they were contemplating the potential hazards of incorporating an anti-communist town within the confines of their communist-led Chinese state, however, Beijing's leaders learned about colonialism's various ways of producing "safe" outcomes and reliable parliamentary majorities. There were intermediate solutions short of independence after all, and these proved especially useful in designing constitutional arrangements for the "one country, two systems" experiment. Hong Kong's 1984 incremental reform plan included several such ingenious devices for introducing limited electoral representation and China borrowed freely from all of them.

The Beijing-led Basic Law Drafting Committee was formed in 1985, with 36 mainland members and 23 from Hong Kong. When the law was promulgated five years later, it revealed a system patterned on Hong Kong's 1984 reform model, albeit with an even more elaborate complex of checks and balances. Lobbying had been intense on all sides throughout the drafting process, with those advocating a faster pace of democra-

18. *South China Morning Post*, Hong Kong, and *Hong Kong Standard*, both 17 September 1984. For a useful collection of early popular views inspired by the 1997 question, see Joseph Y. S. Cheng (ed.), *Hong Kong in Search of a Future* (Hong Kong: Oxford University Press, 1984), *passim*; also, Lo Shiu-hing, *The Politics of Democratization in Hong Kong* (New York: St Martin's Press, 1997), chs 2–4 (pp. 67–176).

19. See, for example, Martin Lee's maiden speech in the Legislative Council (*Hong Kong Hansard*, 27 November 1985, pp. 146–49).

tization striving to make their influence felt on the coalition of business interests, professional conservatives and pro-China partisans that dominated the committee. Meanwhile, China had warned Britain repeatedly that it should not create before 1997, a political system incompatible with China's post-1997 plans. Britain accepted the principle of convergence and postponed further democratic reform until after the Basic Law's scheduled 1990 promulgation.[20]

In Hong Kong, however, China's 1989 crackdown on student protesters gave a tremendous boost not just to the demand for self-government as a safeguard against Chinese interference, but also to the more "subversive" corollary that Hong Kong's only real protection was the democratization of China itself. Hong Kong's most active democrats, including Martin Lee and teachers' union leader Szeto Wah, formed a new group at this time, the Hong Kong Alliance in Support of the Patriotic Democratic Movement in China. Beijing's leaders quickly dubbed the alliance subversive in its aims which were, and remain, dedicated to that corollary. Yet even Hong Kong's conservative establishment was now tempted by its logic. So intense were the emotions generated by Tiananmen that conservative and liberal wings of the Legislative and Executive Councils' non-official members (the colonial term "unofficials" was dropped during the mid-1980s) reached an unprecedented consensus in July 1989. Implicitly acknowledging popular representation as a guarantee of autonomy, councillors called for a third of all legislators to be directly elected in 1991, at least half by 1995, and suggested also direct election of the chief executive, as the governor was to be called after 1997. By these standards, the Basic Law was indeed a disappointment, although perhaps not quite the "shameful act of surrender" proclaimed by some democrats.

As future sovereign, China's fears loomed overall. These were addressed first and foremost by the overriding powers granted to the chief executive vis-à-vis the legislature, and by the multiple constraints drawn around its directly elected members. The Basic Law typically consigned application of the Joint Declaration's most liberal principles to the far distant future or checked and balanced them against someone else's safeguards. Thus it stipulated universal suffrage to be the "ultimate aim" for electing both the chief executive and all Legislative Council members (articles 45 and 68), and the executive authorities were still accountable to the legislature (article 64). But the councillors' 1989 consensus in favour of a 50–50 division between directly and indirectly elected representation was postponed until the third SAR legislature (2003–

---

20. Also evoking memories of the past was the Hong Kong government's manipulation of its promised reform review in 1987. This conformed to long-standing colonial precedent whereby petitions for reform were dismissed as "unrepresentative." On the controversy surrounding the 1987 exercise, see Mark Roberti, *The Fall of Hong Kong: China's Triumph and Britain's Betrayal* (New York: John Wiley, 1996, rev. ed.), ch. 17 (pp. 197–210); Norman Miners, *The Government and Politics of Hong Kong* (Hong Kong: Oxford University Press, 1991, 5th ed.), pp. 26–27; and, Jonathan Dimbleby, *The Last Governor* (London: Warner Books, 1998), pp. 129–130.

2007), with built-in constraints against the realistic possibility of progressive development thereafter (annex II).

The first SAR legislature would be allowed only 20 directly elected members in a 60-seat chamber, with a "safe" majority of 40 including 30 seats to be filled by the functional constituencies and ten by an electoral college of complex origin. The electoral college was itself to consist of 800 members, also elected mostly by the functional constituencies but with the mandatory inclusion as well of all Hong Kong's deputies to China's National People's Congress plus a selection of Hong Kong representatives to the Chinese People's Political Consultative Conference (annex I). The latter two groups were intended to guarantee places for members of Hong Kong's pro-China community who dominated local representation on the national bodies and would also provide an otherwise unacknowledged direct link between them and Hong Kong's local legislature. Basic Law drafters had obviously mastered the British colonial art of "safe" constitutional design.

The Patten finale. Perhaps it was because Britain's 150-year stewardship over Hong Kong had been one of such unmitigated equivocation on the matter of electoral reform, that Prime Minister John Major decided to make one last grand gesture. With documentation still not available, however, this decision remains as obscure as the initial shift that occurred some time between March 1979 and June 1980. Presumably, considerations in 1992 were mostly strategic. Hong Kong had been traumatized by Tiananmen, which in turn hastened the new elite consensus for democratic reform, and if the wider public had ever been truly apathetic it was no more. Since the Basic Law permitted 20 directly elected seats in the first SAR legislature, Hong Kong was now free to introduce such a change and had begun with 18 Legislative Council seats in the 1991 poll. Democratic politicians ultimately won 17 of the seats, surprising only conservative pundits too slow to catch the changing public mood. They predicted among other things that the novice Chinese electorate would not demonstrate partisan preferences. Its size overall was also growing – from 342,700 votes cast in the first May/September 1982 District Board elections, to half a million in the 1985 district polls and 750,000 for the Legislative Council in 1991.

Although restrictions on overt political organizing remained, electioneering was allowed and 1980s-style pressure groups eased into the role of political parties.[21] Several such groups sponsored candidates in 1991. Most popular was the United Democrats of Hong Kong formed in 1990, after Lee, Szeto and others from the Hong Kong Alliance decided to separate its (potentially dangerous) China-support activities from those of Hong Kong politicking. This group grew into the Democratic Party after

21. On Hong Kong's early 1990s political evolution, see, Louie Kin-sheun, "Political parties," in Sung Yun-wing and Lee Ming-Kwan (eds.), *The Other Hong Kong Report, 1991* (Hong Kong: Chinese University Press, 1991), pp. 55–75; Donald H. McMillen and Michael E. DeGolyer (eds.), *One Culture, Many Systems: Politics in the Reunification of China* (Hong Kong: Chinese University Press, 1993), part one, *passim.*

restrictions were finally lifted a few years later. Despite the political fragmentation, however, Hong Kong voters demonstrated a clear preference for candidates belonging to the "democratic camp." These were easily distinguished by their platforms advocating directly elected representative government as the best guarantee for Hong Kong's future autonomy. As a rough rule-of-thumb, the more outspoken candidates were in this respect, the more votes they won. This new maxim was epitomized in the 1991 victory and ongoing popularity of journalist-turned-politician Emily Lau.

Besides the new mood in Hong Kong, however, a second consideration for London must have been the massive shift in international power and public opinion following the collapse of communism between 1989 and 1991. Given the enormity of this new world trend, it seemed evident that China would not be able to escape its impact. Presumably for all these reasons, then, London decided to turn Hong Kong's final five-year gubernatorial term into a crash course on democratic institution-building and citizenship.[22] Whether by accident or design, the effect of that decision was enhanced by John Major's choice for governor since all previous incumbents had had conventional colonial and foreign service backgrounds. By contrast, Conservative Party politician Chris Patten possessed an acerbic wit and had the licence to use it, which fitted perfectly with Hong Kong's new mood of defiance. The reforms Patten introduced were as much about style as substance and he was clearly at ease in his new role. Walkabouts, radio phone-in talk shows, town hall meetings and Legislative Council question time all became regular features of his repertoire. One aim of this new gubernatorial style was to court public opinion for his cause; a second was part of that cause itself, namely, to set an example in promoting more open and responsive government. The second would eventually come to be appreciated by almost everyone, including both those who applauded his overall purpose of strengthening democratic reform and those who did not.

The nature of Patten's assignment was not announced in advance, however, nor did London trouble to consult Beijing. Concerning substance, what came to be known as the Patten reform package was unveiled in his first policy address at the start of the 1992–93 legislative year.[23] Although advertised as a modest pre-1997 preface for the Basic Law's post-1997 programme, Patten's plans actually entailed a thorough overhaul of Hong Kong's governing institutions. The aim was to make them as fully and directly elected as possible while keeping within the letter of the Basic Law by exploiting its loopholes and grey areas. For example, the Basic Law did not even deal with the District Boards and municipal councils (local shorthand for the Urban and Regional Coun-

---

22. Although couched in careful parliamentary prose, these reasons for London's 1992 shift are evident, in "Relations between the United Kingdom and China in the period up to and beyond 1997," Foreign Affairs Committee, House of Commons, 23 March 1994.

23. Patten's address seems to be the only document outlining his programme in full. See, "Our next five years: the agenda for Hong Kong," *Hong Kong Hansard*, 7 October 1992, pp. 14–49.

cils), referring to them as consultative bodies and not "organs of political power." As of 1992, about one-third of their members were still appointed. Under the new plan, all these bodies were to become fully and directly elected by universal suffrage, as the basic building blocks of Hong Kong's new democratic government.

The Legislative Council presented a greater challenge since the Basic Law specified its make-up in some detail and the principle of convergence between pre- and post-1997 arrangements had been accepted by both Britain and China. The 20 directly elected seats therefore remained unchanged, but Patten essentially ignored the cumbersome Basic Law-style electoral college (responsible for filling ten LegCo seats). Instead, he adapted Hong Kong's 1985 body, except that now all the District Board members who would make up the electoral college were themselves to be directly elected. There remained the 30 seats which the Basic Law had allocated to the functional constituencies. By the 1991 election, Hong Kong's functional constituency seats had been expanded to 21, but the constituencies themselves were still small and narrowly based on professional divisions of labour. The Patten plan retained these 21 old-style seats, although the complicated voting methods were reformed somewhat to replace corporate with individual balloting. Additionally, nine new large constituencies were created, designed to represent not just employers and professionals but all working people in Hong Kong. Only the unemployed and retirees did not qualify to claim a second vote through one of them. The net result of these changes was to create, in effect, nine new directly elected seats, plus ten elected by District Board members who would themselves be directly elected. Hence, with 19 seats filled from Hong Kong's "grassroots," in addition to the 20 directly elected seats, the Basic Law's carefully crafted safe majority was safe no more.[24]

In China's eyes, therefore, Patten's transgressions were multiple and varied.[25] Playing to the fears of post-Tiananmen audiences both local and international, he had produced one last grand electoral design to counter China's own Basic Law adaptation. In 1993, after Beijing's leaders realized the new governor could not be deflected from his purpose, they declared his plans to be in violation of the Basic Law. Any attempt to implement them would be invalidated in 1997. Instead of co-operating on the so-called "through-train" of convergence between institutional developments before and after 1997, the two principals then went their separate

24. For Patten's perspective on the reforms, see, Dimbleby, *The Last Governor*, *passim*; for another view: Steve Tsang, *Hong Kong: Appointment with China* (London: I.B. Tauris, 1997), ch. 9 (pp. 181–208).

25. British Foreign Office regulars generally took exception to the Pattern reform package on the grounds that China would never accept it. Hence potential risks in terms of Chinese retribution might well outweigh short-term gains. The old hands also knew more than did Patten about the effort to win China's acceptance for directly elected LegCo seats which, due to the convergence agreement, had been the subject of considerable discussion between Britain and China during the Basic Law's final drafting stage. In the acrimonious dispute that followed, China forced the release of relevant 1990 correspondence between the British and Chinese foreign ministers, which everyone on the British side allegedly "forgot" to share with Patten. The correspondence was published in *Renmin ribao (haiwaiban)* (*People's Daily*, overseas edition) and *China Daily*, both 29 October 1992.

ways. China began laying the foundations for Hong Kong's post-1997 Basic Law government, Patten implemented his reform package, and the stage was set in Hong Kong for a clear partisan confrontation. Democrats united in support of Patten's reforms while a coalition of pro-China loyalists and business people rallied behind Beijing's strict constructionist interpretation of the Basic Law.[26]

Yet despite China's wrath and the lack of consensus – or perhaps because of both – Hong Kong's commitment to electoral reform seemed to strengthen as the sequence of council elections proceeded under Patten's rules in 1994 and 1995. Although not an uncritical champion of those rules, Allen Lee exemplified the new norms when he decided to contest a directly elected seat in 1995. As founder of the new pro-business Liberal Party, he was mindful of its members' dependence on the functional constituencies and said he wanted the additional authority that only a popular mandate could bring. Even more significant was a similar decision by Hong Kong's patriotic community. After the Basic Law authorized directly elected seats for the SAR legislature, Beijing together with Hong Kong's pro-China leaders decided that the community's leaders must enter Hong Kong's brave new world of electoral politics or lose any chance of exercising popularly accepted authority therein. Some pro-China candidates did join the 1991 contest but could not compete with prevailing anti-China sentiments so soon after Tiananmen. They persevered nevertheless and in 1992 established a political group of their own, the Democratic Alliance for the Betterment of Hong Kong (DAB). Many of its members were concurrently active in the Federation of Trade Unions.

Pro-China candidates and sympathizers then did reasonably well in the small District Board constituencies in 1994, since residential patterns gave them an edge in several urban and suburban areas. Like everyone else, they learned fast and were soon campaigning about grassroots concerns and the need to elect local leaders not antagonistic to China. Additionally, the pro-China community was able to adapt its traditional "united front" tactics to the new situation and encouraged alliances mostly with sympathetic business people in town and "rural" conservatives in the suburbs. Such new supporters opposed the democrats' aggressive demands that, by the mid-1990s, included a wide range of long-overdue civil, social and economic legislation. Yet the new supporters did not share a complete identity of interests with the DAB, which represented primarily the traditional patriotic left and labour. Hence the New China News Agency's political staffers encouraged the formation of other pro-business pro-China groups which later merged to become the Hong Kong Progressive Alliance (HKPA).

Looking to the future, the 1995 election's partisan results thus provided a good illustration of Hong Kong's developing political spectrum, as well as the checks and balances built upon its complex mix of political and social interests. The turnout rate was still not impressive. At only 36 per

26. See, for example, *Hong Kong Hansard*, 29 June 1994, pp. 4690–5049.

cent of all registered voters, it seemed to vindicate the conclusions of conservative analysts still guided by assumptions about Hong Kong's political apathy. But in absolute terms, the number of votes cast had continued to rise: from 750,000 in 1991 to 920,500 in 1995, among 2.57 million on the final registrar's list, in a city of six million. Pro-democracy candidates again topped the poll. They included like-minded independents such as Emily Lau and members of the new Democratic Party. These candidates took something over 60 per cent of the one million votes cast for the 20 directly elected seats and won 14. Pro-China candidates and their declared allies won about 30 per cent of the popular vote, demonstrating the extent of public support for this sector in a way that had never before been possible.[27] But it won only two of the directly elected seats. Of the remaining four, two went to another small democratic party, the Association for Democracy and People's Livelihood (ADPL), which was more moderate than others on the question of confronting China. The other two were filled by the pro-business Liberal Party and an independent.

Pro-China forces were nevertheless successful in exploiting their support at the District Board level and won six of the ten electoral college seats, as well as an additional eight in the functional constituencies. By contrast, democrats won only a handful of additional seats in these two categories combined. Pro-business candidates did poorly in all the directly elected contests, but recouped their losses in the functional constituencies, to reach a total of ten seats (not including those who overtly declared for the pro-China side). Overall, 25 seats were solidly in the democratic camp (19 Democratic Party and six others); the pro-China coalition won 16; and pro-business candidates, ten. The balance was held by a few "true" independents and four ADPL legislators, who usually voted with the democrats.

Reconstructing Hong Kong's Post-1997 Political Order: Colonial Frame, Mainland Fixtures, Hong Kong Style

As Beijing promised, Patten's designs were all deactivated during the early hours of 1 July 1997. Formal preparations proceeded on schedule from December 1995, and by late 1998 the new system was essentially complete. Since the transition back to Chinese sovereignty overall was far smoother than anyone dared hope beforehand, with all of Hong Kong's basic rights and freedoms remaining unchanged, the impact of its new governing arrangements was minimized. Nevertheless, the imposition of Basic Law rule was carried out with a determination that belied the

27. Calculations are my own based on the official election results (*South China Morning Post*, 19 September 1995). One pro-China source estimated 34% of the popular vote in the geographic constituencies for its candidates and 61% for the democrats (*Wenhui bao*, 22 September 1995). Patten claimed that democrats received about 60% of the popular vote both in 1991 and 1995 (*South China Morning Post*, 2 October 1995); depending on candidate categorization, some calculations placed the democratic camp's share of the vote as high as 65–66%.

smiling face and political inexperience of Hong Kong's first SAR chief executive, Tung Chee-hwa.

Whereas Patten had exploited opportunities to enlarge the scope for direct elections and thereby enhance the exposure of Hong Kong's most popular politicians, now the opposite aim was pursued with every bit as much vigour. Towards that end, additional loopholes and grey areas were found in the Basic Law that had previously gone almost unnoticed. The net result is a system more checked than balanced, that will probably never grow into a workable amalgam without major revision. Hence, driven by an updated version of Hong Kong's oldest contradiction – between the need to maintain "liberal" appearances and the fear of liberal consequences – Patten's successors seemingly adapted all the devices at their disposal in deference to three overarching concerns. Those aims were to curb democratic impulses, enhance conservative corporate power and safeguard Chinese sovereignty. This last, however, had to be maintained without overt recourse to the equivalent of direct colonial rule from London, given Beijing's repeated promise of autonomy for Hong Kong's own rulers under the "one country, two systems" formula. The reconstruction of Hong Kong's post-1997 government proceeded to follow both in letter and spirit the Basic Law's prescriptions for achieving these aims.

Dismantling Patten's designs. Between 1996 and 1998, Hong Kong looked on as its sovereign-to-be introduced rules that shifted the costs of partisan confrontation dramatically, giving long-ignored patriotic neighbours a central role within the emerging political power structure. In this way, while new governing bodies were being created, Hong Kong also saw the first direct application, for local use, of what soon came to be dubbed "mainland political culture." Along with the experience came a realization that the separation-of-systems ideal was already compromised since two political cultures were already competing for influence *within Hong Kong itself.* The contrast was thus sharply drawn in public commentary, which carried on as before, between mainland and Hong Kong styles. One relied on pre-ordained shortlists and unanimous votes in stacked committees where pro-China partisans were guaranteed not just safe but overwhelming majorities. The other was held up as the antithesis in all respects.

The sequence of bodies responsible for bringing this contrast into clear public focus was the Preparatory Committee, which created the Selection Committee, which in turn selected the chief executive, the provisional legislature and Hong Kong's new delegation to the National People's Congress. The provisional legislature then passed new election laws which coloured in the Basic Law's grey areas with China red to replace Patten's Tory blue and create, via a special mid-term election held in May 1998, a new Legislative Council more strictly in keeping with Beijing's original intentions.

The Preparatory Committee (PC) was empowered to prepare all the foundations for Hong Kong's first SAR government, including personnel and policy recommendations. The 150 members were appointed by Beijing in December 1995, with 94 Hong Kong representatives and 56 from China. Most heavily represented among the latter contingent were the two bodies most directly responsible for transitional work, the Hong Kong and Macau Affairs Office (HKMAO) of the State Council in Beijing and the New China News Agency's Hong Kong branch. HK-MAO director, Lu Ping, headed the all-important PC secretariat, while Vice-Premier and Foreign Minister Qian Qichen was named committee chairman.

Hong Kong's 94 members represented the embryo of its future leadership and about 50 were business people, typically those with cross-border economic interests. The remainder were a mix, mostly of professionals. Prevailing orientations were conservative and pro-China, the latter to varying degrees that might be roughly categorized as: traditional or "old left"; "new left," indicating recently declared associations; and more peripheral "united front" commitments. Among old and new left categories, the status of some 30 individuals was reinforced by concurrent membership in one or the other of China's two national representative bodies, the National People's Congress (NPC) and the Chinese People's Political Consultative Conference (CPPCC). These delegates henceforth became mainstays in all the transitional Hong Kong bodies.

None of Hong Kong's most popular politicians was represented, however, and the democrats were noticeable by their absence. The Democratic Party's status was especially problematic because of its overlapping membership with the "subversive" Hong Kong Alliance. Some PC members, however, blamed specifically the democrats' unequivocal support for Patten's reform package as the reason for their exclusion. Among Hong Kong democrats, only the ADPL was granted representation, with two PC seats. The pro-business Liberal Party was allocated four seats. Shipping magnate Tung Chee-hwa, already being groomed as Hong Kong's new post-1997 chief executive, was named a PC vice-chairman.[28]

The Selection Committee (SC) was authorized to select the SAR's first chief executive only. Forming a provisional legislature was added to SC responsibilities only after Beijing's leaders decided to dissolve the Legislative Council elected in 1995 and replace it with an interim body as of 1 July 1997, to sit for about one year until fresh elections could be held. This decision was formalized in March 1996 by the PC which then proceeded to create the 400-member SC in accordance with stipulated proportions of 25 per cent each for four broad functional categories: business, industry and finance; professionals; labour and grassroots; and political figures including specifically all Hong Kong's incumbent NPC delegates and a selection of its CPPCC representatives as well.

Creating such a committee actually required far more organizational precision than any of Britain's old colonial formations. Formal criteria

28. *Wenhui bao*, *South China Morning Post* and *Hong Kong Standard*, all 29 December 1995.

were now overtly introduced to underline the political cost of supporting Patten's arrangements: all SC candidates had to acknowledge the legitimacy of the provisional legislature, which all but the ADPL among Patten's supporters refused to do. Ultimately, 5,700 people were accepted as candidates, but these were quickly reduced by the PC. Its secretariat produced a shortlist of 409 candidates, divided into the four categories, and even ranked candidates in order of preference. This left little for the 150 PC members to do at their 2 November 1996 plenary meeting but check the first 340 names on the list. The remaining 60 seats necessary to produce the 400-member SC were reserved for NPC and CPPCC delegates.[29]

The results were thus a foregone conclusion and the SC emerged as an enlarged replica of the PC. Two-thirds of the 400 SC members had direct links with mainland bodies, including a core bloc of 92 who were members of either the NPC or CPPCC (some of the latter were elected from other SC functional categories). Additionally, about 50 members were concurrently delegates in different provincial people's congresses and consultative conferences, mostly in Guangdong and Fujian. The pro-China establishment's electoral wing was rewarded with some 60 SC seats. These went to the two organizations (the DAB and the Federation of Trade Unions) that had fielded candidates in Hong Kong's recent directly elected contests. With its 70 seats, however, the Chinese Chamber of Commerce secured the largest bloc held by a single Hong Kong organization.[30]

Once the SC itself had been formed, the rest was relatively easy and organizers thereafter took refuge in Hong Kong's oldest political shadow play. In trying to maintain some semblance of "liberal appearances," however, they began adapting mainland rules for Hong Kong use and such rules once adapted were never quite the same again. The Basic Law stipulated that Hong Kong's first SAR chief executive must be chosen by the SC through "local consultations or through nomination and election after consultations." In fact, extensive consultation had continued informally for months. Tung Chee-hwa, who was also a member of Patten's Executive Council, had emerged by late 1995 as virtually the only choice more-or-less acceptable to everyone including China, Britain and the international business community. Nevertheless, a mini-selection campaign was organized in late 1996, rumoured to have been promoted by Chinese authorities concerned about the negative image being generated by their consultation and elite consensus methods. Ultimately, three other contenders emerged and everyone went through their paces "Hong Kong style," generating much media attention with platform presentations, press conferences and community walkabouts. In the end, of course, the SC performed as expected and Tung Chee-hwa emerged victorious in

29. A few Chinese-language newspapers printed the secretariat's ranked shortlists, e.g. *Xianggang jingji ribao* (*Hong Kong Economic Daily*), and *Xingdao ribao* (*Sing Tao Daily*), both 2 November 1996.

30. *Wenhui bao, South China Morning Post* and *Hong Kong Standard*, all 3 and 4 November 1996.

mid-December. His managers were nevertheless at least able to score one telling point over their critics since the new selection process was clearly more open to prior public scrutiny and comment than all past appointments of British governors had been.

Creating a substitute Legislative Council was more difficult to finesse, despite repeated assertions that it was the creation of Hong Kong's own SC and not by appointment from Beijing. The appearance of continuity was achieved by promising seats to as many incumbent legislators as were willing to cross over. Here the precision of pre-ordained committee voting was clearly demonstrated by an almost perfect score: 34 incumbents declared their candidacy and 33 were "elected" in SC balloting on 21 December. Except for ADPL members, however, no democratic councillors were willing to make the switch. Among the incumbents who were willing, almost all came from the conservative and pro-China camps including a total of only six who had been directly elected (DAB, 2; ADPL, 2; Liberal Party, 1; independent, 1). This result reinforced the existing division between popularly elected democrats and indirectly elected others, since the great majority of cross-over incumbents were also those who won their seats in 1995, via the old functional constituency or electoral college routes.

In this manner, if the SC emerged as a larger replica of its PC founder, the 60-member provisional legislature appeared as a concentrated version of both, notable primarily for its overlapping and concurrent memberships. Of the 60 provisional legislators, 54 had worked in the various Beijing-appointed transitional committees, including 51 who were SC members and had therefore simply selected themselves. More significant in terms of compromising the "one country, two systems" principle, however, were the overlapping memberships with China's own government bodies. Thus, the first direct link between Hong Kong's new legislative apparatus and China's counterpart was established in the form of nine provisional councillors who were concurrently incumbent members of either the NPC or CPPCC.[31]

Yet however complex, the edifice was still only in a preliminary stage of construction and the SC had not completed its labours. An unanticipated decision issued on the overriding authority of the NPC Standing Committee gave the SC one additional extra-Basic Law task, namely that of selecting the SAR's first NPC delegation. Members had previously been tapped by the local branch of the New China News Agency from within Hong Kong's pro-China community, and attached to the delegation of neighbouring Guangdong province. As a mark of its return to Chinese sovereignty, Hong Kong would have its own separate delegation, conveniently timed to coincide with the start of the new 1998–2003 term in March 1998. Following national practice, the delegation should have been elected indirectly by the provincial congress, but as Hong Kong's Legislative Council equivalent was still very much "in transition," the SC method was deemed an appropriate substitute. The SC itself was ex-

31. *Hong Kong Standard*, 22 December 1996.

panded slightly for the purpose, to 424 members, and rechristened an Electoral Conference.

By the time the exercise ended in December 1997, Hong Kong had hosted the most open and competitive election for China's NPC in that body's history, with NPC and local NCNA officials improvising step-by-step as they adapted Beijing conventions to Hong Kong's new political work style. By the time delegates took their places in Beijing, however, it was also clear that new boundaries were being drawn, as unyielding as those Hong Kong had formerly drawn against its own patriotic community. The lines and limits would now be enforced to curb Hong Kong's democratic impulses both within the NPC and in Hong Kong, where one of the mechanisms for doing so would be this same NPC delegation together with its CPPCC companion.

Although the clash between mainland and Hong Kong political cultures had been evolving in principle since 1982, the dynamic in practice had usually moved in other ways. Now for the first time, the clash was face-to-face on Hong Kong soil and the point of contact was a heretofore purely mainland institution. Multiple conflicts and controversies, including those both angry and humorous, unfolded during the month-long campaign to select Hong Kong's delegates. Most important was an abortive rapprochement with the Democratic Party.

Ultimately, the 36-member delegation was formed, in the image of its parent body, using the same kind of rank-ordered candidate lists to which the latter had grown accustomed. But official protestations to the contrary notwithstanding, the delegates' most important tasks seemed to be in Hong Kong not Beijing. Altogether, 19 of the delegates who formed Hong Kong's new teams for the NPC and CPPCC in March 1998 were concurrently members of Hong Kong's Provisional Legislative Council, occupying almost one-third of its 60 seats. Among the ten NPC and nine CPPCC delegates holding dual positions was Rita Fan who had been elected president of the provisional Hong Kong body.[32]

Keeping up appearances: Hong Kong's Basic Law government. Hong Kong's new post-1997 government naturally carried forward much from its colonial past. Most striking, however, is the continuing anomaly created by a free and open society and unfettered economy, combined with so restrictive a form of governance. Despite everyone's apprehensions and the potential for Beijing's interference, none materialized – except in the realm of government and politics. Hong Kong's new SAR government proceeded to enforce, from its first hours in office, all the institutional checks and balances prescribed by the Basic Law, and many partisan political decisions besides. The ensuing shift would have been comparable to that in an adversarial two-party parliamentary system

32. See Suzanne Pepper, "Hong Kong joins the National People's Congress: a first test for one country with two political systems," *Journal of Contemporary China*, Vol. 8, No. 21 (July 1999), pp. 319–343.

when ins and outs trade places, had the change not also entailed new rules designed to ensure the democrats would remain indefinitely marginalized

The democratic camp is therefore free to protest, lobby, contest elections and win a majority of the direct popular vote. Even the Hong Kong Alliance continues unhindered, despite continuing charges of "subversive" intent against it in the local pro-China press. Alliance members contest elections under the Democratic Party's banner along with everyone else. Yet the Basic Law's prescriptions are such that democratic legislators can occupy no more than about one-third of LegCo's 60 seats and therefore cannot win passage of any bill without conservative support. Nor indeed can any councillor introduce substantive legislation without executive consent. Additionally, Hong Kong's most popular politicians are denied any role within the all-powerful executive branch which keeps contact between it and them to an absolute minimum.

In fact, the Tung Chee-hwa administration soon gained a reputation for overall inexperience and indecision, which has yet to be surmounted three years later. Only its complex political agenda was orchestrated with dispatch, in a process that began, under Beijing direction, with the formation of all the inter-locking mainland-style committees. The single most ambitious undertaking thereafter was the May 1998 special election to create a new post-Patten Legislative Council. Only after its results were registered was the new edifice complete, since only then did the tripartite divisions of Hong Kong's new Basic Law political system assume their full and final shape. A few key details will suffice by way of illustration.[33]

The provisional legislature's preliminary January-to-June 1997 sittings were devoted to readying, on Preparatory Committee recommendation, a list of bills for passage beginning soon after midnight on 1 July 1997. Among these early pieces of new legislation, and certainly the most complex, was the Legislative Council Bill, prescribing in minute detail the May 1998 election rules. These seemingly left no loophole in the effort to reduce democratic margins of victory. Besides adhering to a strict constructionist interpretation of the Basic Law, the Preparatory Committee and Provisional Legislative Council added several extra touches of their own.[34] Most significant was proportional representation. Not content with the near 40-seat conservative and pro-China majority the Basic Law design guaranteed, new rules mandated proportional representation for all directly elected seats instead of the simple majority voting method used in 1995. The rules also stipulated that a full 100 seats

33. On the 1998 elections and related developments, see Richard Baum's article in this issue.

34. See "Chouweihui guanyu Zhonghua renmin gongheguo Xianggang tebie xingzhengqu diyi jie lifahui de juti chansheng banfa" ("The Preparatory Committee's concrete methods for producing the first Legislative Council of the Hong Kong SAR, of the People's Republic of China"), passed by the PC's ninth plenary meeting, 23 May 1997, in Yuan Qiushi (ed.), *Xianggang guodu shiqi zhongyao wenjian huibian* (*A Compilation of Important Documents on Hong Kong's Transition Period*) (Hong Kong: Sanlian, 1997), pp. 304–307; and Legislative Council Ordinance, in, *Government of the Hong Kong Special Administrative Region Gazette*, Legal Supplement, No. 1, 3 October 1997, pp. 435–621.

on the 800-strong Election Committee be reserved for NPC/CPPCC incumbents. The NCNA then persevered in its management of this group by organizing a get-out-the-vote campaign when a preliminary functional constituencies election was held in April, to choose the 800-member Election Committee which was responsible for filling ten LegCo seats.

Once all the scores were settled and tallies finalized in May, Basic Law drafters could rest content that their complicated colonial-mainland design with Hong Kong characteristics had fulfilled its purpose. The democratic voting majority not only held but public commitment to electoral politics actually seemed to strengthen with an unprecedented 53 per cent turnout on election day, of which more than 60 per cent again went to democratic candidates. They were nevertheless limited to a proportionally correct 14 of the 20 directly elected seats, while pro-China candidates won five. The latter also won a majority of the ten Electoral Committee seats, and business candidates swept the functional constituencies losing only five of those seats to the democratic camp. Thus despite taking over 60 per cent of the popular vote, democratic candidates occupied only 19 of LegCo's 60 seats.[35]

Of the 19 legislators in concurrent Provisional Legislative Council and NPC/CPPCC positions, ten remained after the 1998 election. Among them was council president Rita Fan who the democrats tried but failed to dislodge, given the council's overwhelming conservative and pro-China majority. Nor could democrats muster sufficient votes to prevent the Tung government from restoring a 25 per cent non-elected membership to the District Boards. Similarly, the government declared both the Urban and Regional Councils redundant and abolished them at the end of 1999, with LegCo endorsement, thereby eliminating entirely Hong Kong's middle tier of elected offices. The belated colonial effort to establish a territory-wide council system, accountable to Hong Kong's voting public, has thus been effectively negated.

Whither Hong Kong's new democracy? By the second year under Chinese rule, then, all pre-1997 hyperbole about Hong Kong serving as a democratic bridgehead across the 1997 divide was but a distant memory. As for the "one country, two systems" design, it was often difficult to determine where one system ended and the other began. The defensive lines of protection demanded by all concerned had been established, but the dynamic seemed overwhelmingly in China's favour. Thus, after Hong Kong's new Basic Law government emerged in the form China intended, two key aims stood out that did not obtrude quite so clearly before. One was the determination to check Hong Kong's democratic politicians, achieved through the three-way Legislative Council division into directly elected, corporate and mainland-style representatives. The other aim was to create in Hong Kong a system that replicated

35. Official election results in, *South China Morning Post, Hong Kong Standard* and *Wenhui bao*, all 26 May 1998.

China's own ponderous movement toward Communist Party-led political reform.

These consequences were not unintended but only obscured by the Basic Law's complex origins. Hence Britain's colonial legacy had actually been adapted for use within an intricate "Chinese" design. The British legacy included paramount gubernatorial leadership augmented by a partially elected and marginally empowered legislature designed to produce safe majorities for all occasions. The functional constituency option came specifically from Hong Kong's own colonial past and was essentially the same solution identified by Grantham in 1950 as the most appropriate form of representation for Hong Kong's legislature. Additionally, however, from post-1949 China came the concurrent positions and interlocking organizational memberships of democratic centralism. This feature, which provided a living link between the Chinese and Hong Kong legislatures, was not spelled out in the Basic Law but only appeared after the system took final shape.

China had therefore insisted on an all-powerful executive for Hong Kong's government, while relegating the legislature to simple supervisory and debating society functions. Such a design places Hong Kong on a parallel course with the reforms being introduced in China's own congress system – which grant it new powers to supervise, inspect and assist governments at various levels, but not actually to initiate legislation. Even LegCo's division between directly elected and functional constituency members has an important mainland counterpart, reflecting their common origins. These lie in long-forgotten pre-1949 Chinese experiments with constitutional reform, which Grantham's advisors must have been aware of in 1950. China's CPPCC is thus organized on a functional basis, while the NPC derives from geographic divisions where reforms are also moving China, like Hong Kong, at a snail's pace towards directly elected local assemblies.

Within this grand constitutional design, both Hong Kong's new executive and the Chinese sovereign are playing strictly by the Basic Law rule book, albeit interpreting its provisions with clear partisan intent so as to reduce democratic margins for manoeuvre wherever possible. Here the consequences are undoubtedly not intended, however, since the impact has been to perpetuate and strengthen the main pro-democracy/pro-China divide that shaped Hong Kong's emerging spectrum during the 1980s. Its post-1997 equivalent is the liberal/conservative division being reaffirmed daily over matters of policy and practice to create, in effect, a multi-party system governed by adversarial "two-line" politics. The challenge for Hong Kong democrats, then, is to maintain their partisan strength within a system that has relegated them to the status of a permanent powerless opposition.

In terms of political resources and possibilities, of course, the democrats are not powerless, which is why the new regime has stacked the deck so heavily against them. They know, for example, that history and "world trends" are on their side. More specifically, Hong Kong democrats know it was not just the impersonal force of 20th-century trends and historical circumstances that finally compelled the break-through over British inertia and Beijing's objections. That opportunity might have passed them by again, as in 1949, but for the political movement that local activists themselves began building in the 1980s, around their demands for representative government. Thereafter the idea took hold that the power of political leaders should derive, via electoral mandates, from the people governed. The old silent majority with its alleged apathy and distaste for partisan politics has consequently given way to a self-conscious political culture, which is argumentative, demanding and alert to the full range of civil rights issues even if not necessarily effective in promoting them. That culture has also produced a new 1.5 million electorate with voters who demonstrate a continuing majority preference for candidates committed to Western-style democracy. This was promoted initially as a form of protection against mainland interference, and more recently as an alternative to autocratic rule whatever its origins. Within this culture, it is also a commonplace that Hong Kong has its own activist movement to thank, along with Britain's latter-day efforts and China's beneficence, for Hong Kong's post-1997 political tranquillity.

If they value history and their voters so highly, however, it is because Hong Kong democrats currently have few other resources with which to counter the strength of the national and local forces ranged against them. Should their loyal public begin to defect, in other words, the democrats' movement will recede accordingly. That particular aim, to counter ongoing democratic demands for stronger rather than weaker institutions of representative government, is in fact now being openly promoted by some of Hong Kong's leading businessmen. With the power balance having shifted so clearly in their favour, these tycoons are speaking out unapologetically for the first time since a local consensus formed against them in 1989, invoking the same mix of conservative elitism and economic self-interest as in pre-1989 days.

Predictions as to who will prevail in this contest between populists and political-economic elites are thus premature. Nor should the presence of so many "objective" conditions typically associated with a successful transition to representative self-government weigh too heavily in this equation. Hong Kong's open society and thriving economy were never sufficient in themselves to challenge the constraints maintained by a British-run company town, which served simultaneously as a trading centre and refugee haven at China's sufferance. Probably more important in calculating Hong Kong's political future, then, are the specific barriers that have recently been surmounted. Fear of direct elections was as old as the colony itself, reinforced after 1949 by the legacy of China's civil war living on beneath the surface of Hong Kong's émigré society. China was therefore as apprehensive as Britain had ever been about introducing electoral politics in Hong Kong, since it meant the long-suppressed confrontation there between communist friends and foes was inevitable. Yet once China had accepted Hong Kong's demands for directly elected LegCo representation and for "eventual" universal suffrage, it also had no choice but to allow its partisans to join the competition – whereupon both barriers were quickly surmounted without incident. The legacy of Hong Kong's fearful past is, of course, now carved in Basic Law stone. Barring some Draconian crackdown, however, the current competition between democrats and conservatives should be sufficient to sustain its dynamic, perhaps even until such a time as all the principals have learned to fear each other less.

Democracy Deformed: Hong Kong's 1998 Legislative Elections – and Beyond

Richard Baum

"Would it be good for Hong Kong to hold general elections? I don't think so ..."
Deng Xiaoping (April 1987)

Electoral democracy has been defined as "a system of government in which the principal positions of effective government power are filled, directly or indirectly, through meaningful, regular, free and fair ... elections."[1] By this criterion, Hong Kong today falls short of being an electoral democracy. There are periodic elections, and there is a 60-seat Legislative Council (LegCo), at least some of whose members are chosen by universal adult suffrage. There are also a number of organized, highly articulate political parties whose legislative members are frequent, outspoken critics of the government and its policies. And there is a system of transparent electoral laws and procedures administered by a professionally neutral civil service, ensuring that elections remain free and fair. Yet for all its manifest electoral virtues, democracy in post-handover Hong Kong is highly constrained and confined, as noted in the previous article by Suzanne Pepper.

The Legislative Council has little power to initiate or enact legislation. The non-democratically selected chief executive is effectively immune from LegCo oversight and accountability. Opposition parties, though vocal, are largely impotent. Ordinary citizens, while exercising the right to vote, lack any regular, institutionalized mechanism for ensuring governmental responsiveness. And finally, there is the ever-present "China factor" – the giant shadow cast over all political life in Hong Kong by the physical proximity and sovereign prerogatives of the People's Republic of China. Because of these factors, and because a clear institutional disconnect separates Hong Kong's semi-democratic electoral *forms* from its executive-dominated governmental *essence*, the Hong Kong Special Administrative Region (SAR) today presents a curious case study of democratic deformity, a case where elections are free, fair and regular – but not particularly meaningful.[2]

This article examines the institutional framework, socio-economic context and outcome of Hong Kong's first post-handover legislative elections of May 1998. The aim is to elucidate the effects of the disconnect between political participation, political representation and political power in the new SAR. The article concludes by exploring the

---

1. Larry Diamond, "Limited elections and the development of democracy," paper presented to the conference, Elections in Taiwan, Hong Kong, and China: Does Limited Democracy Lead to Democracy? Hoover Institution, 5–6 March 1999, p. 7.
2. In H.C. Kuan's apt phrase, elections in Hong Kong are "without political clout." See Kuan Hsin-chi, "Election without political clout," in Kuan Hsin-chi, Lau Siu-kai, Louie Kin-sheun and Wong Ka-ying (eds.), *Power Transition and The Legislative Elections in Hong Kong SAR* (Hong Kong: The Chinese University Press, 1999).

implications of this disconnect for the long-term health and stability of Hong Kong's political system.

The Institutional Framework: "Executive-Led Government"

The Basic Law. Under the guiding principle of "one country, two systems," the drafters of the 1990 Hong Kong Basic Law retained many of the key institutional features of the late colonial regime, including a strong, appointed chief executive and a weak, mainly advisory/consultative legislature, an arrangement popularly referred to as "executive-led government." To dilute the democratic impulse, the Basic Law stipulated that in the first post-handover election two-thirds of Hong Kong's legislators (40/60) would be indirectly chosen, either in functional constituencies or by a small, pre-screened Election Committee whose members were themselves drawn from functional constituencies; only one-third (20/60) would initially be directly elected by universal suffrage in geographical constituencies.[3] Elections would be held every four years. Political parties, which did not exist in Hong Kong at the time of the Basic Law's promulgation in 1990, received no mention whatever in that document.

To disarm lingering local fears of China's anti-democratic intentions – fears that were particularly intense in the aftermath of the 1989 Tiananmen Square debacle – the framers of the Basic Law reluctantly agreed to introduce a timetable for the progressive expansion of the democratic franchise for LegCo elections. Under an annex to the Basic Law, the number of directly elected seats was to increase from 18 to 20 in the legislative term that commenced in 1995, to 24 in the second term (1999–2003), and to 30 – one-half the total number of seats – in the third term (2003–2007).[4] Over the same 12-year period, the ten LegCo seats initially set aside for selection by an indirectly chosen Election Committee would be phased out entirely, leaving LegCo, by the year 2007, equally divided between 30 directly elected geographical constituencies and 30 indirectly elected functional constituencies (annex II). It was further stipulated that the "ultimate aim" was the election of *all* LegCo members through "universal suffrage" (articles 45, 68). Though no specific mechanism or timetable for achieving this goal was included in the Basic Law, the SAR government has promised to hold a plebiscite in the year 2007 to solicit the views of the Hong Kong people on the question of creating a wholly democratic LegCo. The results of the plebiscite would be non-binding, however, since any proposal to elect directly all 60 legislators would require a two-thirds majority vote in

3. The text of the Basic Law appears in Ming K. Chan and David J. Clark (eds.), *The Hong Kong Basic Law: Blueprint for "Stability and Prosperity" under Chinese Sovereignty?* (Armonk NY: M.E. Sharpe, 1991).

4. China's agreement to allow the legislature elected under British colonial auspices in 1995 to finish its four-year term beyond the 1997 retrocession date comprised the essence of the "through train" concept, designed to ensure basic institutional continuity across the 1997 divide.

LegCo as well as endorsement by the chief executive. The changing size and composition of LegCo are shown in Table 1.

Executive–legislative relations. Notwithstanding its promise of democratization by degrees, the Basic Law narrowly circumscribed the constitutional powers of LegCo.[5] Indeed, the document's framers intended that LegCo should be unambiguously subordinated to a dominant chief executive, a relationship that closely mirrored the British colonial regime. Asserting the PRC's sovereign prerogative in the matter of choosing Hong Kong's first chief executive, the Basic Law stipulated that both he and all principal officers of his administration would be appointed by the Central People's Government in Beijing, for a term of five years (article 16). However, in a concession to local concern over possible Chinese heavyhandedness, the PRC delegated the task of choosing the chief executive to a local "united front" body, in the form of a hand-picked selection committee made up initially of 400 (later enlarged to 800) prominent – and predominantly "patriotic," pro-Chinese – Hong Kong elites chosen from four main sectors of the society: industry, commerce and finance; the professions; local officials; and labour, social services and religion (annex I).[6] As H.C. Kuan has aptly noted, in this and other key respects the Basic Law represented "a pact between the Chinese government and the business and industrial elites in Hong Kong."[7]

Concerning the selection of future chief executives after the 1997 handover, the Basic Law held out the possibility that democratic procedures might be adopted as early as 2007. However, this prospect was carefully hedged with the requirement that any such procedural change must be endorsed by two-thirds of all LegCo members, by the incumbent chief executive himself, and by the Standing Committee of China's National People's Congress (NPC) – no easy pathway, to say the least (annex I). The NPC was further invested with the exclusive power to interpret and amend the Basic Law, thereby ensuring against a future constitutional coup by democratic forces in Hong Kong (articles 158 and 159).[8]

The constitutional prerogatives of the chief executive are numerous.

5. The following analysis is based on David J. Clark, "The Basic Law: one document, two systems," in Chan and Clark, *The Hong Kong Basic Law*, pp. 36–59; James T.H. Tang, "Executive–legislative relations in Hong Kong," *CSIS Hong Kong Update*, August 1998, pp. 6–9; and Li Pang-kwong, "Executive and legislature: institutional design, electoral dynamics and the management of conflicts in the Hong Kong transition," in Li Pang-kwong (ed.), *Political Order and Political Transition in Hong Kong* (Hong Kong: The Chinese University Press, 1997), pp. 53–78.

6. See "Decision of the National People's Congress on the Method for the Formation of the First Government and the First Legislative Council of the Hong Kong SAR" (4 April 1990), in Chan and Clark, *The Hong Kong Basic Law*, pp. 207–209.

7. Kuan Hsin-chi, "Power dependence and democratic transition: the case of Hong Kong," *The China Quarterly*, No. 128 (1991), p. 785.

8. Amendments to the Basic Law could be proposed by a two-thirds majority vote of LegCo; however, before a proposed amendment could be referred to the NPC for final debate and decision, prior approval by both the chief executive and two-thirds of Hong Kong's NPC delegation was required.

Table 1: The Composition of LegCo, 1984–2007

Year	Ex-officio members	Appointed members	Elected members FC	EC	GC	Total seats	GC electoral mechanism
1984	17	30	–	–	–	47	N/A
1985	11	22	12	12	–	57	N/A
1988	11	20	14	12	–	57	N/A
1991	4	18	21	–	18	60	double-member, plurality
1995*	–	–	30	10	20	60	single-member, plurality
1998**	–	–	30	10	20	60	multi-member, proportional
2000	–	–	30	6	24	60	??
2004	–	–	30	0	30	60	??
2007/8	–	–	??	??	??	??	??

Notes:

FC = functional constituency; EC = Election Committee; GC = geographical constituencies.

* Due to alleged British violations of the Basic Law, the 1995 LegCo election results were overturned at the time of the 1997 handover.

** Originally scheduled for 1999, this election was moved up one year following the dissolution of LegCo in 1997.

Source:

Adapted from Norman Miners, *The Government and Politics of Hong Kong* (5th ed.) (Hong Kong: Oxford University Press, 1995), p. 116.

They include: exclusive power to introduce legislation pertaining to public expenditure, political structure and the operation of government; the power to prevent private members from introducing bills affecting government policy without his consent; and the power to refuse to sign into law any bill deemed "incompatible with the overall interests of the region" (articles 48, 49 and 74). Further strengthening executive dominance over the legislature, the Basic Law required that all bills introduced by private members be approved by concurrent majorities of two separate groups of legislators before being enacted into law: one group comprising corporate members selected in functional constituencies and the other including both directly elected members and members chosen by the appointed Election Committee. In effect, this rather ingenious device meant that a minority of 15 indirectly-elected legislators (one-fourth of the whole) could block the passage of any bill opposed by the chief executive. By contrast, bills introduced by the chief executive required only a simple majority vote of the members present to be enacted into law (articles 74 and 75).

In cases of deadlock between the chief executive and the legislature, the constitutional balance was once again tilted sharply in the executive's favour. Although two-thirds of LegCo members could vote to compel the chief executive to enact a private member's bill, it was the chief executive who held the trump card: by sitting on an unsigned bill for just one month he could force a dissolution of the legislature. Only if the successor legislature once again passed the bill by a two-thirds majority would he then be compelled either to sign it or to submit his resignation (articles 49, 50 and 52). In these and other ways, the Basic Law made it extremely difficult for LegCo effectively to oppose the will of the chief executive.

The Legislative Council. Originally a wholly appointed advisory body with no significant law-making powers, LegCo was designed to bridge the gap between an all-powerful British colonial governor and Hong Kong's emerging economic, social and professional elites.[9] As late as 1984, when the Sino-British Joint Declaration established the basic parameters for Hong Kong's transition to Chinese sovereignty, LegCo was composed entirely of appointed local elites (30) and ex-officio government members (17). In 1985 the Council was enlarged from 47 to 57 members with the addition of a small number of functional constituency seats and an Electoral College made up of local district officials. All seats within these new constituencies were filled indirectly through corporate voting. The underlying British intent in introducing these new corporate constituencies was to augment local home rule without at the

---

9. The origins and early development of LegCo are examined in Steve Tsang (ed.), *A Documentary History of Hong Kong: Government and Politics* (Hong Kong: Hong Kong University Press, 1995).

same time overly antagonizing China by introducing direct legislative elections, which were considered anathema to Beijing.[10]

Although LegCo continued to function primarily as a sounding board for the colonial administration until the 1997 handover, by the early 1990s it had became the focal point of mounting Sino-British tension. Following the outbreak in Hong Kong of massive anti-China street demonstrations protesting against the 1989 Tiananmen Square crackdown, Britain came under mounting local pressure to strengthen the representative nature and democratic composition of LegCo.[11] Caught squarely in the middle between popular agitation for rapid democratization and Chinese insistence on going slow, Hong Kong's last British governor, Chris Patten, moved to broaden LegCo's popular base by eliminating all remaining appointed and ex officio seats and – most controversial of all – dramatically enlarging the popular franchise in functional constituencies.

Under new electoral rules introduced by Patten for the 1995 LegCo elections, corporate voting in functional constituencies, which had disproportionately empowered a small number of elites drawn from key business, industrial and professional sectors, was greatly curtailed. At the same time, nine new functional constituencies were created, within each of which the franchise was extended to all ordinary members and employees. At a single stroke, Chris Patten thus enlarged the eligible electorate in the functional constituencies from less than 70,000 to more than 1.1 million. The Chinese government vigorously protested at Patten's unilateral action, claiming that it violated past Sino-British agreements and was contrary to the intent, if not the letter, of the Basic Law. Undeterred by Beijing's threat to annul the 1995 election results, dissolve LegCo and install a provisional legislature at the stroke of midnight on 1 July 1997, Patten went ahead with his reforms – thereby setting the stage for a major constitutional crisis.[12]

Political parties. Hong Kong's first distinctive political interest groups emerged only in the 1980s, their formation catalyzed by growing public concern over the mechanics and consequences of the transition process. Although a number of professional and civic associations had existed in Hong Kong at least since the early 1950s – some of which had become intermittently politicized in the 1950s and 1960s – it was only after the 1982 Beijing visit of British Prime Minister Margaret Thatcher confirmed

10. Note Deng Xiaoping's blunt rejection of direct elections, quoted in the epigram at the head of this article. On Britain's reluctance to antagonize Beijing in the late 1980s, see Mark Roberti, *The Fall of Hong Kong: China's Triumph and Britain's Betrayal* (New York: John Wiley & Sons, 1994), ch. 17 *et passim*; also Lo Shiu-hing, *The Politics of Democratization in Hong Kong* (London: Macmillan Press, 1997), ch. 2.

11. When martial law was imposed in Beijing in May 1989, one million Hong Kong people – almost 20% of the population – took to the streets to protest against the Chinese government's actions.

12. The controversy over Patten's electoral reforms is examined in Jonathan Dimbleby, *The Last Governor: Chris Patten and the Handover of Hong Kong* (London: Little, Brown, 1997), chs. 13–17.

the "writing on the wall" for Hong Kong that a participant political culture began to emerge. Between 1982 and 1986 at least ten new political organizations were formed in the territory, with membership ranging from a dozen or less to several hundred. Among other activities, these groups began mobilizing voters for the 1985 district board elections, the first direct elections ever held in Hong Kong.[13] In their political agendas and platforms, these early proto-parties diverged widely, ranging from strong support for China's recovery of sovereignty to equally strong opposition; from neo-authoritarian endorsement of executive-led government to populist demands for rapid, extensive democratization.[14]

In the late 1980s a loose constellation of democratic interest groups began to coalesce under the leadership of two prominent critics of China, teacher's union leader Szeto Wah and British-trained barrister Martin Lee Chu-ming. Szeto and Lee had actively participated in the early work of the Basic Law Drafting Committee. However, they broke with the pro-China majority on that committee when they openly criticized Britain's failure to introduce direct legislative elections in 1988.[15] Thereafter, a pro-democratic popular backlash began to emerge in Hong Kong, one which propelled Szeto, Lee and a handful of other vocal critics of Sino-British "collusion," including Emily Lau Wai-hing, willy-nilly into leadership roles in Hong Kong's nascent democracy movement.[16] It was this movement – further fuelled by massive local reaction to the Tiananmen crackdown – that spawned Hong Kong's first pro-democratic political parties in the early 1990s.

When the handover from British to Chinese sovereignty took place on 1 July 1997, the first official act of the new regime – as promised – was to dissolve the elected legislature and install a hand-picked provisional body in its place.[17] But the dissolution did not take place quickly enough to prevent ousted legislators from coming within a single vote of passing a defiant resolution condemning the provisional LegCo as a puppet of the

13. District boards constituted the bottom layer of Hong Kong's three-tiered governmental structure. They were responsible primarily for providing local recreational, cultural and public health services. The intermediate layer of government was made up of Urban and Regional Councils. The evolving structure of local government in Hong Kong is examined in Norman Miners, *The Government and Politics of Hong Kong* (5th ed.) (Hong Kong: Oxford University Press, 1995).

14. For details and analysis, see Lo Shiu-hing, *The Politics of Democratization*, ch. 4.

15. Shortly after the 1984 promulgation of the Sino-British Joint Declaration, the Hong Kong colonial government issued a white paper promising gradually to introduce democratic reforms during the run-up to 1997 – beginning with limited elections in 1985 to fill several newly-created functional constituency seats on the Legislative Council, to be followed by the introduction of "a very small number" of directly elected LegCo seats in 1988. Under intense pressure from China, however, Britain ultimately reneged on this pledge, drawing the ire of many Hong Kong people, including Szeto and Lee. See Roberti, *The Fall of Hong Kong*, pp. 118–120.

16. *Ibid.* chs. 17–19

17. In preparation for the dissolution of LegCo, a Provisional Legislative Council had been set up at China's initiative late in 1996, its members chosen by the same 400-person selection committee entrusted to pick the SAR's first chief executive.

Chinese government.[18] To assuage Hong Kong's angry democrats, who constituted a highly vocal and potentially influential opposition group, the new SAR government promised to hold fresh legislative elections within a year.

The 1998 Legislative Elections

With the provisional LegCo widely stigmatized as illegitimate,[19] little legislative initiative was displayed in the first year of the new SAR. From the 1 July handover until 24 May 1998, when the promised elections were held to replace the provisional body, the legislature served primarily as a rubber stamp for the chief executive, Tung Chee-hwa, duly endorsing his conservative, China-friendly agenda, which in this early period consisted largely of rolling back a number of pro-democratic, pro-labour and pro-human rights initiatives passed by the colonial legislature from 1991 to 1997.[20]

Election rules. Reflecting Beijing's determination to reverse Chris Pattern's 1995 electoral reforms, the 1998 LegCo elections were held under substantially altered voting rules. While the total number of seats and their internal apportionment remained the same as in the 1995 elections – 20 members directly elected in geographical constituencies, 30 indirectly selected in functional constituencies and ten chosen by an Election Committee (see Table 1) – the voting rules used within each type of constituency were dramatically altered in an attempt to dilute the electoral strength of pro-democratic parties and correspondingly to augment the corporate potency of Hong Kong's generally conservative business and professional elites.[21]

In place of the system used in 1995 in the geographical constituencies – direct elections in single-member districts, with victory going to the candidate securing a simple plurality of votes ("first past the post") – the 1998 elections saw the introduction of proportional representation with party-list voting in multi-member geographical districts. According to the conventional political wisdom, single-member districts with a simple plurality requirement tend to over-represent major parties while making it extremely difficult, if not impossible, for minor parties to gain a legislative foothold; conversely, proportional representation in multi-member

18. The resolution was defeated by a vote of 23 to 22. See Frank Ching, "China–Hong Kong relations," in Joseph Y.S. Cheng (ed.), *The Other Hong Kong Report 1997* (Hong Kong: The Chinese University Press, 1997), p. 33.

19. Public opinion surveys throughout the first half of 1997 showed that only a minority of Hong Kong people – between 40% and 45% in various polls – approved of either the existence or the performance of the provisional legislature. See, e.g., Worthlin Worldwide, "Attitudes toward the transition of Hong Kong," 18 June 1997; *Pop Express* (University of Hong Kong, Social Sciences Research Centre), January 1997, p. 4.

20. See Suzanne Pepper's article in this volume.

21. Changes in the 1998 electoral rules and procedures are examined in Suzanne Pepper, "Hong Kong's first elections under Chinese rule: democracy across the 1997 divide," *CSIS Hong Kong Update*, April 1998, pp. 9–12.

districts is held to be conducive to the fragmentation of party systems insofar as it allows smaller parties the possibility of at least some electoral success in proportion to their share of the popular vote. At the same time, the use of party-list voting in a proportional representation system putatively strengthens voters' identification with party platforms as a whole at the expense of their identification with particular local issues or individual candidates.[22]

In the 1995 LegCo balloting, the conventional wisdom proved essentially correct. The system of single-member, "first-past-the-post" elections enabled the dominant pro-democratic coalition, capitalizing on widespread fears of heavy-handed Chinese intervention after 1997, to turn a 60 per cent share of the popular vote into an 85 per cent legislative majority within the geographical constituencies. The lesson was not lost on the SAR's new leaders. In the 1998 elections, a proportional representation system with voting by party lists was adopted. Under this system Hong Kong was divided into five large districts instead of 20 small ones, with voters in each district choosing three to five legislators from candidate lists submitted by the various political parties.[23]

In the event, the new system did precisely what it was designed to do: spread the fruits of victory among the various parties roughly in proportion to their share of the popular vote, thereby diluting the electoral strength of the majority democrats. As a result, Hong Kong's pro-democratic parties and their allies, who once again collectively gained just over 60 per cent of the popular vote, saw their share of directly elected legislative seats shrink from 85 per cent (17/20) to 65 per cent (14/20). By the same token the leading pro-China party, the Democratic Alliance for the Betterment of Hong Kong (DAB), which had suffered from legislative under-representation under the single-member plurality system, now picked up one seat in each of the multi-member geographical districts, for a total of five directly elected seats for its 25 per cent share of the popular vote.[24]

Seeking to counteract the majority-diluting effects of the new system, pro-democratic parties in some cases adopted a strategy of encouraging split voting among their supporters. For example, in the New Territories East, Martin Lee's Democratic Party reportedly advised its supporters to split their family members' votes between the Democratic Party and the politically liberal Frontier in order to help ensure the election of a third

22. See Maurice Duverger, *Political Parties* (London: Methuen, 1954); and Richard Katz, *A Theory of Parties and Electoral Systems* (Baltimore: Johns Hopkins University Press, 1980).

23. For an analysis of the process by which proportional representation was introduced into the 1998 LegCo elections, see Lau Siu-kai, "The making of the electoral system for the 1998 Legislative Council elections," in Kuan *et al.*, *Power Transition and The Legislative Elections*.

24. Election results are taken from Lo Shiu-hing, "The 1998 Legislative Council election in Hong Kong," paper presented at the conference on The Hong Kong Transition: One Year Later, UCLA, 6 June 1998. For analysis of the effects of the new proportional representation system on the outcome of the 1998 elections, see Ma Ngok, "Party competition pattern under the new electoral system," in Kuan *et al.*, *Power Transition and The Legislative Elections*.

pro-democracy candidate. Similar strategic electoral behaviour occurred on Hong Kong Island, where the Democratic Party picked a relatively unknown candidate to occupy the third slot on its party list, a move reportedly intended to help Christine Loh of the pro-democratic Citizen's Party to finish ahead of the rival DAB's second candidate.[25]

Notwithstanding the introduction of proportional representation in geographical constituencies, perhaps the most significant change in voting procedures in 1998, in terms of its impact upon the election's outcome, was the restoration of corporate voting in all functional constituencies. This reduced the number of eligible voters in these constituencies by almost 90 per cent, from over 1.1 million in 1995 to fewer than 140,000 in 1998. Moreover, among the 30 functional constituencies there were vast disparities in the number of eligible voters, ranging from highs of approximately 50,000 in the education sector and 20,000 in the health services sector to lows of a few hundred or less in the agricultural, transport, insurance and urban/regional councils sectors.[26] On election day, some 77,813 voters (65 per cent of those eligible) cast ballots in the 20 functional constituencies in which the names of two or more candidates appeared on the ballot. Candidates in the other ten functional constituencies ran unopposed and no vote tallies were recorded. Reflecting a built-in conservative bias in the majority of functional constituencies, pro-government parties and their unaffiliated allies captured more than twice as many seats (17) as pro-democratic parties and individuals (eight), with a handful of independents making up the balance.[27]

The third component of Hong Kong's three-legged electoral stool was the 800-member Election Committee, successor to the 400-member selection committee which in 1996 picked the SAR's first chief executive and the provisional legislature. Reflecting the united front design and composition of the committee, with its predominant representation of conservative, pro-Beijing business, industrial and professional elites, eight of the ten Election Committee seats went to pro-government candidates, with the other two captured by independents. No democrats were elected in this constituency.

Voter turnout. Confirmation of the skewed pattern of representation resulting from the new electoral mechanism is found in aggregate voting data. Whereas on average 74,000 voters cast ballots for each available seat in the geographical constituencies, there were only 2,600 voters per seat in the functional constituencies, and a mere 80 voters per seat in the Election Committee. Yet notwithstanding either the obvious anti-democratic bias of this three-legged electoral system or its extraordinary complexity, which led many experts to predict a low turnout on election

25. I am indebted to Suzanne Pepper and Ming K. Chan for calling my attention to such patterns of strategic co-operation among pro-democratic parties.
26. Data in this section are drawn from the website of the Hong Kong Government Information Office, http://www.info.gov.hk/election/524-e.htm (25 May 1998).
27. See Lo Shiu-hing, "The 1998 Legislative Council election," p. 5.

Table 2: LegCo Election Results, 1998 and 1995 Compared

Party (1998 votes)	Geographical constituencies		Functional constituencies		Election Committee		Total seats		Percent popular vote	
	1998	1995	1998	1995	1998	1995	1998	1995	1998	1995
DP (633,835)	9	12	4	5	0	2	13	19	42.9	42.3
DAB (373,428)	5	2	3ª	3	2ª	2	10	7	25.2	15.6
Frontier^b (187,134)	4^c	n/a	0	n/a	0	n/a	4	n/a	12.6	n/a
ADPL (59,034)	0	2	0	1	0	1	0	4	4.0	9.6
LP (50,335)	0	1	9	9	1	0	10	10	3.4	1.7
Citizens^b (41,633)	1	n/a	0	n/a	0	n/a	1	n/a	2.8	n/a
HKPA^d	n/a	0	2	0	3	3	5	3	n/a	2.9
Independents (91,739)	1	2	11	11	4	1	16	15^e	6.2	21.0
Others (31,207)	0	1^f	1^g	1	0	1	1	2	2.1	6.4
Total: (1,479,440)	20	20	30	30	10	10	60	60	99.2	99.5

Notes:

[a] Includes one member running under banner of Federation of Trade Unions (FTU).

[b] The Frontier and Citizens parties were founded in 1996.

[c] Includes one member running under banner of Neighbourhood and Workers Service Centre (NWSC).

[d] Did not enter candidate lists in geographical constituencies in 1998

[e] Includes United Ants and future members of Frontier (4) and Citizens (1)

[f] Liberal Democratic Federation (LDF)

[g] Confederation of Trade Unions (CTU)

Key to parties:

DP: Democratic Party

DAB: Democratic Alliance for the Betterment of Hong Kong

ADPL: Hong Kong Association for Democracy and People's Livelihood

LP: Liberal Party

HKPA: Hong Kong Progressive Alliance

Sources:

Adapted from *Hong Kong Voice of Democracy* (Internet edition), May 1998 (http://www.democracy.org.hk/pastweek/may.htm); and Elaine Chan and Rowena Kwok, "Democratization in turmoil? Elections in Hong Kong," paper presented at the annual meeting of the Association for Asian Studies, Washington D.C., 26–29 March 1998, table 4.

day, an unexpected rush to the polls occurred on 24 May, easily surpassing the previous high of 920,000 voters (36 per cent) recorded in 1995. Braving torrential rains and flash flooding, almost 1.5 million people – 53.3 per cent of those registered – cast ballots in the geographical constituencies.[28] Although the heavy turnout favoured the democrats and their independent allies, the electoral system worked in precisely the opposite direction, ensuring a conservative, pro-government majority in LegCo, and thereby setting the stage for future legislative acrimony. The election results are summarized and compared with the 1995 outcome in Table 2.

Interpreting the results. Observers offered various explanations to account for the unexpected surge of voter interest in 1998. Democrats were quick to conclude that the election constituted a popular referendum on the need to speed up the democratization process.[29] Even the head of the most popular pro-China party, the DAB, acknowledged that the high turnout probably meant that the pace and tempo of democratization should be accelerated somewhat. On the other hand, Chief Executive Tung Chee-hwa attributed it not to any frustrated popular demand for democratization, but rather to people's strong sense of civic duty and their putative desire to support the "one country, two systems" concept.[30] Other observers took a rather more cynical view of such "civic duty," noting that many people had evidently voted in order to take advantage of an election-day advertising promotion run by the Hong Kong government in conjunction with a local clothing retailer, wherein all those who cast a ballot received a souvenir card which entitled them to a 40 per cent discount on a polo shirt.[31]

At first glance, both the high turnout rate and the 60 per cent vote share gained by pro-democratic parties seemed to confirm the democrats' interpretation of the 1998 elections as a resounding rebuff to the provisional legislature and a clear affirmation of the need for accelerated democratization. However, closer scrutiny of mass electoral behaviour and patterns of partisan support reveal a more complex, multi-dimensional reality. For one thing, while it is certainly true that the democrats

28. For pre-election predictions of low voter turnout, see "Hong Kong election raises concerns," Associated Press (Hong Kong), 8 May 1998; and "Turnout may be below '95 poll," *Hong Kong Standard*, 15 May 1998. According to one pre-election survey, 88% of Hong Kong residents polled admitted to knowing "little or nothing at all" about the new electoral system, while only 6.6% could name the proportional representation mechanism as the one to be employed in the May election. See "Hong Kong election raises concern: poll finds most people still ignorant of electoral system," *Hong Kong Standard*, 19 March 1998.

29. Democratic Party chairman Martin Lee thus claimed that "a very clear signal has been given by Hong Kong people to our leaders ... that Hong Kong people want and deserve democracy." In a similar vein, one Hong Kong public opinion analyst stated: "What this means is that people have overwhelmingly rejected the notion of an appointed legislature ... They've come out in massive numbers in favor of direct elections." Michael DeGolyer, cited in *The Washington Post*, 25 May 1998.

30. *Hong Kong Standard*, 27 May 1998.

31. See Lo Shiu-hing, "The 1998 Legislative Council election," p. 12; and Byron Weng, "Impact of the first LegCo elections," *CSIS Hong Kong Update*, June 1998.

continued to get a boost from their popular image as outspoken defenders of "little Hong Kong" against the putative predatory impulses and appetites of "big China," such David-versus-Goliath imagery was no longer so potent in 1998 as it had been in previous elections. By the time of the 24 May balloting Chinese self-restraint during the first post-handover year had done much to calm popular fears of heavy-handed interference. Indeed, opinion surveys conducted during the run-up to and immediately following the elections confirmed that fear of China was no longer a predominant concern among voters. Thus, for example, whereas on the eve of the 1995 LegCo elections 62 per cent of people expressed dissatisfaction with the way Beijing was handling the Hong Kong transition, by the late spring and summer of 1998 that figure had dropped to just 11 per cent. Moreover, by the spring of 1998 fully 64 per cent of respondents in one poll expressed the opinion that reunification with China was the "best arrangement" for Hong Kong.[32] Clearly, fear of China was now much diminished.[33]

Nor was antagonism toward the provisional legislature, the new SAR government or Chief Executive Tung Chee-hwa – three more-or-less constant targets in the campaign platform of most pro-democratic candidates in 1998 – a potent motivating factor for the electorate as a whole. Indeed, discontent with the provisional LegCo, while certainly widespread, ranked only eighth in importance among 13 motivational factors mentioned by voters. Even lower, in eleventh place, was voters' desire to "express my discontent with the SAR government." Indeed, the two most frequently-named factors were "to exercise my rights as a citizen" and "to have someone in LegCo watch out for my interests."[34] This tends to confirm the hypothesis that the concept of active, involved citizenship was an important motivating factor in the 1998 elections. Indeed, one post-election survey found that 60 per cent of people interviewed went to the polls primarily to fulfil their responsibility as citizens.[35]

The diminishing importance of the China factor in the 1998 elections served to underscore a major shift in Hong Kong's political landscape. Ever since Tiananmen, attitudes towards China (and later towards Governor Patten and the provisional LegCo) had constituted the primary axes of political conflict and electoral competition in Hong Kong. Now, with Patten gone, with the provisional legislature on the verge of extinction

32. Data from surveys by the Hong Kong Transition Project, as reported in Michael DeGolyer, "Public opinion and participation in the 1998 LegCo elections: pre/post colonial comparisons," in Kuan *et al.*, *Power Transition and The Legislative Elections*.

33. On China's self-restraint in the immediate post-handover period, see Richard Baum, "Enter the dragon: China's courtship of Hong Kong, 1982–1999," *Communist and Post-Communist Studies*, Vol. 32, No. 4 (December 1999).

34. See Robert Ting-yiu Chung, "Voter participation: explaining the record turnout rate," in Kuan, *et al.*, *Power Transition and The Legislative Elections*.

35. *Ibid.* An even higher percentage – 87.7% – indicated that the fulfilment of civic responsibility had been an "important factor" in their decision to vote, while a desire to demonstrate support for democracy had been important to 78% of voters in this same survey. See "Voters driven by freedom, democracy," *Hong Kong Standard*, 19 June 1998.

and with the China factor receding in importance, new issues and orientations began to assume increased political salience.

The Emerging Political Landscape

Issue orientations in the 1998 elections. For the first time the 1998 LegCo elections were fought mainly over something other than the handover itself. With fear of China receding, and with reverberations from the deepening Asian financial crisis now being widely felt in Hong Kong, economic issues rose to the forefront of voter concerns. The magnitude of this change was clearly revealed in pre-election public opinion surveys which showed that the percentage of Hong Kong people concerned mainly about their economic prospects and living standards had jumped from 19 per cent at the time of the handover to 50 per cent by early 1998.[36] In another survey shortly after the May elections, more than half of all voters (51.5 per cent) indicated that the state of the SAR's economy was the most important single factor affecting their choice of candidates, followed by concern over class-based issues of wealth distribution (18 per cent), concern for socio-political stability (12 per cent) and the China factor (8 per cent).[37] With economic issues thus ranking both first and second in importance among voters, and – equally important – with almost two-thirds of residents (63.7 per cent) now subjectively locating themselves below Hong Kong's median income on a scale of relative economic well-being,[38] the political landscape shifted noticeably.

Pro-democratic parties were quick to sense the electoral implications of this shift. Although they were unrelenting in their criticism of the government of Tung Chee-hwa, they now began to de-emphasize the China factor and to stress instead the current regime's administrative incompetence, pro-business bias and lack of concern for the welfare of ordinary citizens. Maintaining a posture of principled opposition to the provisional LegCo, they supplemented this with criticism of Tung's cosy ties to Hong Kong's billionaire tycoons and with attacks on the government for its inept handling of the "bird flu" and "red tide" outbreaks of late 1997.[39] As the campaign wore on, democrats increasingly portrayed the government as the willing captive of a plutocratic elite-tycoon axis. In doing so, the democrats sought to position themselves as defenders of the "silent majority" of ordinary, middle-class voters.

Despite their 60 per cent plurality in the 24 May elections, the democrats' successful campaign masked a number of emerging problems and vulnerabilities. For one thing, the proportional representation system of list voting for the first time pitted pro-democratic parties directly

36. See Sonny Lo Shiu-hing, "Hong Kong's changing public opinion," *CSIS Hong Kong Update*, February 1998.
37. See Timothy Ka-ying Wong, "Issue voting in the 1998 Legislative Council election," in Kuan *et al.*, *Power Transition and The Legislative Elections*.
38. *Ibid.*
39. On the government's handling of the bird flu crisis, see Yi-zheng (Joseph) Lian, "Tung's Hong Kong in distress," *CSIS Hong Kong Update*, January 1998.

against one another in at least some geographical constituencies. Consequently, the pro-democratic coalition forged in the early 1990s showed signs of strain, as democrats in some cases openly criticized one another.[40] Secondly, although the Democratic Party benefited from strong voter identification in 1998,[41] this was based largely on its track record of opposition to Beijing and the provisional LegCo, rather than its proposals for dealing with current economic problems. With Democratic Party (and other pro-democratic) candidates generally avoiding staking out clear, explicit policy positions on such increasingly salient local concerns as housing, immigration, employment and social welfare, the party's support base – while still quite broad – showed signs of incipient erosion. Indeed, there was evidence of a growing disconnection between the Democratic Party and its voter base, as almost 20 per cent defected in the 1998 elections to vote for other parties.[42] Other pro-democratic parties and candidates suffered even larger voter defections. Thus, the Association for Democracy and People's Livelihood (ADPL) managed to capture just 72 per cent of the votes cast by its own partisan identifiers, in the process failing to win a single LegCo seat. By the same token, Emily Lau's Frontier held on to just 63 per cent of its partisan base.[43]

Somewhat surprisingly, the party that most effectively mobilized its support base in 1998 was the left-wing unionist, pro-China DAB, led by Jasper Tsang Yok-sing. With more than 87 per cent of its partisan identifiers voting for its candidates, the DAB managed to capture five seats in the geographic constituencies together with five additional seats in the functional and Election Committee constituencies. Benefiting from the same anti-tycoon voter backlash stirred up by the democrats, the DAB successfully positioned itself as champion of the working masses. Finally, ranking last among the parties in terms of partisan faithfulness was the politically conservative, pro-business Liberal Party, which managed to hold on to just 44 per cent of its party identifiers.[44] Although it made a strong showing within business-oriented functional constituencies, where it captured ten seats, the party suffered a serious setback within the geographical constituencies, winning no seats at all, including an embarrassing defeat suffered by party chairman Allen Lee Peng-fei.

Non-party political organizations. In addition to the six political parties that fielded candidate lists in the geographical constituencies in 1998 – in descending order of popular votes: Democratic Party, DAB,

40. Ma Ngok, "Party competition pattern."
41. Party identification among all voters rose from 25% in 1995 to 70% in 1998. Among Democratic Party voters the increase was even greater, rising to 86% in 1998. See Milan Tung-wen Sun, "Hong Kong party identification re-examined: retrospective or prospective voting," in Kuan *et al.*, *Power Transition and The Legislative Elections.*
42. *Ibid.*
43. *Ibid.* The ADPL's defeat at the polls was widely attributed to party chairman Frederick Fung's controversial 1996 decision to participate in the provisional LegCo, a decision that split the organization's rank-and-file and alienated Hong Kong's other pro-democratic parties and groups.
44. *Ibid.*

Frontier, ADPL, Liberal Party and Citizens – a number of other political organizations competed for electoral support within the functional and Election Committee constituencies. Most prominent among these were the tycoon-dominated, pro-Beijing Hong Kong Progressive Alliance (HKPA), arguably the most staunchly conservative of Hong Kong's political groups, which captured five seats in non-geographical constituencies; and the leftist-oriented Federation of Trade Unions, closely aligned with the DAB and loyal to Beijing but increasingly alienated from the pro-business stance of the SAR government, which secured two seats in indirect elections. A rival, pro-democratic union organization, the Confederation of Trade Unions, gained one directly-elected seat in LegCo in the person of Lau Chin-shek, who campaigned under the banner of the Democratic Party.

With Hong Kong's post-handover political landscape becoming more complex, the political spectrum began to reflect a more nuanced distribution of voter opinion on localized socio-economic issues. Figure 1 depicts the post-handover policy alignments of the major political parties and non-party organizations that participated in the 24 May elections. Two major policy axes are represented in this schematic diagram: the (old) axis of support for democratization versus loyalty to Beijing, and the (new) axis of pro-business versus pro-welfare economic orientations.

Figure 1: **Hong Kong Political Matrix, 1998**

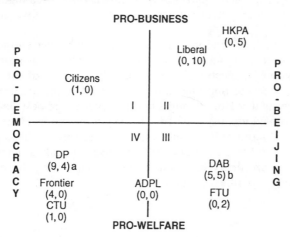

Notes:

Numbers in parentheses represent LegCo seats captured in direct and indirect elections, respectively, in May 1998.

a Includes one concurrent member of the Confederation of Trade Unions (CTU).

b Includes two concurrent members of the Federation of Trade Unions (FTU).

Sources:

Adapted by the author from a schema suggested by Michael DeGolyer, "Sticking your neck out, the first ten years of the HKSAR: a study in unintended consequences," unpublished paper, Hong Kong University, July 1997, p. 11.

A few tentative inferences can be drawn from the political topography depicted in Figure 1. First, while pro-Beijing parties and groups clearly dominated indirect elections within both the functional constituencies and the Election Committee (quadrants II and III), the coherence – and hence the potency – of this artificially contrived legislative majority was dramatically undercut, or at least cross-cut, by the unexpected weakness of voter support for parties and groups endorsing the Hong Kong government's traditional pro-business, laissez-faire economic orientation (quadrants I and II). Indeed, it is striking that in 1998 not a single member of a pro-business party was popularly elected in a geographical constituency. By contrast, 18 out of 20 directly elected LegCo members came from parties or groups supporting welfare economics and increased governmental intervention in the economy (quadrants III and IV). Given the rising salience of economic concerns and class-based redistributive issues among the voting public, noted earlier, this suggests the existence of a gaping – and potentially critical – political disconnect between the *legislative* majority and the *popular* majority.

A second, related inference to be drawn from Figure 1 is that the curious coalition between "patriotic" capitalists and left-wing unionists that formed the principal base of support for Tung Chee-hwa's new SAR government has begun to suffer substantial electoral decay. The fact that the pro-welfare DAB won 25 per cent of the popular vote (and a similar proportion of LegCo seats) in the five geographical constituencies, while the pro-business Liberal Party and the tycoon-dominated HKPA failed to capture a single seat in those same constituencies, suggests that the "new politics" of class and socio-economic interest-based voting in Hong Kong is seriously eroding the dominance of the traditional government-business coalition.[45]

Finally, the distribution of parties in political space shown in Figure 1, when viewed in conjunction with the rising rate of partisan defections in the 1998 LegCo elections, the decreasing salience of the China factor, and the increasing importance of class-based economic issues and interests, suggests that Hong Kong's political parties are now undergoing their first full-blown identity crisis. It also suggests that as Hong Kong moves closer to a more fully democratized legislature in elections currently scheduled for 2000, 2004 and 2007, partisan appeals to narrow economic self-interest are likely to increase, thereby hastening the realignment of Hong Kong's political parties.[46]

45. For an examination of the political significance of the emerging, mass-based pro-welfare constituency in Hong Kong, see David Zweig, "Eye on the ball: the politics of welfare in Hong Kong," *CSIS Hong Kong Update*, November 1997.

46. The shifting fault lines of partisan cleavage that underlay such a realignment were first noted by a handful of observers before the 1997 handover. See, for example, Suzanne Pepper, "China and Hong Kong: the political economy of reunification," in Christopher Hudson (ed.), *The China Handbook* (Chicago & London: Fitzroy Dearborn Publishers, 1997), p. 46.

Local Politics since 1997: "It's the Economy, Stupid"

While the above inferences were drawn from one-off election results and thus remain largely conjectural, they are supported and reinforced by a striking array of collateral evidence. Immediately after the May elections, the worsening Asian financial crisis pushed the economic concerns of Hong Kong citizens to the forefront of the political arena. As late as November 1997, four months after the handover, fully 72 per cent of Hong Kong's citizens had shared an optimistic assessment of the SAR's future economic prosperity.[47] By the late spring of 1998, however, the deepening impact of the Asian crisis was clearly reflected in the performance of Hong Kong's stock market, which by mid-year had lost almost 50 per cent of its pre-handover value, and in the property market, which declined by 45 per cent in the same period. With tourism falling off dramatically, retail shops closing their doors at an accelerating rate, GDP growth declining to − 3 per cent, unemployment doubling to top the 5 per cent mark and public confidence in Hong Kong's economic future dipping below 50 per cent for the first time, alarm bells began to ring.[48]

One of the earliest signs of political fallout from the economic crisis was the forging of an unprecedented post-election agreement among Hong Kong's seven political parties, for the purpose of pressing Chief Executive Tung Chee-hwa to take a more active, interventionist role in addressing Hong Kong's economic problems. Following an economic policy roundtable convened by the Democratic Party at the end of May, the seven parties put forward a set of common proposals calling, among other things, for stepped-up public spending and tax relief; creation of a fund to help middle-class families meet mortgage payments; and reduction of rates payments and public transportation fees.[49]

In response to such surprisingly unified, Keynesian proposals – and to public opinion polls which showed the chief executive's level of popular support sagging noticeably[50] – Tung announced in June a US$5.6 billion relief package designed to shore up Hong Kong's free-falling property market and to provide mortgage assistance and rate rebates for at least some members of the SAR's hard-pressed middle classes.

The decline of civility. In the event, Tung's emergency measures were

---

47. Hong Kong Government poll, cited in Frank Ching, "Political and social impact of the Asian financial crisis on Hong Kong," *CSIS Hong Kong Update*, December 1997.

48. On the impact of the Asian crisis on Hong Kong's economy in the first half of 1998, see Byron Weng, "Weathering a growing discontent," *CSIS Hong Kong Update*, August 1998, pp. 4–6.

49. "Democrats call parties to economic meeting," *Hong Kong Standard*, 29 May 1998.

50. In a poll taken in June 1998, only 46% of respondents expressed satisfaction with Tung's performance as chief executive. See DeGolyer, "Public opinion and participation in the 1998 LegCo elections."

widely dismissed as "too little, too late."[51] And as the economic crisis worsened over the summer of 1998, the seven-party LegCo coalition came unglued. Differences between (as well as within) the parties now emerged on such benchmark economic issues as the supply of new housing, the relaxation of barriers against imported Chinese labour, unemployment relief, deficit spending, and a controversial stock market intervention by the SAR government which, in August 1998, purchased US$10 billion in local blue-chip securities in an effort to repel international hedge-fund speculators and boost investor confidence. Within LegCo, voices of opposition to government economic policies now grew more numerous – and more strident.

Lacking the constitutional power either to initiate meaningful legislation or to amend the Basic Law to remedy legislative impotence, and unable to muster a working majority in LegCo because of systemic bias in the electoral mechanism, Hong Kong's pro-democratic legislators went sharply negative in the second half of 1998. Democrats and their allies turned increasingly to trench warfare, directing a series of scathing verbal attacks against Tung and his administration. The emergency relief measures were dismissed as "woefully inadequate";[52] the stock market intervention was called "disruptive";[53] the Hong Kong Monetary Authority was berated for doing a "really bad job";[54] a sudden freeze on new housing construction was derided as "ridiculous";[55] a cargo-handling débâcle at the newly-opened Hong Kong International Airport at Chek Lap Kok was blamed on governmental incompetence and perfidy;[56] and a proposal by the government to reintroduce a one-fourth minority of appointed members to the district boards and to eliminate altogether the elected Urban and Regional Councils (the middle layer in Hong Kong's three-tiered system of representative government) was attacked as a thinly-veiled attempt to roll back democratization and suppress the *vox populi*.[57] There were even suggestions from some angry legislators that – notwithstanding daunting constitutional obstacles – impeachment proceedings might be initiated against Tung Chee-hwa.[58]

---

51. "Government action too little too late," *Hong Kong Standard*, 30 May 1998. One local commentator likened Tung's modest relief measures to "painting [a picture of] a pancake to ease hunger." See "$2b offer for small businesses described as 'useless'," *South China Morning Post*, 23 June 1998.

52. See "Tung must apologize for bungles," *South China Morning Post*, 29 June 1998.

53. See "Economy in turmoil: conflicting cries from parties," *South China Morning Post*, 29 August 1998.

54. "Politicians better than civil servants," *South China Morning Post*, 17 August 1998.

55. "Hong Kong land freeze draws ire," *Wall Street Journal*, 25 June 1998.

56. On the airport fiasco and its effects see Weng, "Weathering a growing discontent," pp. 4–6.

57. In December 1998, all 13 Democratic Party members of LegCo staged a walkout over the government's proposal to increase the number of appointed and ex officio seats on reconstituted district boards. Shortly thereafter, The Frontier's Emily Lau claimed that the government's plan constituted a violation of the International Covenant on Civil and Political Rights. See *Hong Kong Standard*, 17 December 1998, and 12 February 1999.

58. "Don't abuse power to dump Tung, legislators warned," *Hong Kong Standard*, 8 August 1998.

Key members of Tung's administration were now subject almost daily to legislative barbs. Secretary of Justice Elsie Leung Oi-sie was criticized, among other things, for refusing to indict a local publishing tycoon whose newspaper had illegally inflated its circulation figures.[59] Financial Secretary Donald Tsang Yam-kuen was accused of a number of failings, from enabling wealthy cronies to profit from government stock purchases, to failing vigorously to implement a promised programme of employment stimulation through public works spending, to covering up the airport fiasco at Chek Lap Kok.[60] Constitutional Affairs Secretary Michael Suen Ming-yeung – arguably Hong Kong's most pro-Beijing senior civil servant – was scolded for allegedly referring to LegCo's democrats as an "extreme minority" and for saying that Hong Kong people were "not interested in democracy."[61] In early autumn, four legislators from The Frontier issued a blanket condemnation of the Tung administration, accusing it of "protecting the rich but paying little attention to the public."[62] And when Tung gave his annual policy review in early October, a rising chorus of critics blasted him for his vacillation, inconsistency and weak leadership.[63] Adding insult to injury, democrats in LegCo managed to vote down the customary legislative motion of thanks for his policy address.[64] Not even the much-revered Chief Administrative Secretary Anson Chan – the most popular member of Tung's government – could escape the wrath of the aroused legislators, as LegCo judged her to have been primarily responsible for the Chek Lap Kok airport fiasco.[65]

The DAB was also beginning to part company with the chief executive and his pro-business administration on key economic issues. The most potent areas of disagreement were immigration and housing supply. While the tycoon-dominated HKPA favoured the relaxation of immigration restrictions in order to permit large numbers of low-paid mainland Chinese labourers to work in the SAR's depressed construction industry, the pro-unionist DAB was principally concerned with protecting the jobs and wages of Hong Kong workers.[66] By the same token, while both the HKPA and Liberal Party – representing property-owning upper and middle-class members of Tung's support base – lobbied heavily for severe restrictions on the supply of new housing (to counteract a precipi-

59. Dow Jones Newswires, 21 May 1998; *Hong Kong Standard*, 5 February 1999; and Byron Weng, "Whither the rule of law in the HKSAR?" *CSIS Hong Kong Update*, April 1998.
60. "Jobs creation way off target," *Hong Kong Standard*, 10 September 1998; and "Tsang blows his top at tormentors," *Hong Kong Standard*, 10 December 1998.
61. The allegations were denied by Suen, who nevertheless continued to antagonize the democrats by claiming that only 5% of Hong Kong people had expressed support for accelerated democratization in the May LegCo elections. See *South China Morning Post*, 12 January 1999.
62. *Hong Kong Standard*, 26 September 1998.
63. "Tung feels mounting heat amid Hong Kong's woes," *Wall Street Journal*, 12 October 1998.
64. "Tung brushes off LegCo vote of no thanks," *Hong Kong Standard*, 5 November 1998.
65. "Tung 'sorry' as LegCo blames Chan," *Hong Kong Standard*, 28 January 1999.
66. DAB legislators attributed the sharp rise in local unemployment to the importation of Chinese workers by mainland-based "red chip" firms operating in Hong Kong. See "Unions brace for feared 6pc jobless figure," *Hong Kong Standard*, 20 February 1999.

tous decline in housing prices), the DAB, defending the interests of working class and non-homeowning middle-class people, pushed for a rapid expansion of the housing supply. Indeed, the frequency with which legislators from the formerly pro-government DAB now took issue with Tung's backers within the business community led one frustrated conservative member of the Executive Council to disparage *all* legislators as "the opposition."[67]

Fragmentation, polarization and paralysis. As popular dissatisfaction with Tung's government mounted in the second half of 1998, pro-democratic legislators floated a number of initiatives designed to strengthen LegCo's hand vis-à-vis the executive branch. To speed the process of democratization, Democratic Party legislators introduced a bill calling for direct election of all LegCo members in the year 2000 and direct popular election of the chief executive in 2002. To no one's surprise, the bill was defeated by conservative legislators from the functional constituencies.[68] In an attempt to make it more difficult for the chief executive to muster the simple majority of votes needed to pass government-sponsored bills in LegCo, democratic legislators now proposed to count abstentions as votes. The same legislators proposed to use the device of offering amendments to government bills to get around the Basic Law's prohibition against private members introducing bills pertaining to government policy, public expenditure or government structure. Both proposals elicited strenuous constitutional objections from Solicitor-General Daniel Fung Wah-kin on the grounds that they violated the NPC's exclusive right to interpret and amend the Basic Law, and were thereby mooted. A related initiative by Christine Loh of the Citizen's Party to call a constitutional convention for the purpose of amending the Basic Law was also rejected out of hand, and for the same reason.[69] In response to such persistent executive stonewalling, a frustrated Martin Lee publicly charged the government with seeking a "rubber stamp" legislature.[70] Commenting on the legislature's increasingly adversarial relations with the government, one observer noted that "taking autonomy from LegCo does not mean a compliant LegCo, but one that is forced to go to extremes."[71]

Democracy Deformed: The Chickens Come Home to Roost

By the end of 1998, the political consequences of Hong Kong's unbalanced institutions of governance were becoming clear. The polariza-

---

67. Cited in James T.H. Tang, "Hong Kong's confidence crisis," *CSIS Hong Kong Update*, August 1998, p. 7.
68. "Democracy camp loses first LegCo battle," *Hong Kong Standard*, 16 July 1998.
69. "Complete overhaul of Basic Law needed," *Hong Kong Standard*, 10 July 1998.
70. "Constitutional crisis threat," *Hong Kong Standard*, 10 July 1998; "Rules in line with Basic Law, say legislators," *Hong Kong Standard*, 22 July 1998; "Opposition leader: government wants 'rubber stamp' legislature," Dow-Jones Newswires, 26 July 1998.
71. Weng, "Weathering a growing discontent," p. 6.

tion of LegCo – and the rising sense of political impotence shared by a substantial number of its members – had reached the point where younger, more radically-inclined members of the Democratic Party's legislative contingent proposed permanently walking out of both LegCo and the 18 local district boards, taking their dispute with the government directly into the streets and urging a party boycott of the 2000 LegCo elections.[72] The threatened walkout split the Democratic Party's leadership, prompting two of its core members – newly-elected vice-chairman Lau Chin-shek (who also represented the Confederation of Trade Unions) and former vice-chairman Cheung Bing-leung – to resign from their party posts.[73] In the wake of the resignations, speculation mounted about an imminent rupture in the Democratic Party and the possible formation of a new labour party in Hong Kong.[74]

In early January 1999 the Democratic Party held a day-long conference to discuss its future as a parliamentary opposition party. In the end, a moderate faction under Martin Lee prevailed, and the party elected to keep its members inside LegCo and the district boards – thus narrowly averting a political crisis. Backing away from the brink of open rebellion, the party issued a five-point communiqué in which it pledged to fulfil its electoral mandate to serve as a responsible opposition voice within the assemblies.[75] Meanwhile, a nervous Tung Chee-hwa, in a symbolic gesture intended to assuage the rising frustration of the democrats, consented to hold only his second meeting with Democratic Party leaders since the May elections. The meeting, held on the eve of the party's day-long strategy conference, failed to produce any agreement.[76]

As 1999 – the Year of the Rabbit – began, Hong Kong's political parties faced a mounting crisis of identity. Lacking either legislative power or responsibility, they chafed at their own impotence. They were frustrated with the chief executive's lack of forthright, hands-on leadership, and were increasingly, and at times almost reflexively, critical of his government.

Without a significant China threat or a provisional LegCo to attack, the unity displayed by the Democratic Party for the better part of a decade was now seriously frayed, as were its working relations with other democratic parties and groups. Symptomatic of a growing intra-party malaise was the acknowledgment by Democratic Party leaders that they would have difficulty fielding a full list of candidates for the 1999 district board elections.[77] At the other end of the political spectrum the pro-Beijing DAB, which had emerged as principal electoral rival to the fractious democrats, was also distancing itself from the chief executive

72. See "Democrats at the crossroads," *South China Morning Post*, 30 December 1998.
73. "Resignations rock democrats," *Hong Kong Standard*, 18 December 1998.
74. "Democrats at the crossroads."
75. "Democrats decide to play by the rules," *South China Morning Post*, 12 January 1999.
76. According to Martin Lee, "Mr Tung was not the least bit swayed by our conversation." *Ibid.*
77. "Democrats doubt full show of strength for elections," *Hong Kong Standard*, 6 January 1999.

and his administration. Even the Liberal Party, reeling from its over-whelming defeat in the geographical constituencies in the May elections, began to reposition itself, championing middle-class (as opposed to strictly business-class) interests. Among the political parties only the arch-conservative, tycoon-dominated HKPA – with no popularly elected legislators within its ranks – remained unswervingly loyal to the chief executive. Meanwhile, Tung's job approval ratings continued to slide, reaching a new low of 32 per cent in January 1999.[78]

Conclusion

With LegCo hamstrung, with executive–legislative relations at an impasse and with few prospects of an early reduction of tension in sight, it is tempting to conclude that Hong Kong's democratic deformity is destined to be a permanent condition. The SAR's political institutions – which have been characterized as semi-democratic in form but neo-auth-oritarian in essence – continue to present students of comparative demo-cratic process with a profound puzzle. As one long-time observer of Hong Kong politics has noted:

The continued use of the term ["representative government"] is misplaced, since according to the Basic Law the Legislative Council does not determine the formation of government ... Members of the Council are severely circumscribed in their ability to play an active role in legislation or to share responsibilities in the making of policies ... The design of the constitution was aimed precisely at containing the hypothetically "harmful" effects of electoral politics in terms of "radical," "populist" policy demands ... The functional constituencies in Hong Kong were designed not to protect vulnerable minorities, but to substitute for the appointment system in the past, through which socio-economic elites gained access to political influence ... Does it follow that elections [do not] matter? The answer hinges on the standard we employ to measure an election ...[79]

This brings the issue back to the central question posed by the editors of this volume; for if electoral democracy is a process by which citizens choose their most important leaders in regular elections that are free, fair and meaningful, then Hong Kong clearly does not qualify as an electoral democracy. Raising the number of directly elected legislators from 20 to 30 over the next half decade, as scheduled, will certainly enhance the SAR's "democraticness"; but in the absence of a popularly elected chief executive, and with the retention of functional constituencies and split voting within the Legislative Council, progress toward real democracy will necessarily be slow and halting. And while the Basic Law holds out the promise of reopening the question of an all-directly-elected LegCo in the year 2007, there are substantial constitutional blocks in the way of such an outcome. Not least of these is the institution of an indirectly chosen chief executive, beholden to Beijing, who, in conjunction with China's National People's Congress, retains effective veto power over

---

78. "Government still out of favour says poll," *Hong Kong Standard*, 2 February 1999.
79. Kuan Hsin-chi, "Election without political clout."

critical phases of the democratization process, including constitutional amendment.

Yet for all its democratic deformity, Hong Kong is not exactly a "pseudodemocracy" either, if by that term is meant a process by which the political centre controls the election process to achieve its goals.[80] Despite serious structural imperfections, elections in Hong Kong are relatively free, unfettered, competitive affairs, while political parties are vigorous and (for the most part) organizationally autonomous.[81] By the same token, an emergent "civic culture" of rising (though not yet particularly high) political awareness and citizen activism is also in evidence, as shown by the unprecedented voter turnout for the 1998 LegCo elections and the enormous (and ultimately effective) public pressure brought to bear on Tung Chee-hwa to ameliorate economic suffering in response to the 1998 market crash. The problem, then, lies not in any glaring shortage of civic virtue, political awareness or party organization in Hong Kong. On the contrary, the problem is essentially a constitutional one. By deliberate design, the Basic Law's architects fashioned electoral and legislative mechanisms that guaranteed an effective institutional disconnect between political participation, political representation and political power. It is this disconnect – sometimes referred to as "birdcage democracy"[82] – which lies at the very heart of Hong Kong's democratic deformity, rendering predictions of a future democratic transition uncertain at best.[83]

Notwithstanding such uncertainty, a few emerging trends are discernible. A repolarization of political life appears to be occurring. The principal axis of political cleavage in the pre-handover era, defined by a bipolar distribution of attitudes towards China, has given way to a new, class-based axis of socio-economic cleavage pitting pro-business elitists against pro-welfare populists. With the deepening of Hong Kong's post-handover recession, this cleavage appears also to be deepening. If this trend continues, politicians hoping to win a plurality of popular votes in direct elections (within LegCo's expanded geographical constituencies and in the newly reconstituted district boards) will find themselves under

80. Definition suggested by Larry Diamond and Ramon H. Myers in the original project memorandum.

81. One partial exception to the rule of organizational autonomy is the DAB, which has reportedly maintained close links with the Hong Kong and Macau Affairs Office of the Chinese Communist Party.

82. See Byron Weng, "The first year of the HKSAR: changes in the political institutions," *CSIS Hong Kong Update*, 1998 July pp. 1–4.

83. A rather different conclusion has been reached by H.C. Kuan and Lau Siu-kai in their study of recent trends in Hong Kong's political culture. Focusing on the effects of "intermediation environments" such as primary social networks, secondary associations and the mass media on the political awareness and mobilization of Hong Kong people, Kuan and Lau found that a majority of SAR residents surveyed in 1999 were only weakly, if at all, embedded in (or affected by) these politicizing environments, thus raising doubts about claims of increased citizen activism. Their findings tend to reinforce earlier (pre-Tiananmen) observations concerning the political apathy of Hong Kong people and thus carry negative implications for the success of the democratic transition in Hong Kong. See Kuan Hsin-chi and Lau Siu-kai, "Intermediation environments and election in Hong Kong," *Democratization* (spring 2000).

increasing pressure to respond to voters' immediate economic concerns. Those parties and politicians that are able successfully to adapt to the electoral vicissitudes of the "new economic populism" will do well at the polls; those that cannot will not. Based on recent experience, the winners in such a repolarization are likely to be the DAB, Frontier and the radical-unionist wing of the Democratic Party; the losers are likely to be the Liberal Party, the HKPA and the moderate wing of the Democratic Party. A further realignment of political parties would not be unlikely in such a situation, such as a split within the Democratic Party leading to the creation of a new labour party, and/or a new coalition among "patriotic" pro-business parties and groups. While the DAB would initially benefit from the rise of economic populism, the need to respond to the immediate socio-economic concerns of Hong Kong voters would inevitably place added strain on its pro-Beijing orientation.

If this picture proves generally accurate, LegCo can be expected to become increasingly obstructionist; the SAR government will come under increasing popular and legislative pressure to accelerate the process of democratization; and the chief executive – whoever it might be – will be forced to choose between endorsing major institutional reforms (thereby upsetting both Beijing and his own local big-business constituency) and holding the line on democratization (thereby alienating Hong Kong's middle-class and working-class voters). This will not be a comfortable choice.

On the other hand, if Hong Kong's post-handover recession should level out soon and give way to a broad-based recovery, with unemployment (which reached a new high of 6.2 per cent in March 1999) receding, real wages rising and a modicum of sanity restored to Hong Kong's volatile property and securities markets, then the phenomenon of class-based political mobilization might well be slowed down. This would mean, in turn, that populist pressures for accelerated democratization would abate somewhat, giving the chief executive additional time and political breathing space within which to forge a new governing coalition and mount a more effective defence of the SAR's neo-authoritarian institutions.

Amid all this uncertainty, one thing is sure. Regardless of the outcome of the current economic crisis, the genie of democratic participation, released from captivity over the past 15 years, is not likely to crawl meekly back into the jar of executive-led government. Elections do matter, even if they are limited in scope and impact. Consequently, challenges to Hong Kong's constitutionally-deformed political institutions will continue to be felt for years – and perhaps decades – to come.

Accommodating "Democracy" in a One-Party State: Introducing Village Elections in China*

Kevin J. O'Brien and Lianjiang Li

When residents of a few Guangxi villages decided to elect their own leaders in late 1980 and early 1981, none of them could have known they were starting a historic reform. What began as a stopgap effort to fill a political vacuum, after much debate and two decades of uneven implementation, is now enshrined in a national law. Procedures for holding elections have been spelled out and implementing regulations are being formulated at all levels. Voting is now mandatory every three years in every village, bar none.

Meanwhile, insofar as they bear on the nation's democratic prospects, village (and now township) elections have become one of China's most talked-about political reforms. Scholars examine them to gauge the likelihood of regime transition. Journalists visit villages to see if this experiment with political competition is real. Prominent political figures in the West have applauded Beijing's willingness to subject some officials to the people's will. Even China's top leaders, after years of relative silence, have praised "villagers' self-government" (*cunmin zizhi*) as one of the "great inventions" of Chinese farmers.[1]

Where and how did village elections begin? What was at stake and why were they so controversial? Who took part in the spread of elections and what role did they play? Using interviews, leadership speeches and archival materials, this article describes the origins and implementation of villagers' self-government. After tracing various ups and downs, it offers some thoughts on whether villagers' committee (VC) elections have brought real democracy to China's countryside.

Origins

The earliest villagers' committees emerged in two Guangxi counties (Yishan and Luocheng) in late 1980 and early 1981. Formed without the knowledge of local authorities, these somewhat makeshift organizations were created by village elders, former cadres and community-minded villagers. Their purpose was to address a decline in social order and a broader political crisis that was fast becoming apparent as family farming took hold and brigades and production teams stopped functioning. At this early stage, VCs were called "leadership groups for village public security" (*cun zhian lingdao xiaozu*) or "village management committees" (*cun guan hui*). The term "villagers' committee" (*cunmin weiyuanhui*) only

* For generous financial support, we would like to thank the Asia Foundation, the Henry Luce Foundation, The Research and Writing Program of the John D. and Catherine T. MacArthur Foundation, the Pacific Cultural Foundation, and the Research Grants Council of Hong Kong.

1. For remarks by President Jiang Zemin, see *Renmin ribao* (*People's Daily*), 19 October 1998, p. 1.

appeared in Luocheng county in spring 1981. Within a matter of months, county administrators in Yishan and Luocheng had reported this development to their superiors in Hechi prefecture and had recommended its popularization. The prefectural Party committee then decided to establish VCs throughout the region and reported its plan to the provincial government, which in turn reported it to Beijing.[2]

In the early 1980s, villagers' committees were genuine, if circumscribed, organs of self-government. Committee members were elected (though rather informally), and their responsibilities were confined to managing neighbourhood affairs in natural villages (*ziran cun*). VCs at this point were free-standing and relatively autonomous non-governmental bodies that did not take part in the allocation of state resources such as land or quotas. Typical undertakings included enacting codes of conduct banning gambling and theft, maintaining irrigation ditches, paving roads and repairing bridges, and mediating disputes. VCs might also raise funds and mobilize labour to rebuild schools, run day-care centres, and look after the poor, the elderly and relatives of soldiers.[3] They were not, however, expected to help township governments enforce state policies (such as birth control and tax collection), nor did they rely on township assistance to conduct their work. If two farmers rejected a VC's efforts to settle a dispute, for example, the committee might invite all adults in the village to assemble and decide (by secret ballot) who was in the right. Both parties would be required to pay a deposit before the hearing began; whoever received a two-thirds majority of the ballots cast would then receive his or her money back plus a portion of the loser's deposit. The remaining funds would be used to compensate the "jury" for their time and efforts.[4]

2. Yu Xiangyang, "Woguo nongmin de weida chuangju" ("A great invention of Chinese peasants"), *Kexue shehuizhuyi cankao ziliao* (*Reference Materials on Scientific Socialism*), No. 14 (1984), pp. 26–27; also *Guangxi ribao* (*Guangxi Daily*), 30 December 1987, p. 3. For more on these early experiments, see Wang Zhongtian, "Zhongguo nongcun de jiceng minzhu fazhan yu nongmin de minzhu quanli baozhang" ("The development of grassroots democracy in the Chinese countryside and the guarantee of farmers' democratic rights"), paper presented at the Conference on the Construction of Village-Level Organizations in Mainland China, Chinese University of Hong Kong, 8–9 October 1998, p. 1. For brief mentions of Luocheng and Yishan, see Amy B. Epstein, "Village elections in China: experimenting with democracy," in U.S. Congress, Joint Economic Committee, *China's Economic Future*, (Washington D.C.: Government Printing Office, 1996), p. 406; Xu Wang, "Mutual empowerment of state and peasantry: grassroots democracy in rural China," *World Development*, Vol. 25, No. 9 (1997), p. 1436. In some sources, Luocheng county is mistaken for the non-existent Luoshan county.
3. Yu Xiangyang, "Cunmin weiyuanhui banle shier jian da shi," ("Villagers' committees do 12 jobs"), *Neibu wengao* (*Internal Manuscripts*), No. 20 (1983), pp. 17–24; also Xu Wang, "Mutual empowerment," p. 1436; Epstein, "Village elections," p. 406. On proto-VCs in Sichuan, Hebei, Henan, Shandong, Yunnan and other provinces, see Wang Zhongtian, "The development of grassroots democracy," p. 1; Bai Gang, "Zhongguo cunmin zizhi fazhi jianshe pingyi" ("Discussing legal construction concerning villagers' self-government in China"), *Zhongguo shehui kexue* (*Social Sciences in China*), No. 3 (May 1998), p. 88; and Liu Cheng and Dong Junming, "Dalemu cun minzhu xuanju cunzhang de diaocha" ("An investigation of the democratic election of village chiefs in Dalemu village"), *Nongcun jingji wenti* (*Rural Economic Issues*), No. 8 (1982), pp. 38–39.
4. Yu Xiangyang, "A great invention," p. 21. The author did not explain what would happen if the vote did not produce a two-thirds majority.

When Guangxi's report on VCs reached Beijing, Peng Zhen, then vice-chairman of the National People's Congress Standing Committee (NPCSC), praised villagers' committees as the perfect vehicle for practising grassroots democracy. So impressed was Peng, he instructed the NPC and the Ministry of Civil Affairs (MoCA) to send investigators to Guangxi to find out what was going on. At the same time, he encouraged other provinces to experiment with VCs.[5] In a short time committees spread widely, especially in areas that had taken the lead in abolishing communes and establishing township governments. Reports suggest that pace-setting provinces included Anhui, Beijing, Fujian, Gansu, Hebei, Jiangsu, Jilin, Shandong and Sichuan.[6]

In December 1982, thanks mainly to Peng's urging,[7] villagers' committees were written into the Constitution as elected, mass organizations of self-government (article 111). A 1983 Central Committee circular also instructed that elected VCs should be set up, that they should actively promote public welfare and assist local governments, and that implementing regulations should be drawn up in light of local conditions.[8] These directives generated some controversy, but opposition at this point was relatively muted. For one thing, the early 1980s were a time when far-reaching changes were taking place in all walks of political life. For another, the Party leadership was busy exploring political reform. In 1979, Deng Xiaoping had remarked that "we have not propagated and practised democracy enough, and our systems and institutions leave much to be desired."[9] A year later, Deng specifically called for "practising people's democracy to the full," especially at the grassroots.[10] And in June 1981, The Resolution on Certain Questions in the History of Our Party announced that it was the Party's aim to "gradually realize direct popular participation in the democratic process at the grassroots of political power and community life."[11]

The 1980s were not the first time that the Party had experimented with basic-level elections. As early as the Jiangxi Soviet (1931–34), popular assemblies had been established to draw villagers and "enlightened gentry" into local government. Later, after the Japanese invasion, the so-called "three-thirds system" (*san san zhi*) had also played some part in

5. Bai Yihua, *Zhongguo jiceng zhengquan de gaige yu tansuo (Reform and Exploration of China's Basic-Level Governance)* (Beijing: Zhongguo shehui chubanshe, 1995), p. 284.

6. See Mi Youlu, "Villager participation in autonomy and its evaluation," paper presented at Conference on Local Self-Government in Mainland China, Hong Kong and Taiwan, Duke University, 2–3 May 1997, p. 3.

7. Bai Yihua, *Reform and Exploration*, pp. 284–85.

8. "Party Central Committee and State Council 'Circular on separating government administration and commune management and setting up township governments'," *Chinese Law and Government*, Vol. 19, No. 4 (1986–87), p. 36.

9. Deng Xiaoping, *Selected Works of Deng Xiaoping, 1975–1982* (Beijing: Foreign Languages Press, 1984), p. 183.

10. *Ibid.* p. 304. See also, Allen C. Choate, "Local governance in China: an assessment of villagers committees," Working Paper No. 1 (San Francisco: The Asia Foundation, 1997), p. 6.

11. In Harold C. Hinton (ed.), *The People's Republic of China 1979–1984* (Wilmington: Scholarly Resources, 1986), p. 108.

reducing the gap between leaders and led, making cadres accountable to their constituents and encouraging attention to the mass line.[12] In most of the communist-controlled districts, however, elections were first and foremost a device for winning over converts to the struggle against the Kuomintang and local power-holders. Making a show of granting country people political rights was designed to undermine the traditional elite, rein in the Party's ideologically suspect allies, and draw attention to the contrast between border region governments and the Kuomintang's "one-party dictatorship."[13] For the Communists, war-time elections were state-building exercises in which controlled polarization and community building co-existed with democratization. Affording villagers a smidgeon of power served the Party's overriding aim of cementing its supremacy and deepening penetration into rural communities.[14]

Under these circumstances, popular assemblies in the border regions were inevitably "feeble and fleeting institutions" that were overshadowed by smaller, more efficient governing committees and the bureaucracy. The assemblies formed in Shaan-Gan-Ning, for example, met infrequently and offered little guidance to the permanent organs of state. Moreover, Party domination of elected bodies predictably increased as one approached the real locus of power.[15]

Peng Zhen's singular enthusiasm for grassroots elections and villagers' committees can be traced to this era and his experiences in the Jin-Cha-Ji Border Region.[16] In a report delivered to the Politburo in 1941, Peng

12. Yung-fa Chen, *Making Revolution* (Berkeley: University of California Press, 1986), pp. 256–57; also Mark Selden, *China in Revolution* (Armonk, NY: M.E. Sharpe, 1995). On assemblies in the Jiangxi Soviet, see Kevin J. O'Brien, *Reform Without Liberalization* (New York: Cambridge University Press, 1990), pp. 20–21. The three-thirds system required that Party representation in assemblies be no more than one-third of the total, and that two-thirds be made up of "non-Party left-wing progressives" and "middle-of-the-roaders."

13. On various border regions, see Chen, *Making Revolution*, p. 223; Pauline B. Keating, *Two Revolutions* (Stanford: Stanford University Press, 1997), pp. 131–35; Tetsuya Kataoka, *Resistance and Revolution in China* (Berkeley: University of California Press, 1974), p. 241; Steven I. Levine, *Anvil of Victory* (New York: Columbia University Press, 1987), pp. 111–13; Peng Zhen, "Report on the work of the party and specific policies in the Jin Cha Ji border region," in Tony Saich (ed.), *The Rise to Power of the Chinese Communist Party* (Armonk, NY: M.E. Sharpe, 1996), p. 1035.

14. On Shaanbei, see Keating, *Two Revolutions* pp. 130–146. On "controlled polarization" more generally, see Chen, *Making Revolution*, pp. 11–12, 230; Although "strengthening the grip of the party over the entire region" is not his focus, see also Selden, *China in Revolution*, p. 128. In a first-person report that stresses the Party's democratic achievements, Jack Belden, *China Shakes the World* (New York: Harpers, 1949), p. 88, also notes: "in some villages, the various planks of all candidates contained a resolution to 'Support the Communist party and follow Mao Tze-tung,' illustrat[ing] clearly enough that the Communists are trying to establish not so much a utopian democracy as a support for themselves."

15. This paragraph is drawn from Selden, *China in Revolution*, p. 117; Apter and Saich, *Revolutionary Discourse*, pp. 206, 214; Chen, *Making Revolution*, pp. 255–56; and Keating, *Two Revolutions*, pp. 134–36. The quoted text refers to Suide and appears in Keating, p. 136.

16. Peng Zhen, "Cunmin weiyuanhui zuzhifa shi guojia zhongyao falü zhi yi" ("The organic law of villagers' committees is one of the nation's important basic laws"), speech at the 20th group meeting of the Sixth NPCSC, 16 March 1987, in *Peng Zhen tongzhi guanyu cunmin weiyuanhui jumin weiyuanhui de zhongyao jianghua* (*Important Speeches of Comrade Peng Zhen on Villagers' Committees and Residents' Committees*), unpublished compilation (Beijing: Minzhengbu jiceng zhengquan jianshesi, 1990), p. 10. Peng's comments on the 1930s are also alluded to in Foreign Broadcast Information Service: *Daily*

explained why and how local elections had been held and suggested establishing "district and village assemblies" (*qu cun daibiaohui*) to oversee elected, village cadres. In Peng's view, elections were not only compatible with Party rule; they were the right instrument for tightening the Party's grip in areas where its dominance was still uncertain.[17] A measure of mass participation, in other words, would generate support for the Party's revolutionary mission while serving its state-building aspirations. "Democracy" and governmental power could develop together.

In the years after the People's Republic was founded, Peng continued to show interest in basic-level, mass organizations. In the early 1950s, for instance, Mao had ordered that urban residents who did not belong to work units should be organized. Peng, then deputy director of the Central Committee's Political-Legal Committee and mayor of Beijing, suggested forming "residents' committees" (*jumin weiyuanhui*). These would be "mass autonomous organizations, not political [i.e. government] organizations." Their tasks, according to Peng, would centre on improving public welfare, popularizing policies and laws, mobilizing participation in state-sponsored activities, and reflecting opinions to grassroots officials. Members of residents' committees were to be elected and to accept the guidance of urban, basic-level authorities. Peng's proposal was later ratified by the Party's Central Committee and residents' committees became an established feature of the urban landscape.[18]

Peng's later experience as one of the first victims of the Cultural Revolution only reinforced his commitment to "socialist democracy" and prompted him to consider how it might be built in China.[19] According to him, inasmuch as China had almost no tradition of self-government, democratic habits had to be cultivated among both Party leaders and ordinary citizens. Realizing socialist democracy thus involved a two-pronged approach. For the leadership, respect for democracy would be nurtured by strengthening people's congresses; for the masses, democratic ways of thinking would be instilled through self-government. The focus of "democratic training" in the countryside would be the construction of villagers' committees. By electing their own leaders and participating in grassroots decision-making, 800 million Chinese villagers would learn how to manage their community's affairs. After rural people

---

footnote continued
Report (China) (hereafter, FBIS-CHI), No. 79 (1987), p. K10. On Peng and "filtered democracy" in Jin-Cha-Ji, see Pitman B. Potter, *From Leninist Discipline to Socialist Legalism* (Hong Kong: Hong Kong Institute of Asia-Pacific Studies, 1995), p. 14.

17. See Peng Zhen, "Report on the work," pp. 1017–38; Apter and Saich, *Revolutionary Discourse*, pp. 212–13.

18. See Benkan Jizhe, "Cujin nongcun minzhuhua jianshe de zhongyao falü" ("An important law that promotes rural democratic construction"), *Liaowang* (Haiwaiban) (*Outlook* (Overseas Edition)), No. 51 (1987), p. 17.

19. Tianjian Shi, "Village committee elections in China: institutionalist tactics for democracy," *World Politics* Vol. 51, No. 3 (1999), p. 329. Peng said in 1987: "We suffered greatly from failing to construct socialist democracy after the founding of our state. During the Cultural Revolution there was so-called big democracy, but in fact there was no democracy." Peng Zhen, "The organic law," p. 10.

became skilled at running their own villages, Peng argued, they might then move on to govern townships and counties.[20]

Controversy, 1983–1987

From the very beginning, many local administrators harboured doubts about the role VCs might come to play. As early as 1983, questions were raised regarding the degree to which villagers' committees would become autonomous from Party branches and township governments. While everyone agreed that Party branches ought to lead VCs, some sceptics felt that committee members should seek Party approval for each and every decision they made, while others thought the branch could exercise leadership merely by checking if a committee had strayed from the Party's line and policies.[21] As for the relationship between VCs and township governments, some rural leaders thought informal "guidance" (zhidao) would suffice, but others (including many grassroots cadres), favoured hierarchical, "leadership" (lingdao) relations. Township officials had an especially large stake in this debate: many believed that without tight control over VCs and an ability to issue direct commands, village cadres would be tempted to ignore state interests and disregard township instructions. Elected VC members might, in a word, be inclined to take their cues from below rather than above. This could interfere with tax collection, grain procurement and enforcing the birth control policy, and might ultimately cripple township authority.[22]

Out of fears that committees would become "independent kingdoms," some critics of self-government even recommended transforming VCs into full-blown state organs.[23] Common proposals included turning them into "village administrative offices" (cungongsuo) or setting up administrative offices alongside them. These offices would be directly responsible to townships and their appointed heads would presumably be more

---

20. Peng Zhen, "Qunzhong zizhi shi fazhan shehuizhuyi minzhu de zhongyao yi huan" ("Mass autonomy is an important link in the development of socialist democracy"), speech at the chairmanship meeting of the Sixth NPCSC, 23 November 1987, in *Important Speeches*, p. 25. See also Cai Dingjian, "Tuijin nongcun de minzhu jianshe" ("Advance democratic construction in the countryside"), *Zhengzhi yu falü* (*Politics and Law*), No. 4 (1989), pp. 16–17.

21. Yu Xiangyang, "Villagers' committees," p. 24; Yu Xiangyang, "A great invention," p. 28. On Party branch leadership of VCs, see Daniel Kelliher, "The Chinese debate over village self-government," *The China Journal*, No. 37 (1997), pp. 81–83, 85.

22. Cai Dingjian, "Advance democratic construction," p. 18; Yu Xiangyang, "Villagers' committees," p. 24; Yu Xiangyang, "A great invention," pp. 28–29; Chen Guanglong, "Guanyu 'cunmin weiyuanhui zuzhifa' de youguan wenti tantao" ("Exploration of issues related to the 'organic law of villagers' committees' "), *Fazhi yuekan* (*Legality Monthly*), No. 6 (1987), pp. 39–40. On a similar debate over leadership versus guidance relations in the legislative realm, see Kevin J. O'Brien and Laura M. Luehrmann, "Institutionalizing Chinese legislatures: trade-offs between autonomy and capacity," *Legislative Studies Quarterly*, Vol. 23, No. 1 (1998), pp. 91–108.

23. Yu Xiangyang, "Villagers' committees," p. 24; Yu Xiangyang, "A great invention," pp. 28–29.

receptive to township orders than elected committee directors.[24] Some less ardent foes of self-government proposed a compromise: they recommended that if village administrative offices could not be established, a "specially appointed agent" (*tepaiyuan*) should be sent to every village to represent the township.[25]

Reservations about VCs also existed at the top. Premier Zhao Ziyang suggested that replacing brigades with VCs could reduce the reach of townships and that large townships might find it beneficial to set up village administrative offices.[26] Although these remarks have led some to conclude that Zhao was "the leading opponent of the reform,"[27] the story is more complex. In fact he agreed that elected, autonomous committees should be established. However, while on an inspection tour in November 1986 he had concluded that VCs should not always take the place of brigades, because many brigades, particularly those in south China, were composed of up to a dozen natural villages. Zhao preferred forming VCs in natural villages, large or small, irrespective of whether previously the natural village had been a brigade or a production team.[28] (This approach, incidentally, owed much to the Guangxi model of the early 1980s.) In this regard, rather than undermining self-government, Zhao's plan would have better enfranchised residents of small, remote settlements, who otherwise might find it difficult to win a seat on a committee based in a bigger "core village" (*zhu cun*).

In spite of these disputes, VCs replaced brigades nearly as fast as family farming had replaced collective agriculture. In Yunnan and Guangdong, VCs took the place of production teams; in all other

24. See Deng Minjie, "Guangxi shixing cungongsuo de xianshi dingshi" ("Guangxi's experimentation with village administrative offices"), in Zhongguo jiceng zhengquan jianshe yanjiu hui *et al.* (eds.), *Shijian yu sikao* (*Practice and Reflection*) (Shenyang: Liaoning daxue chubanshe, 1989), pp. 126–133. On *cungongsuo* thwarting the intent of the Organic Law, see Tyrene White, "Political reform and rural government," in Deborah Davis and Ezra Vogel (eds.), *Chinese Society on the Eve of Tiananmen* (Cambridge, MA: Harvard University Press, 1990), p. 57.

25. Minzhengbu and Guowuyuan fazhiju, "Guanyu dui 'Zhonghua renmin gongheguo cunmin weiyuanhui zuzhifa' youguan tiaowen xiugai yijian de baogao" ("A report on revisions of some articles of the organic law of villagers' committees of the People's Republic of China"), mimeo (Beijing: Quanguo renda changweihui bangongting, 11 November 1987), p. 2.

26. "Zhao zongli zai shiyiyue waichu shicha qijian dui ruogan juti wenti de zhishi" ("Premier Zhao's instructions on several concrete issues while on inspection tours in November [1986]"), unpublished transcript. Critics of Zhao, however, argued that establishing village administrative offices was unconstitutional and would enervate VCs. They also regarded his proposal to be impractical because the government could not afford to add several million cadres to the state payroll. Interviews, Beijing, January 1997.

27. Shi, "Village committee," p. 393. Zhao's alleged conflict with Peng has been mentioned in a number of sources. See, for example, Lin Changsheng, *Dalu nongcun cunmin zizhi zhidu yanjiu* (*A Study of the Villagers' Self-Government System on the Mainland*) (Taipei: Xingzhengyuan dalu weiyuanhui, 1995), p. 40. We ourselves wrote that Zhao Ziyang "in fact had no great sympathy for grassroots democracy." Lianjiang Li and Kevin J. O'Brien, "The struggle over village elections," in Merle Goldman and Roderick MacFarquhar (eds.), *The Paradox of China's Post-Mao Reforms* (Cambridge, MA: Harvard University Press, 1999), p. 132. Based on a transcript of Zhao's remarks (rather than our original interviews), we now regard this to be an oversimplification.

28. "Premier Zhao's instructions," p. 1.

provinces they supplanted brigades.[29] By the end of 1984, some 700,000 brigades had been transformed into nearly 950,000 villagers' committees. The transition proceeded smoothly because, at this point, it was little more than a change in name. Constitutional provisions notwithstanding, most committees were still appointed rather than popularly elected. Prior to 1987, although VCs were called "mass autonomous organizations," they were effectively extensions of township government.[30]

Shortly after receiving the 1983 Central Committee circular on VCs, Tianjin and six other provincial-level units (Beijing, Inner Mongolia, Shanxi, Heilongjiang, Zhejiang and Ningxia) took the lead in enacting rules concerning the responsibilities, composition and election of villagers' committees.[31] The Ministry of Civil Affairs dutifully collected and reviewed these regulations, and in August 1984 it produced the first draft of the Organic Rules on Villagers' Committees.[32] At this stage, the main sticking point continued to be whether relations between township governments and committees should be ones of leadership, guidance or some combination of both. Some provincial officials (particularly from Hebei and Jiangsu) favoured turning VCs into cogs in the administrative machine, while legal drafters in the MoCA, citing the Constitution, defended autonomy and the status of VCs as elected, mass organizations.[33]

As the Ministry solicited opinions in the course of revising the Rules, there was also some discussion of elections. Until officials from Sichuan, Jiangxi, Heilongjiang and Shaanxi pointed out that it was unconstitutional, one MoCA draft had permitted a murky mixture of elections, appointment and self-selection. Under this plan, a list of VC members would be popularly elected; then, from among the successful candidates, VC leaders would be "selected" (*tuixuan*) – perhaps by the township, perhaps by committee members themselves. Scholars and local administrators also found fault with draft articles dealing with recall procedures

---

29. Fa Gong Wei, "Quanguo cunmin weiyuanhui jiben qingkuang" ("Basic information on villagers' committees throughout the country"), mimeo (Beijing: Renda changweihui bangongting, March 1997), p. 1.

30. Cai Dingjian, "Advance democratic construction," p. 15; Tang Jinsu, "Woguo cunweihui jianshe zhuangkuang yu zhanwang" ("Current conditions and prospects for construction of our country's villagers' committees") *Shehuizhuyi yanjiu* (*Studies in Socialism*), No. 6 (1992), p. 42. Wang Zhenyao, "Village committees: the basis for China's democratization," in Eduard B. Vermeer, Frank N. Pieke and Woei Lien Chong (eds.), *Cooperative and Collective in China's Rural Development* (Armonk, NY: M.E. Sharpe, 1998), p. 243.

31. Quanguo renda changweihui bangongting, "Qi ge sheng, zizhiqu, zhixiashi zhiding de 'cunmin weiyuanhui gongzuo jianze' qingkuang" ("Seven provinces, autonomous regions and cities have enacted working rules on villagers' committees"), mimeo, (Beijing: Quanguo renda changweihui bangongting, 12 January 1987), pp. 2–3.

32. Bai Yihua, *Reform and Exploration*, p. 287.

33. Minzhengbu, Minzhengsi, "Ge di, ge bumen dui cunmin weiyuanhui zuzhi tiaoli (cao gao) de xiugai yijian" ("Suggestions on revision of the organic law of villagers' committees (draft) from all places and departments"), in Minzhengsi (comp.), *Qingkuang fanying* (*Reflecting the Situation*), No. 11 (1985), p. 2. This issue also featured prominently in NPCSC deliberations. See Bai Yihua, *Reform and Exploration*, pp. 291–95; also, more generally, Choate, "Local governance," p. 8.

and the length of VC terms, and some even proposed that committee members be subject to term limits.[34]

Opposition to villagers' self-government turned out to be unexpectedly strong when the Ministry submitted its 13th draft of the Rules to the NPC in 1987. At the plenary session that spring, a number of legislators rose to argue that the time was not "ripe" for a full-fledged law to be passed. More than a few deputies said that Chinese villagers lacked the "democratic consciousness" to govern themselves. Others were concerned that the bill did not clarify (or even mention) the relationship between Party branches and villagers' committees. Speaking as long-time administrators, many deputies openly doubted whether township guidance of VCs would be enough to guarantee state interests in the countryside.[35]

Although electoral matters did not receive much attention at the 1987 NPC, scepticism about enfranchising villagers lay just below the surface of many comments. Some critics questioned whether "cadres who truly work conscientiously will get elected" and instead supported combining "evaluation by higher-level authorities" with voting by villagers. Several deputies warned that cadres who did the township's bidding would certainly be defeated and that "complex problems will arise if cadres are selected merely through elections." Most opponents recommended that the draft be revised; some, echoing the anxiety of detractors outside the legislature, went so far as to advise that the Constitution be amended so that VCs were converted into government organs led by appointed directors.[36]

Supporters of more autonomy argued the opposite. They thought that "the bill did not go far enough in empowering village cadres against the encroachments of township officials," and some "wanted to add a provision stipulating the right of village cadres to turn down any assignment not covered by the bill."[37] These legislators were concerned that township work would crowd out village concerns and preferred Guangxi-style, free-standing VCs to administrative appendages. The Law Department at the People's University even advised the NPC that any organization that assigned VC members administrative work should pay them for doing it.[38]

As the chief justification for self-government, supporters of the Law argued that passing the bill would help curb arbitrary and predatory

34. Minzhengbu, Minzhengsi, "Suggestions on revision," pp. 4–5.
35. This paragraph is drawn from FBIS-CHI, No. 79 (1987), pp. K10–12; FBIS-CHI, No. 71 (1987), p. K24; FBIS-CHI, No. 66 (1987), p. K7; FBIS-CHI, No. 68 (1987), p. K17. Two NPCSC members also called for enhancing villagers' "educational and scientific level" before enacting the law. FBIS-CHI, No. 224 (1987), pp. 12–13.
36. Bai Yihua, *Reform and Exploration*, pp. 296–97; Interviews, Beijing, September 1993; also FBIS-CHI, No. 79 (1987), p. K11; FBIS-CHI, No. 71 (1987), p. K24. Quoted text in FBIS-CHI, No. 66 (1987) p. K7; FBIS-CHI, No. 68 (1987), p. K17.
37. Tyrene White, "Reforming the countryside," *Current History*, Vol. 91, No. 566 (1992), pp. 275–76. For the amendment suggested by Law Committee members, see FBIS-CHI, No. 47 (1987), pp. K3–4.
38. Minzhengbu, Minzhengsi, "Suggestions on revision," p. 2.

behaviour by rural cadres. They agreed that township leaders had to execute policies that villagers did not understand and did not readily accept, but stressed that this did not justify recourse to threats and coercion.[39] In their view, even the least popular measures (such as birth control and tax collection) could be implemented through persuasion and the mass line – things elected cadres would be more inclined to practise than township appointees. Proponents said that NPC deputies should show a little more faith in the masses and that villagers would not turn self-government into anarchy.[40] They also suggested that worries about the draft failing to mention the Party's role in the village were over-reactions. Party leadership had already been affirmed in the Constitution. "It would make the Party appear weak," a MoCA official who participated in drafting the Rules said, "if we had to place this mass organization under Party branch leadership."[41] A confident Communist Party had no reason to fear that village self-government would lurch out of control.

The debate was so heated that Peng Zhen found it necessary to make three speeches within 48 hours to drum up support among NPC leaders.[42] Peng's lobbying was characterized by nostalgic memories of how close Party–villager relations had been before 1949 and a warning that rural rebellion was possible if self-government was put off. In a speech to the heads of the NPC's provincial delegations, which according to MoCA officials "played a key role in unifying deputy thinking,"[43] Peng argued that village democracy was a matter of "life and death" for the Party. He acknowledged that self-government might "make rural cadres' life a little harder" (that is, it might complicate policy implementation in the short term), but insisted that it would not "produce chaos" (*gao luan*) because "the masses accept what is reasonable."[44] Clearly distressed and drawing on all his prestige as a Party elder, Peng went on to lament how relations between cadres and villagers had deteriorated over the years, noting that some rural cadres "resorted to coercion and commandism" while not a few had become corrupt and high-handed "local emperors" (*tu huangdi*). If such trends were not reversed, he cautioned, villagers would "sooner or later attack our rural cadres with their shoulder poles." To prevent further erosion in cadre–mass relations, Peng claimed that top-down supervision was not enough: "Who supervises rural cadres? Can we supervise

39. For arguments that bullying and violence were counterproductive, see Kelliher, "The Chinese debate," p. 73.

40. Bai Yihua, *Reform and Exploration*, pp. 296–97. For more on the NPC debates, see Kevin J. O'Brien, "Implementing political reform in China's villages," *The Australian Journal of Chinese Affairs*, No. 32 (1994), pp. 36–39. On the belief that "mass consciousness" was high enough that dutiful cadres would not be voted out, see Kelliher, "The Chinese debate," p. 74.

41. Interviews, Beijing, September 1993.

42. Bai Yihua, *Reform and Exploration*, pp. 298–302.

43. Zhongguo nongcun cunmin zizhi zhidu yanjiu ketizu, *The Legal System of Village Committees in China* (English version) (Beijing: Zhongguo shehui chubanshe, 1996), p. 23.

44. Peng Zhen, "Fandui qiangpo mingling, jianchi qunzhong zizhi" ("Against coercion and commandism, uphold mass autonomy"), speech at the fifth joint meeting of delegation leaders and members of the Law Committee of the Sixth NPC, 6 April 1987, in *Important Speeches*, p. 20.

them? No, not even if we had 48 hours a day." The only solution, Peng proclaimed, was to promote self-government so that China's rural masses could themselves select and oversee village cadres.[45]

Despite Peng's impassioned words, opposition lingered on. As the session closed, the NPC Presidium decided it was "improper to force the draft law through the legislative procedure"[46] and instead recommended that deputies approve the Law in principle and authorize the Standing Committee to make further revisions before promulgating it. This motion was accepted and eight months later, in November 1987, after further spirited debate and over the opposition of Standing Committee members who felt it was still premature, a trial Organic Law was passed.[47]

Although opponents in the NPC could not prevent the Law from being enacted, they did stir up worries that village elections might undermine policy implementation and jeopardize social order. This caused even the most steadfast supporters of self-government to agree that test sites should be developed before the programme was put in force nation-wide. Peng himself, on the day the Law was passed, warned against enforcing it where conditions were not "ripe," on the grounds that hasty implementation would set back self-government and ruin the reputation of the Law. He announced that so long as local officials worked toward creating a setting conducive to villagers' autonomy, they would not be considered derelict for failing to carry out the Law in the near future.[48] Peng's preference for either good implementation or none at all provided just the opening that the many critics of self-government needed. They promptly shifted their efforts to blocking the trial Law's implementation.

Implementation and Indecision, 1988–1990

The same Ministry of Civil Affairs that had been in charge of drafting the Organic Law was entrusted with its execution. For this purpose, the Department of Basic-Level Governance was set up in early 1988, a few months before the Law went into effect. As a new department in a low-ranking ministry, it at first did little to promote villagers' autonomy, which it knew was quite controversial. The earliest circular it prepared (26 February 1988), for instance, stressed that VCs should become genuinely autonomous and that experiments with self-government should be conducted; but it did not say anything specific about elections.[49]

45. Peng Zhen, "Against coercion and commandism," p. 20. For excerpts, see Bai Yihua, *Reform and Exploration*, pp. 294–306. On this more generally, see Epstein, "Village elections," p. 411. For Peng's understanding of the relationship between Party leadership, democracy and law, see Potter, *From Leninist Discipline*.

46. FBIS-CHI, No. 79 (1987), p. K12.

47. On remaining opposition, see FBIS-CHI, No. 224 (1987), pp. 12–13.

48. Peng Zhen, *Lun xin shiqi de shehuizhuyi minzhu yu fazhi jianshe* (*On the Construction of Socialist Democracy and Legal System in the New Period*) (Beijing: Zhongyang wenxian chubanshe, 1989), p. 371.

49. "Guanyu guanche zhixing Zhonghua renmin gongheguo cunmin weiyuanhui zuzhifa de tongzhi" ("Circular on carrying out the People's Republic of China's organic law

The first elections under the Law took place without much guidance from the MoCA. In some places, county administrators held elections after provincial civil affairs departments selected their counties for trial implementation of the Law.[50] In other places, voting was introduced by county and township officials on their own, because they believed that popular involvement in cadre recruitment would turn up individuals who could lead a village to prosperity.[51] In still others, elections began after villagers (who had somehow heard about the Law) pressured townships to let them nominate and vote for VC members.[52] These local experiments attracted the attention of MoCA officials in Beijing. At a conference in July 1989, a member of the Liaoning provincial civil affairs department, while reviewing the record of an early test site for competitive elections, argued that a "key link" (*guanjian*) in implementing the Law was holding elections. By the year end, MoCA Deputy Minister Lian Yin was using precisely the same language to urge provincial civil affairs officials to convene elections, particularly for VC chairs.[53]

That the MoCA decided to make popular elections the heart of self-government was, ironically, occasioned by a conservative attempt to kill off the reform. After the suppression of the 1989 protest movement, opponents of villagers' autonomy had demanded that the Organic Law be repealed because it "was far ahead of its time." Some even alleged that the Organic Law was an example of the "bourgeois liberalization" condoned by disgraced Party General Secretary Zhao Ziyang.[54] To deter-

---

footnote continued

of villagers' committees"), Ministry of Civil Affairs Document No. 7 (1988), reprinted in Bai Yihua, *Reform and Exploration*, pp. 270–71. See also Zhongguo nongcun cunmin zizhi zhidu yanjiu ketizu, *Legal System*, p. 132.

50. Bai Gang, " 'Liangpiaozhi' xuanju moshi fawei" ("An analysis of the 'two-ballot system' "), paper presented at the Conference on Construction of Village-Level Organizations in Mainland China, Chinese University of Hong Kong, 8–9 October 1998, p. 2. On the role of local civil affairs' bureaus, see Pei Minxin, " 'Creeping democratization' in China," *Journal of Democracy*, Vol. 6, No. 4 (1995), p. 75.

51. Liaoning sheng minzhengting diaochazu, "Jingzheng xuanju cunji ganbu tuidong nongcun shenhua gaige" ("Elect village cadres competitively and advance rural reforms"), *Zhongguo minzheng* (*Chinese Civil Affairs*), No. 6 (1989), p. 4. The MoCA has also stressed how elections serve economic development. See Jude Howell, "Prospects for village self-governance in China," *The Journal of Peasant Studies*, Vol. 25, No. 3 (1998), pp. 91–92; Kelliher, "The Chinese debate," pp. 68–70. On the perceived need for self-rule in less developed villages, see Susan V. Lawrence, "Democracy, Chinese style," *The Australian Journal of Chinese Affairs*, No. 32 (1994), p. 67; Jean C. Oi, "Economic development, stability and democratic village self-governance," in Maurice Brosseau, Suzanne Pepper and Tsang Shu-ki (eds.), *China Review 1996* (Hong Kong: Chinese University Press, 1996), pp. 127–28, 131; Epstein, "Village elections," pp. 411, 414–15.

52. See Lianjiang Li and Kevin J. O'Brien, "Villagers and popular resistance in contemporary China," *Modern China*, Vol. 22, No. 1 (1996), pp. 44–45; Kevin J. O'Brien and Lianjiang Li, "The politics of lodging complaints in rural China," *The China Quarterly*, No. 143 (1995), pp. 765–66; Kevin J. O'Brien, "Rightful resistance," *World Politics*, Vol. 49, No. 1 (1996), pp. 38–39.

53. For the Liaoning official's remarks, see Hu Ke, "Tan guanche cunmin weiyuanhui zuzhifa de guanjian" ("The crux of implementing the organic law of villagers' committees"), in *Practice and Reflection*, pp. 134–36. On Lian Yin, see Zhongguo nongcun cunmin zizhi zhidu yanjiu ketizu, *Legal System*, pp. 133–34.

54. See Tang Jinsu, "Current conditions," p. 44; Sun Youfu, "Jianshe zhenzheng lüxing zizhi zhineng de cunweihui" ("Build villagers' committees that genuinely perform the

mine whether the Law should essentially be scrapped, the NPC, the Central Organization Department, the MoCA and the Ministry of Personnel dispatched a team of investigators to report on the performance of village political organizations. But the team could not reach a consensus. Only a small majority favoured implementing the Law, while the rest suggested that VCs be replaced by administrative offices or "share a sign board" (*liang kuai paizi, yi tao renma*) with such offices. With no agreement in sight, the NPC asked the MoCA to prepare a second report *on its own*, advising what should be done.[55]

Now the ministry was in a stronger position to promote self-government. Under Minister Cui Naifu's supervision, MoCA staff members drew up a set of recommendations. Based largely on what they had found in Heilongjiang, where VCs were operating quite well, the investigators concluded that introducing village elections was the best way to reduce cadre–mass tensions and to prevent "an even larger crisis." Merely reorganizing Party branches or establishing village administrative offices, they argued, did not suffice or worked only for a short time.[56]

Around this time, Peng Zhen, nearly 90 years old and retired, also returned to the fray. In February 1990, according to accounts by two MoCA officials, Peng called Minister Cui Naifu to his home. When Cui reported that there was still much opposition to the Law, Peng purportedly sprang to his feet and asked what was Cui's "attitude" towards self-government. Cui answered that he was "absolutely committed" to it. Peng was relieved and restated his case for grassroots democracy. He then went a step further than he had on earlier occasions: he said he regretted failing to shepherd an Organic Law of Township Government through the NPC so that township officials would be subject to mass supervision, too.[57]

Then a second Party elder, Bo Yibo, intervened and spoke up in favour of self-government. After his staff obtained the MoCA report praising elections, Bo read it and called it "brilliant."[58] As one of the "eight immortals" and a close ally of Deng Xiaoping, Bo's backing proved decisive. Shortly after he added his voice to Peng's, Politburo Standing

---

footnote continued

function of self-government"), *Zhongguo minzheng*, No. 2, (1992), p. 7. Interviews, Beijing, September 1993, January 1997.

55. Li Xueju, *Zhongguo cheng xiang jiceng zhengquan jianshe gongzuo yanjiu* (*Research on Construction of Grassroots Governance in Urban and Rural China*) (Beijing: Zhongguo shehui chubanshe, 1994), pp. 69–72.

56. For a synopsis, see Wang Zhenyao and Wang Shihao, "Guanjian zaiyu jishi tiaozheng dang he guojia yu nongmin de zhengzhi guanxi" ("The key is to adjust the political relationship between the party, state and peasants"), *Shehui gongzuo yanjiu* (*Research in Social Work*), No. 3 (1990), pp. 12–14.

57. Bai Yihua, *Reform and Exploration*, pp. 223–24; also see Li Xueju, *Research on Construction*, p. 72. On Peng summoning (unnamed) opponents to his home to complain about foot-dragging on implementation, see White, "Reforming the countryside," p. 277; also Shi, "Village committee," n. 37.

58. Interviews, Beijing, November 1993, January 1997. On Bo Yibo's role, see also Anne F. Thurston, *Muddling Toward Democracy* (Washington, D.C.: United States Institute of Peace, 1998), pp. 11–12; Choate, "Local governance," p. 8; Wang Zhenyao, "Village committees," p. 244.

Committee member Song Ping finally ended all the indecision. At a conference held in Laixi in August 1990, Song instructed that the Law should be implemented rather than debated.[59] The conference report, which was later issued as Central Committee Document No. 19 (1990), decreed that each of China's counties should establish "demonstration villages" (*shifan cun*) in areas that had "good working conditions," thereby seconding a 1989 MoCA decision to focus on better-off communities where cadre–mass relations were presumably reasonably harmonious.[60] Document No. 19 also accepted the MoCA's interpretation that popular elections were a key link in realizing self-government.

MoCA officials moved swiftly to use the Central Committee's endorsement to push self-government forward. Only six weeks after the Laixi conference report was written, the ministry issued a circular directing that election showcases should be established throughout the nation. Moreover, it ignored the modest quota of pilot programmes in "several or a dozen villages in every county" set in the conference report and instead instructed that full-scale demonstration townships and counties should also be set up.[61] At this point, the MoCA also underscored the importance of elections, and enriched what Thomas A. Metzger, Larry Diamond and Ramon H. Myers call the "ideological marketplace," by redefining the core of villagers' autonomy from "self-government, self-service, and self-education" to "democratic elections, democratic decision-making, and democratic management."[62]

On the Ground: The Role of Local Officials

It was one thing for MoCA officials to decide that elections were a key link, but another to induce local authorities to hold free and fair votes.[63]

59. Interview, Beijing, January 1997. For Song Ping's remarks, see also Li Xueju, *Research on Construction*, p. 73.

60. See "Quanguo cunji zuzhi jianshe gongzuo zuotanhui jiyao" ("Summary report of the national workshop on constructing village-level organizations"), in Minzhengbu jiceng zhengquan jianshesi nongcunchu (comp.), *Cunmin zizhi shifan jiangxi ban shiyong jiaocai* (*Teaching Materials for the Study Group on Villagers' Autonomy Demonstration*) (Shandong: Laixishi niuxibu caiyinchang, 1991), p. 7. The ministry, at this point, was still permitting experimentation with village administrative offices in "economically backward areas where village organizations are paralysed." See Zhongguo nongcun cunmin zizhi zhidu yanjiu ketizu, *Legal System*, p. 132. For an argument that these initial elections seem to have improved "congruence" between cadres and villagers, see Melanie F. Manion, "The electoral connection in the Chinese countryside," *American Political Science Review*, Vol. 90, No. 4 (1996), pp. 736–748.

61. Minzhengbu jiceng zhengquan jianshesi, "Guanyu zai quanguo nongcun kaizhan cunmin zizhi shifan huodong de tongzhi" ("Circular on launching demonstration of villagers' self-government nation-wide"), in *Teaching Materials*, pp. 19–21. For the quoted text, see "Summary report of the national workshop," pp. 11–12.

62. See Li Xueju, *Research on Construction*, pp. 53–55. On the notion of an "ideological marketplace," see the introduction to this issue of *The China Quarterly*.

63. On the state's "becoming weak in protecting villagers, disciplining its agents and effectively implementing its policies," see Lü Xiaobo, "The politics of peasant burden in reform China," *The Journal of Peasant Studies*, Vol. 25, No. 1 (1997), pp. 116, 134; also Kevin J. O'Brien and Lianjiang Li, "Selective policy implementation in rural China," *Comparative Politics*, Vol. 31, No. 2 (1999).

Many local administrators were loath to let villagers select grassroots cadres. Like earlier critics of reform, they suspected that elections would interfere with policy execution, aggravate factional rivalries and intensify lineage conflict.[64] When Xi'an began its experiments with the Organic Law in 1988, only one of its 13 counties agreed to participate. One county Party secretary even cautioned that anyone who dared popularize the Law would be held responsible for causing chaos in the countryside.[65] Township officials tended to be even more antagonistic. A 1989 survey in Shandong revealed that over 60 per cent of township leaders disapproved of self-government, while a 1991 survey of 150 township administrators in Hequ county, Shanxi showed that two-fifths opposed village elections.[66] In Hebei, one township official bluntly told a Xinhua reporter: "presently, villagers don't know how to govern themselves. They don't even know what it means to govern themselves. And we won't let them govern themselves!"[67]

After the Central Committee endorsed the demonstration programme in 1990, most local officials stopped attacking self-government, but quite a few continued to delay or rig elections. Noting the trial status of the Law, some county leaders in Shandong claimed that they had the authority to decide if their counties were ready for villagers' self-government.[68] Township administrators, for their part, often took advantage of the Law's vagueness concerning election procedures to restrict voters' freedom of choice. Among other tactics, they monopolized nominations, conducted snap elections, demanded that Party members vote for hand-picked nominees, banned unapproved candidates from making campaign speeches, annulled elections if the "wrong" candidates won, and insisted that voting be conducted by a show of hands.[69]

64. See Zhou Zuohan, "Guanyu cunmin weiyuanhui jianshe de jidian sikao" ("Some thoughts on the construction of villagers' committees"), *Hunan shifan daxue shehui kexue xuebao* (*Social Science Journal of Hunan Normal University*), No. 5 (1987), p. 18; Tang Jinsu, "Current conditions," p. 44; Sun Youfu, "Build villagers' committees," p. 7. This has also been a major theme for Western analysts. See O'Brien, "Implementing political reform," pp. 37–38, 51–58; Kelliher, "The Chinese debate," pp. 78–84; Xu Wang, "Mutual empowerment," p. 1436.

65. Li Buying, "Lintong xian Baimiao cun shixing cunmin zizhi caifang jishi" ("A report on the implementation of villagers' autonomy in Baimiao village of Lintong county"), *Zhongguo minzheng*, No. 4 (1989), p. 8. On opposition and feigned compliance in Shaanxi, Jiangxi and Hubei, see Kelliher, "The Chinese debate," pp. 79–81.

66. On Shandong, see Yang Xuejun and Sun Xinmin, "Lishun xiang zhengfu yu cunmin weiyuanhui zhijian de guanxi" ("Rationalize relations between township governments and villagers' committees"), in *Practice and Reflection*, p. 113. On Shanxi, see Zuo Guocai and Liu Wenji, "Cunmin he jiceng ganbu dui cunmin zizhi de fanying ji qi fenxi" ("An analysis of the reaction of villagers and grassroots cadres to villagers' self-government"), *Xiangzhen luntan* (*Township Forum*), No. 10 (1991), p. 13.

67. See Bao Yonghui, "Cunmin zizhi fuhe bu fuhe Zhongguo guoqing?" ("Does villagers' autonomy accord with China's conditions?"), *Xiangzhen luntan*, No. 6 (1991), p. 12.

68. Personal communication with a researcher from Shandong, October 1998.

69. See Ma Changshan, "Cunmin zizhi zuzhi jianshe de shidai yiyi jiqi shijian fancha" ("The epoch-making significance and the imperfect practice of building villagers' self-government organizations"), *Zhengzhi yu falü*, No. 2. (1994), pp. 19–20; Fan Yu, "Cunweihui xuanju weifa xu jiuzheng" ("Law-breaking activities in village elections must be corrected"), *Gaige neican* (*Internal Reference on Reforms*), No. 20 (1998), pp. 14–15.

For much of the 1990s, local resistance was, at least in part, a result of the Central Organization Department's (COD) stance towards elections. Suspecting that grassroots democracy would weaken Party branches, and reflecting the low priority that many central leaders attached to village elections, the COD was not remarkably supportive of the Organic Law.[70] This, according to some analysts in Beijing, created a strong disincentive for local authorities to throw their efforts into nurturing self-government. Since the COD controls performance evaluations and decides who is put up for promotion, most cadres are highly attentive to its priorities. "After all," a researcher from the State Council explained, "local officials are most concerned with their own careers. If they figure that promoting village elections will not be rewarded, then they are unlikely to make much effort in this difficult work. And over the last few years, creators of well-known models of village democracy have not received the promotions they deserved."[71]

Owing in large measure to the half-hearted support of top policy makers, which reached local leaders in the form of COD reservations, many county administrators discovered that championing self-government was at best thankless and at worst harmful to their careers.[72] A county official in Jilin who pushed for open nominations and free campaigning acknowledged that he was taking a significant risk. What emboldened him, he said, was that he was not seeking further promotions, because he preferred serving in his home county over being transferred to a higher position elsewhere.[73] Indeed, a notable number of the early adopters of village elections were officials who had peaked in their careers and no longer cared much if the COD liked what they did.[74]

Because it does not control appointments and promotions, even in local civil affairs bureaus, the MoCA is poorly positioned to reward those who co-operate and to motivate those who lag behind. Ministry leaders are aware that they lack meaningful inducements to give out, and have tried to counteract this by urging civil affairs officials to "gain status by producing achievements." In 1995, for example, an MoCA vice-minister suggested that Party and government leaders might start giving local civil

70. Interviews, Beijing, April 1997.
71. Personal communication with a researcher from Beijing, October 1998. On cadre incentive structures, see Shi, "Village committee;" O'Brien and Li, "Selective policy implementation," pp. 171–76; Susan H. Whiting, "Contract incentives and market discipline in China's rural industrial sector," in John McMillan and Barry Naughton (eds.), *Reforming Asian Socialism* (Ann Arbor: University of Michigan Press, 1996), pp. 72–77.
72. Interview, Taiyuan, August 1997.
73. Personal communication, October 1998.
74. Interviews, Beijing, December 1995; Fuzhou, July 1997; Taiyuan, September 1997. Other pioneers professed an ideological justification for their actions: they respected the mass line and shared Peng Zhen's vision of how to realize "socialist democracy." An official in Shandong, for instance, argued that "implementing villagers' self- government is returning power to the people" – a slogan that even an outspoken advocate of self-government in the MoCA deemed "not quite accurate." See Wang Zhenyao, "Cunmin zizhi yu cunweihui xuanju" ("Villagers' self-government and the election of villagers' committees"), in *Teaching Materials*, p. 155.

affairs workers their due if they could show that elections promoted stability, developed the economy and curbed corruption.[75]

Some provincial civil affairs bureaus have also sought to overcome their lowly status by reaching out to more powerful organizations. Leaders of the Fujian civil affairs bureau, for instance, have always regarded the provincial people's congress to be an ally. For over a decade, after each round of elections, they have submitted legislative motions designed to standardize voter registration, nomination and voting procedures, the counting of ballots, and so on. When their proposals have been included in provincial laws, they then use these statutes to goad local leaders into running better elections. In this way, the civil affairs bureau has obtained support from the provincial legislature's leaders, who are delighted to exercise their lawmaking powers and to see their decisions enforced.[76] More recently, the bureau has also made overtures to the provincial Discipline Inspection Commission – which paid off when the Commission realized that corruption tended to be lower where well-run village elections took place. With influential backers working together with civil affairs staff, Fujian has become a national leader in implementing self-government. Among other firsts, it was the first province to require secret balloting, primaries and open nomination for all VC posts.[77]

On the Ground: The Role of Villagers

Apart from obtaining help from other government organizations, the MoCA and its local bureaus have also found an ally in ordinary villagers. Rural people have been quick to recognize that elections provide a means to dislodge corrupt, imperious and incompetent cadres. And when they are deprived of their right to vote, villagers are not always indifferent. Over the past decade, resourceful farmers have frequently turned to what might be called "rightful resistance."[78] Citing the Organic Law as well as provincial regulations, they demand fair elections, boycott rigged votes

75. Yan Mingfu's closing speech in Minzhengbu jiceng zhengquan jianshesi (comp.), *Quanguo cunmin zizhi shifan gongzuo jingyan jiaoliu ji chengxiang jiceng xianjin jiti he xianjin geren biaozhang huiyi wenjian huibian (Collected Documents of the National Conference on Exchanging Experiences of Implementing Villagers' Self-government and Commending Advanced Collectives and Individuals)* (Beijing: Zhongguo shehui chubanshe, 1996), quoted text on pp. 43–44.

76. Interviews, Fuzhou, July 1997. On lobbying provincial people's congresses to close election loopholes, see also Shi, "Village committee," p. 405.

77. Further evidence of the Fujian civil affairs bureau's influence came in 1997, when the bureau head identified, by name and at a provincial conference, several counties that had failed to hold elections in all their villages. Each county rapidly organized make-up elections. Interviews, Fuzhou, July 1997. On Fujian's place "at the forefront of electoral success," see Thurston, *Muddling Toward Democracy*, pp. 33–34; "Report of the Fifth Mission on Chinese Elections" (Atlanta: Carter Center Working Paper Series, 20 June–3 July 1998), p. 4; Kelliher, "The Chinese debate," p. 74.

78. See O'Brien, "Rightful resistance." For what we then called "policy-based resistance," see Li and O'Brien, "Villagers and popular resistance," pp. 40–52. For examples involving election irregularities, see Li and O'Brien, "The struggle over village elections," pp. 137–140; also Howell, "Prospects for village governance," pp. 103–104.

and lodge complaints at higher levels. They adroitly use the language of power to defy "disloyal" local officials and call for scrupulous implementation of existing statutes and leadership promises. Engaging in disruptive but not quite unlawful collective action, rural rightful resisters have made their presence felt at government compounds throughout the nation.

People's congresses and civil affairs bureaus are the most common targets for villagers upset with election irregularities. Provincial civil affairs officials from Shandong, Shanxi, Fujian, Henan and Hebei report that their offices always fill up around election time.[79] Angry villagers sometimes do not stop there but go all the way to Beijing searching for officials who might be willing to champion their claims.[80] In one widely-reported case, after a township in Liaoning prohibited several candidates from running and did not permit secret balloting, over a dozen villagers travelled at their own expense to the county town, the provincial capital and finally Beijing to lodge a complaint. They knew the Organic Law by heart and recited it at each stop while petitioning for a new election.[81]

In the last decade, local civil affairs bureaus and the MoCA have used popular pressure to prod local officials to hold high-quality elections. Provincial civil affairs officials acknowledge that mass complaints often help them detect procedural infractions and enable them to win over reluctant county and township officials by arguing that many appeals are just and cannot be ignored.[82] MoCA officials have also given a sympathetic hearing to some delegations of villagers who seek honest elections. In 1994, for instance, when a group of Hebei farmers came to the capital to protest against a fraudulent vote, an MoCA official shouted "bravo!" (*tai haole*) upon hearing the news. He immediately dispatched two staff members to look into the charges.[83] In the course of a long investigation that ended with the election being annulled, MoCA officials appeared three times on a popular television programme devoted to investigative journalism; in front of a national audience, they openly supported the

79. Interviews, Ji'nan, July 1994; Fuzhou, July 1997. Personal communication with officials from Henan and Hebei, October 1998.

80. See Shao Xingliang, Cui Suozhi, Meng Baolin and Sun Xueliang, "Yi min wei tian" ("Regarding the people as sovereign"), *Xiangzhen luntan*, No. 4 (1994), pp. 10–11; Tian Yuan, "Zhongguo nongcun jiceng de minzhu zhilu" ("The pathway to grassroots democracy in rural China"), *Xiangzhen luntan*, No. 6 (1993), pp. 3–4; and Fan Yu, "Law-breaking activities," p. 14. Survey data from four counties suggests that, when villagers contact officials, about two-fifths of all mentions concern elections. M. Kent Jennings, "Political participation in the Chinese countryside," *American Political Science Review*, Vol. 91, No. 2 (1997), p. 366. Based on a nation-wide survey conducted in 1993, Shi, "Village committee," p. 404, reports that more than 5% of rural residents have lodged complaints against election fraud.

81. See Tian Yuan, "The pathway to grassroots democracy," pp. 3–4. Interviews, Beijing, July 1994. Needless to say, local officials have a strong incentive to keep villagers uninformed. In a case where complainants demanded to see documents that county leaders claimed restricted their rights and superseded the Organic Law, a county official in Hebei "snorted with contempt and said 'you are not county officials, why would you think you have the right to read county documents'." See *Nongmin ribao* (Shehui wenhua tekan), *Farmer's Daily* (Special issue on society and culture), 25 July 1998, p. 1.

82. Interviews, Fuzhou, July 1997; and personal communication with officials from Henan and Hebei, October 1998.

83. Personal observation, Beijing, July 1994.

complainants and warned other local officials to draw the appropriate lesson.[84]

In siding with villagers and insisting that the Organic Law be enforced, MoCA officials have tried to persuade local leaders that infringing villagers' rights could damage their careers. Ministry officials sometimes even raise the spectre of social unrest, the notorious Renshou riots in particular, when trying to convince local officials to conform. Speaking to township officials in Hebei in 1996, one MoCA staff member advised: "I know that many of you oppose village elections. But isn't it mainly because the cadres that you've appointed offer you gifts [i.e. bribes]. If villagers file complaints against these corrupt cadres, they may also bring you down. You know what happened in Renshou. I think it's in your interest to calculate carefully the risks and rewards of refusing to hold good elections."[85]

Appeals by rural people have done so much to spur cadre compliance that some ministry officials place "farmers' active participation" and "mass creativity" uppermost when assigning credit for the spread of village elections.[86] In the opinion of the MoCA official most closely associated with self-government, actions by ordinary villagers are the main reason that elections have not been thwarted by local opponents.[87] Western researchers, interestingly enough, have tended to apportion more credit to the ministry itself.

International Support

MoCA officials have also been adept at obtaining and deploying aid from abroad. In July 1989 the MoCA established a Research Society of Basic-Level Governance. Shortly thereafter, the Research Society won a

84. Interviews, Beijing, December 1995. However, a 1997 documentary about villagers petitioning for their electoral rights was abruptly cancelled, according to one participant, because of fears it would raise unrealistic expectations. *Far Eastern Economic Review*, 6 November 1997, pp. 56–58.

85. Interview, Beijing, January 1997. For another version of these remarks, see Wang Zhenyao, "Zai Hebei sheng di si jie cunmin weiyuanhui huanjie xuanju gongzuo gugan peixun ban shang de jianghua" ("Speech at the training class for key workers in the re-election of villagers' committees in Hebei province"), in Minzhengbu jiceng zhengquan jianshesi nongcunchu (comp.), *1995–1996 Niandu quanguo cunweihui huanjie xuanju ziliao huibian (Collected Materials on the 1995–1996 Re-election of Villagers' Committees Nation-wide)* (Beijing: December 1996), pp. 17–18. For more on Renshou, and a neighbouring county in which a highway levy was successfully collected by elected cadres who had permitted a vote on the tax, see Pei Minxin, "Creeping democratization," p. 76; Epstein, "Village elections," p. 416; Xu Wang, "Mutual empowerment," p. 1439; Shi, "Village committee," n. 38.

86. See, respectively, Wang Zhenyao, "Zhongguo cunmin weiyuanhui de jiben jinzhan yu lilun yiju" ("The basic experience and theoretical grounds of villagers' committees in China"), in Chen Mingtong and Zheng Yongnian (eds.), *Liang'an jiceng xuanju yu zhengzhi shehui bianqian (Grassroots Elections and Political-Social Transformation on Both Sides of the Strait)* (Taipei: Yuedan chubanshe gufen youxian gongsi, 1998), p. 313; Duoji Cairang, "Jinyibu wanshan cunmin zizhi zhidu ba quanguo cunmin weiyuanhui jianshe gongzuo tuixiang xin de jieduan" ("Continue to perfect the villagers' self-government system and advance the construction of villagers' committees to a new stage"), in *Collected Documents*, p. 26.

87. Interview, Beijing, February 1997.

grant from the Ford Foundation to help promote self-government. On the heels of this first major influx of funds, a stream of foreign scholars, journalists and (later) election observers followed. As articles and reports brought China's experiment with "grassroots democracy" to the world, MoCA officials attracted even more overseas help. Since the early 1990s, the Asia Foundation, the International Republican Institute, the Carter Center, the United Nations' Development Agency and the European Union have all joined Ford in offering the MoCA financial and technical assistance.[88] Ministry officials have used these resources to convene a series of international conferences, publish dozens of books on self-government, and reward co-operative local officials (and themselves) with foreign trips, particularly to the United States. Although such visits are one-time perks and do not trump more enduring concerns, they did make lining up in support of elections more appealing to a number of early adopters.[89]

Village elections have also drawn the attention of Western politicians, who in turn have encouraged Chinese leaders to support further democratic reform. In 1997 and 1998, for example, Jimmy Carter and Bill Clinton both lauded village elections in discussions with ranking Chinese officials. Eager to undo bad press about its human rights record and to head off social instability, the Chinese leadership has recently shown much interest in what previously was a low-profile programme left to the MoCA and NPC.[90] On an inspection tour to Anhui in September 1998, General Secretary Jiang Zemin, for instance, praised self-government as Chinese farmers' "third great invention" (along with the household responsibility system and township and village enterprises).[91] Even the usually conservative NPCSC chairman Li Peng has stepped in to foster better village elections. While the Organic Law was being revised in 1998, Li visited a Jilin county known for its open nomination procedures. That same summer he also reportedly instructed *Renmin ribao* to publish the next-to-last draft of the revised Organic Law so that ordinary citizens could offer their comments and suggestions.[92]

Where Implementation Stands

In how many of China's one million villages have democratic elections taken place? Estimates vary widely, as do definitions of what makes an

88. See Thurston, *Muddling Toward Democracy*, pp. iv–v, 45; Epstein, "Village elections," pp. 407–408; Choate, "Local governance," p. 3. For the MoCA using comments by foreign scholars to counter opposition to its efforts to improve election procedures, see Shi, "Village committee," pp. 408–410.

89. For a similar point, see Shi, "Village committee," p. 400.

90. On burnishing China's democratic credentials and fending off foreign critiques of its human rights abuses, see Howell, "Prospects for village self-governance," pp. 87, 92, 103; Kelliher, "The Chinese debate," p. 75.

91. *Renmin ribao*, 25 September 1998, p. 1.

92. On Li Peng's inspection of Lishu county, see *Renmin ribao*, 8 July 1998, p. 1. On Li urging publication of the draft, personal communication with rural researchers from Beijing, October 1998.

election "democratic." Since early 1995, the MoCA has required that in all VC elections voters be offered at least one more candidate than the number of available posts (*cha'e*). Using this standard, the editor of a Chinese magazine that focuses on rural affairs reckoned that "no more than 10 per cent" of Chinese villages had held well-run *cha'e* elections by early 1997.[93] Around the same time, "other experts" and ministry officials estimated that from one-quarter to one-third of China's villages had conducted elections according to the rules (that is, the 1995 MoCA circular) and the Organic Law.[94] And by November 1998, Minister of Civil Affairs Duoji Cairang told a Xinhua reporter that 60 per cent of all villages had convened *cha'e* elections.[95]

Assessments by overseas-based observers vary just as much. Duke University political scientist Tianjian Shi reported that in a 1993 nation-wide survey of 336 villages as many as 51.6 per cent had held *cha'e* elections.[96] X. Drew Liu claimed that in the 1995 round of balloting 30 per cent of villages had allowed open nominations."[97] And the U.S. State Department estimated in 1996 that one-quarter to one-third of China's villagers had "participated in elections that follow, to varying degrees of compliance, the guidelines."[98]

Our research tends to support estimates near the low end of the range. In late 1997 we surveyed 8,302 rural residents from 478 villages in seven provinces (Anhui, Beijing suburbs, Fujian, Hebei, Jiangsu, Jiangxi and Shandong). Respondents were asked if their VCs were elected and, if they were, how candidates were chosen. The research design focused on nomination procedures rather than the number of candidates because "in many ways, the process of nominations is as critical, if not more so, than the elections themselves."[99] Moreover, given the limited degree of competition currently required, *cha'e* elections are readily susceptible to manipulation. An individual who will almost certainly lose, for example, can be listed alongside the incumbents to satisfy the letter of the law. And uncontested elections may not be as undemocratic as they seem. In villages where the final balloting is ostensibly non-competitive, preliminary nominees may become candidates only after winning a

93. Interview, Beijing, February 1997.

94. For these 1996 and 1997 estimates, see "Carter Center delegation report: village elections in China" (Atlanta: Carter Center Working Paper Series, 2–15 March 1998), p. 9; Howell, "Prospects for village self-governance," p. 96; Epstein, "Village elections," p. 410.

95. See *Renmin ribao*, 6 November 1998, p. 1. Duoji Cairang offered a similar estimate in July 1997 while acknowledging that he did not know for certain. Cited in "Carter Center delegation report," p. 9.

96. Shi, "Village committee," p. 386.

97. X. Drew Liu, "A harbinger of democracy: grassroots elections in rural China," *China Strategic Review*, Vol. 2, No. 3 (1997), p. 71.

98. See International Republican Institute, "China's economic future: challenges to U.S. policy," study paper submitted to the Joint Economic Committee, U.S. Congress, August 1996, p. 3.

99. Choate, "Local governance," p. 10. On nomination procedures and their importance, see Jorgen Elklit, "The Chinese village committee electoral system," *China Information*, Vol. 11, No. 4 (1997), pp. 7–9. Anne Thurston, *Muddling Toward Democracy*, p. 26, has also concluded that "the selection of nominees is a vital, but often overlooked, part of the democratic process."

hotly-contested primary in which villagers or their representatives participate.

The resulting data showed that 45 per cent of the individuals surveyed in the 478 villages said that their VC was elected[100] and 26 per cent reported that candidates were selected either by villagers (15 per cent) or villagers' representatives (11 per cent). Correcting for the large number of respondents who happened to be from villages that had primaries, that would mean that approximately 82 of the 478 surveyed villages (17 per cent) had held elections with primaries.[101]

It ought to be noted, however, that our estimate applies only to these 478 villages, not the seven provinces, even less the whole country. The survey was distributed opportunistically in all but two provinces, and no effort was made to construct a nation-wide probability sample.[102] We were not able to include, for example, four provinces that have lagged notably in introducing village elections – Guangdong, Guangxi, Yunnan and Hainan.[103] And even within the seven provinces surveyed, this study suffers from the same problem that all survey research in China faces: on sensitive topics, it is comparatively easy to gain access where all is well but hard to win co-operation where much is awry, particularly when officials suspect that the results might contradict what they have reported to their superiors. For these reasons, we believe that it is more likely that our estimate is high rather than low.

Conclusion

Over the past two decades, village elections have passed through three stages. When villagers' committees first appeared in the early 1980s, elected VCs enjoyed considerable autonomy and operated in what Tang

---

100. Cf. Shi, "Village committee," p. 386. In Shi's 1990 and 1993 nation-wide surveys about 75% of rural residents reported that VC elections had been held in their village.

101. In some provinces, over 100 residents were surveyed in each village, while in others only a dozen or fewer were drawn for interviews. In order to use individual-level responses to estimate the frequency of village elections, we assume that within each province the same number of respondents was drawn from each village.

102. Insofar as the questionnaire touched on a number of sensitive topics, household registration records were not sought from local public security bureaus. In Fujian and Jiangsu, however, the questionnaire was distributed in purposively selected villages. In both these provinces, after two days of intensive training and mock-interviewing, interviewers were dispatched to pre-selected poor, middle income and rich villages, where they interviewed all available adults from a randomly selected villagers' group. Elsewhere, trained interviewers (most of whom were university or rural high school students) were instructed to return to their home villages and to interview available adults.

103. On these four provinces "dragging their feet in introducing village self-government," see Sylvia Chan, "Village self-government and civil society," in Joseph Y.S. Cheng (ed.), *China Review 1998* (Hong Kong: Chinese University Press, 1998), p. 237. Guangdong did not start implementing the Organic Law province-wide until late 1998. Guangxi had the first villagers' committees, but even as recently as November 1995, only 61% of Guangxi's counties had completed converting village administrative offices into VCs. See *Collected Documents*, p. 136. MoCA officials also consider Yunnan and Hainan to be notable laggards. Interviews, Beijing, January 1997.

Tsou once called the "zone of indifference."[104] Although committee members managed important neighbourhood affairs, their responsibilities did not extend to matters of state. During this phase, elections produced a kind of grassroots democracy, but it was uninstitutionalized and had a very limited scope.

This first stage ended when the 1982 Constitution recognized villagers' committees and VCs began to replace production brigades. This new status increased the import of elections many fold, but it also made them more controversial, because committees now had many more responsibilities and resources. Administrators accustomed to the old ways quite naturally feared that letting villagers select cadres would interfere with carrying out unpopular state policies and might even lead to a breakdown of public order. Backers of self-government, on the other hand, felt that elections were a chance worth taking: they were the best way to dislodge second-rate cadres and consolidate Party rule. Neither side was able to persuade the other, and the Law that finally emerged from the NPCSC reflected this stand-off; among other things, it was maddeningly vague about how elections should be conducted. Throughout the next decade, partly through the efforts of the MoCA and partly through the efforts of certain local officials and villagers, voting for VC members has gradually spread through the countryside. Against a backdrop of determined opposition, and worries that self-government would "cut the legs off" township leaders, supporters of elections have been given a chance to prove that enhanced cadre accountability could improve governance without threatening Party rule.

With the passage of the revised Organic Law in November 1998, elections have entered yet another stage. Self-government has finally shed its trial status and the pace of institutionalization has picked up. Election procedures have been clarified. Now, all VC candidates must be directly nominated by villagers, there must be more candidates than positions, and voting must be done in secret (article 14). The revised Law also takes into account continuing bureaucratic resistance and the need to strengthen the coalition pushing self-government. Towards this end, it not only encourages local people's congresses to enact implementing regulations and to do what is necessary to ensure that voters can exercise their democratic rights (articles 14, 28, 29), it also authorizes villagers to combat dishonest elections ("threats, bribes, forged ballots and other improper methods") by lodging "reports" (*jubao*) with local governments, people's congresses and other concerned departments (such as civil affairs offices) (article 15). Each of these clauses should do much to shore up the alliance that has been the driving force behind the spread of elections so far.

Still, successful implementation of the Law remains far from certain. Open resistance to elections may decline, but feigned compliance will almost certainly increase. What is more, even where VC voting is free

104. Tang Tsou, *The Cultural Revolution and Post-Mao Reforms* (Chicago: University of Chicago Press, 1986), p. xxiv.

and fair, there is not yet village democracy. Well-run, semi-competitive elections certainly make it possible to sideline some horribly unpopular cadres. But that says little about Party secretaries who need never face a popular vote. The new Law, in fact, includes one major concession to opponents who have all along said that grassroots democratization is a risk the Party can ill afford to take. Instead of omitting any mention of the Party branch as the 1987 Law did, the 1998 Law stipulates that the Party branch is the village's "leadership core" (*lingdao hexin*) (article 3). As long as VCs do not have final say over village political life, it must be recognized that however much VC election procedures are improved and put into practice, a rethinking of the Party's role must occur before there is real democracy in China's villages.[105]

And if such a rethinking is important for village democracy, it is even more crucial for elections at higher levels. Metzger, Diamond and Myers argue that democratization depends on the emergence of an ideological marketplace that circulates norms and ideas supportive of popular rule.[106] There are tantalizing signs that, in China, such a marketplace is coming into being. Recent experiments with direct township elections, for example, indicate that the bounds of the permissible are being discussed, and that incentives to push elections higher may be growing.[107] Nevertheless, "creeping up" is far from a foregone conclusion. The first open election of a township head, after initial positive reports, was quickly deemed unconstitutional.[108] More fundamentally, many policy makers adamantly oppose democratic entrepreneurship by liberal intellectuals and reform-minded officials at the centre and below. They still feel that holding elections at higher levels is premature – a step that would be likely to create more problems than it resolved.

Democracy may one day appear in China, and an alliance between frustrated citizens and reformist elites may be the force that produces a leadership in which leaders from top to bottom are held accountable via periodic, free elections. But for now, if we limit ourselves to the goals of self-government and put aside unintended outcomes and accidents of history yet to come, Peng Zhen's original vision still rules the day. Elections are designed to increase mass support for the Party, and grassroots democracy is understood to be fully compatible with strong

105. On the role of non-democratically elected Party secretaries, see Oi, "Economic development," pp. 137–39. In over one third of Shanxi's prefectures there have been experiments with subjecting Party members to a popular vote of confidence before permitting them to stand for the Party branch. If this practice was to spread and develop further, the prospects for real village democracy would be greatly enhanced. See Lianjiang Li, "The two-ballot system in Shanxi: subjecting village party secretaries to a popular vote," *The China Journal*, No. 42 (1999), pp. 103–118.

106. See the introduction to this issue of *The China Quarterly*.

107. See *Nanfang zhoumo* (*Southern Weekend*), 15 January 1999, p. 2; *Yangcheng wanbao* (*Yangcheng Evening News*), 28 April 1999, p. 1.

108. For the initial Chinese report on an unapproved election in Buyun township, Suining city, Sichuan, see *Nanfang zhoumo*, 15 January 1999, p. 2. For Western reports, see *New York Times*, 26 January 1999, p. A8; *Washington Post Foreign Service*, 27 February 1999, p. A17. For criticism of the election, see *Fazhi ribao* (*Legal Daily*), 19 January 1999, p. 1.

state control.[109] In this context, the self-government programme is best seen as an effort to rejuvenate village leadership by cleaning out incompetent, corrupt and high-handed cadres, all for the purpose of consolidating the current regime.

109. On similar understandings of "democracy" that trace to the May Fourth era and the *fengjian* tradition, see Keating, *Two Revolutions*, pp. 5–6, 248. On the compatibility of state strengthening and grassroots elections in the 1930s and 1940s, see Apter and Saich, *Revolutionary Discourse*, p. 212, Chen, *Making Revolution*, pp. 240–41; Keating, *Two Revolutions*, p. 133.

The Meaning of China's Village Elections

Robert A. Pastor and Qingshan Tan

"The reform of the political system and the reform of the economic system should depend on and complement each other? In the final analysis, the success of all reforms depends on the reform of the political system." Deng Xiaoping[1]

Direct elections for village leaders have been conducted in China since 1988, but they remain little known or casually dismissed by urban Chinese and the international community. Those who are aware of China's village elections have sharply divergent views as to their genuineness or effectiveness. Some are sceptical that the Chinese Communist Party would ever permit a competitive election that could threaten its grip on power. Others see the elections as a first stage in the building of democracy in China. In many ways, village elections are a kind of Rorschach test, an ambiguous drawing that is interpreted by people according to their predisposition towards China rather than the quality of the elections.

There is a potentially huge data base from which scholars and policy makers should be able to test these contradictory hypotheses. Every three years since 1988, approximately 930,000 villages are required to hold elections for village chairs and committees. Some of these elections have been observed, but the problem with most of the studies is that they use very small samples and often rely on anecdotes. The Ministry of Civil Affairs (MoCA) in Beijing, which is technically responsible for these elections, does not collect data on election results or the process on a systematic or comprehensive basis. There is sufficient information to permit a definition of the parameters of current understanding of village elections, but not enough to derive robust propositions for the entire country.

Relying on our many observations of village elections, interviews, and discussions with central and local election officials from 1996 to 1999, this article first reviews what is known about village elections from reports by the Chinese government and observations of the elections by international non-governmental organizations (NGOs). It describes and assesses the six stages of the village election process. It then identifies criteria to evaluate the elections and explore their meaning for political development in China.

Chinese Assessments and International Observations of Village Elections

In their contribution to this volume, Kevin O'Brien and Lianjiang Li review Western literature on village elections. Many of these studies

1. Cited in Rong Jingben, Cui Zhiyuan, Wang Shuansheng; Geo Xinjun, He Zengke and Yang Xuedong, *Transformation from the Pressurized to a Democratic System of Cooperation* (Beijing: Central Compilation and Translation Press, 1998), pp. 207–208.

produced mixed and even contradictory findings as to whether the elections were successful and what were the critical variables. Studies by the Chinese and NGOs found similar results, although both developed their cases more intensely. The Department of Basic-Level Governance of the MoCA undertook a study, led by its then director, Wang Zhenyao and published in December 1993, that found that in the previous two years, one-half of all provinces, autonomous regions and municipalities completed their second election, but there were vast differences in election procedures. They expressed concern over the role of the local Party cadres, who represented more than half the committee members in six of seven counties/cities, and an even higher percentage of chairs.[2] The group recommended strongly that "local party organizations must not select or nominate candidates. They must respect the selection made by villagers."[3]

In another study, Wang Zhenyao acknowledged that data for the entire country were not available, and that there were substantial variations between provinces on the quality and the results of elections. Nevertheless, he concluded optimistically, "the elections have hatched a new elite with firm roots in local society, which may be able to play an active role in the democratization of Chinese society? The system of democratic self-government is being established in the rural areas of China."[4]

Bai Gang of the Chinese Academy of Social Sciences (CASS) reviewed the progress made in village elections in the decade since the approval of the provisional Law in 1987. Acknowledging that the original Law was quite general, the ministry issued nine circulars to guide its enforcement, and 25 of 31 provincial congresses passed measures for implementing the Law by the end of 1997.[5] Of the 2,141 county-level administrative units (of which 1,696 are counties and 445 are cities of county-level), only 200 (10 per cent) were identified as "model counties." "This shows," declared the CASS report, "how slow the work has progressed in China." Only 20 per cent of the towns have well-written regulations.[6] The report evaluated each stage of the electoral process and noted that private voting booths were "something new" and "mark a fundamental change in the minds of the electorates." New electoral procedures, coupled with the rise in the number of entrepreneurs, caused the people to think differently, and more education and access to television "have made it easy for people to receive new ideas." Another study

2. Wang Zhenyao, "Village committees: the basis for China's democratization," in Edward B. Vermeer, Frank N. Pike and Wei Lien Cheng (eds.), *Cooperative and Collective in China's Rural Development: Between State and Private Interests* (Armonk, NY: M. E. Sharpe, 1998), pp. 247–252.

3. China Rural Villagers Self-Government Research Group, China Research Society of Basic-level Government, *Study of the Election of Villagers Committees in Rural China: Main Report of the Research on Villagers Self-Government* (Beijing, 1 December 1993), pp. iv, 76.

4. Wang Zhenyao, "Village committees," pp. 247–252.

5. Bai Gang, *Report on Improving the Legislation of Villagers' Self-Governance* (Beijing: Centre for Public Policy Research, Chinese Academy of Social Sciences, Working Paper No. 971103, October 1997), p. 52. For a list of the provinces, see p. 55.

6. *Ibid.* pp. 65, 68, 82.

by a different group of Chinese scholars concluded that the "outdated appointment system should be gradually changed to an election system ... democratic reforms in China should not be delayed any more. Some people suspect that the Chinese farmers and rural cadres have too low qualities to practise democracy. The findings in our investigation show the opposite."[7]

In addition to scholarly works on village elections and government papers, a number of international non-governmental and inter-governmental organizations have also studied and observed Chinese village elections since the early 1990s. The Ford Foundation and the Asia Foundation played key roles in supporting studies of village elections. The United Nations Development Programme and the European Union both negotiated extensive projects to assist in the training of newly elected officials, but these projects have been very slow in getting started for numerous bureaucratic reasons on both the Chinese and the donor sides.

The principal evaluations of the village electoral process have been undertaken by two U.S.-based organizations, the International Republican Institute (IRI) and the Carter Center. Both have decade-long experiences in monitoring and evaluating elections internationally, and they use similar techniques, including systematic survey forms that de-compose the electoral process into discrete elements that can be evaluated.

The IRI was the first international team invited to observe village elections, and did so in Fujian in 1994 and 1997.[8] The first mission observed three village elections in different parts of the province and found some striking anomalies. The delegation concluded that the elections it witnessed in Longyan were fairer and less marred by irregularities than the election in Xiamen, where villagers had few opportunities to cast votes secretly. They were also concerned about the potential for abuse in the process of selecting formal candidates. The IRI made 12 recommendations for improving the elections, and its second mission to the same counties (though not the same villages) noted several significant improvements, including the mandatory use of secret ballots and secret voting booths, the abolition of proxy voting, the use of enlarged photographs on campaign materials, and the standardized training of election workers.[9]

In 1995, the Danish embassy in Beijing sent a representative to Sichuan to observe elections for village leaders and the National People's Congress (NPC).[10] The delegation endorsed the "mass voting" style,

---

7. Rong Jingben et al., Transformation from the Pressurized to a Democratic System of Cooperation, pp. 337–348, 413.

8. See International Republican Institute, People's Republic of China Election Observation Report, 15–31 May 1994.

9. International Republican Institute, Election Observation Report: Fujian, People's Republic of China, May 1997.

10. Royal Danish Embassy, Beijing, "Rural village elections," prepared by Franz-Michael S. Melbin, Political Counsellor, December 1995. Although the author refers to NPC elections, villages do not elect representatives to the NPC. What he probably witnessed was a direct election for the township people's congress.

viewing it as a way to allow voters a chance to see the entire process. However, the delegation observed other problems, including the use of open cardboard boxes as ballot boxes, improper handling of unused ballots, and poorly designed ballots for the NPC elections. Although election officials stressed the importance of the secret ballot, voters apparently swamped the booths, making it almost impossible to vote in secret. Proxy voting (one person could vote for three) was permitted. They recommended additional training for election officials and more civic education.

In response to an invitation from the Ministry of Civil Affairs in September 1996 to observe all stages of village elections and advise the ministry on ways to improve them, the Carter Center sent several delegations to China that were led by Robert Pastor and included Qingshan Tan.[11] From 4 to 16 March 1997, a Carter Center delegation observed elections in six villages in Fujian and Hebei. The delegation described problems not dissimilar to those that the IRI encountered and offered 14 specific suggestions on ways to improve the process. These included standardizing rules, synchronizing village elections within a county so as to take advantage of county-wide civic education pro-grammes, taking additional precautions to assure a secret ballot and the correct use of "roving boxes," opening the nomination process, making the election machinery impartial, punishing violations of the election law, encouraging campaigning, and abolishing proxy voting.

Between 2 and 15 March 1998, a second Carter Center delegation observed seven village elections and interviewed officials in two other villages in Jilin and Liaoning provinces. They found that the elections provided voters a reasonably free choice, but there were some procedural problems and other electoral problems related to proxy voting and "roving ballot boxes." The delegation proposed 13 recommendations, which included: added safeguards to ensure the privacy and individuality of the vote, the banning or minimizing of "roving boxes," and the mandating of a methodical and transparent count. The Carter Center observed elections in the south, the north-east and the west, covering about 55 villages in six provinces and one municipality: Fujian, Hunan, Hebei, Liaoning, Jilin, Shandong and Chongqing. The teams found local officials in all the villages ready to share information, and most had quite detailed records of previous elections.

Elements and Stages of the Electoral Process

Based on data from surveys of the elections and interviews, below is a brief summary of some of the patterns and differences found in each of the following stages or elements of the electoral process: election man-

11. For the two Carter Center Reports, see, Carter Center Delegation Report, *The Carter Center Delegation to Observe Village Elections in China*, 4–16 March 1997; Carter Center Delegation Report, *Village Elections in China and Agreement on Cooperation With the Ministry of Civil Affairs, People's Republic of China*, 2–15 March 1998.

agement; registration; nomination and selection; campaign; voting styles and procedures; and the vote count. Discrepancies between the rules and the observed practice are also noted.

Election management. Prior to each election, a village election committee (VEC) is appointed to conduct the registration and election.[12] VEC chairs are sometimes appointed by township officials, sometimes by the village representative assembly and are sometimes self-appointed, but in almost all the cases that the Carter Center observed, they were the Party secretaries of the village. An important, long-term question is whether it is appropriate for the senior representative of the Communist Party in the village to conduct the election as it might be felt that this would bias the process in favour of candidates who were Party members. We posed this question to MoCA and NPC officials and learned that the new village election law (approved in November 1998) mandates that VECs should be selected by the village assembly or by village small groups, not by the Party branch (article 13). Moreover, MoCA officials said that they have instructed the provinces that the chair of the VEC "should not necessarily be the Party secretary."[13] On the other hand, at the last stage in the NPC debate on the new election law, a provision was added that the Communist Party should "play a core role in leadership" of the village. The fairness of the process will be determined, in part, on how these two provisions are reconciled.

The training of election officials is uneven, but with each round, it appears that officials are gaining experience. Most provinces have approved regulations that prohibit a candidate from serving on the VEC, but we saw one case where candidates did not resign from the VEC and a second case where most of the candidates were on the VEC and resigned very late in the process.

Registration. An accurate registration list is necessary to ensure that only citizens with the right to vote in a particular village or precinct are permitted to vote there, and only once. At least 15 days before the election, the VEC should register citizens who are at least 18 years old and are resident in the village. The list is posted usually in the town square or the school courtyard. At the level of the village where everyone knows each other and, in some cases, they are all related, registration is not controversial and, indeed, not taken very seriously. However, the compilation and updating of an accurate registration list will be much more difficult and important for higher-level elections because of people's increasing mobility. In most transitional elections that we have observed, the most serious disputes between political parties often focus

12. The village election committee's function is to prepare for the conduct of the elections for the village committee.
13. Interview with Zhan Chengfu, Rural Areas Section, Ministry of Civil Affairs, Beijing, 14 January 1999.

on the registration list, and whether it enfranchises or disenfranchises a party's supporters.

Nomination and selection of candidates. The process by which candidates are selected for the ballot is a complicated but critical stage in the election. No system can be described as "democratic" if one group or party can select the candidates, as occurs in the indirect elections for township, county, provincial and national executives. In the early rounds of village elections, the Party branch controlled the nomination process. In some places, it still does.

MoCA's decision to encourage other nomination methods was motivated in large part to try to prevent the Party branch from monopolizing the process. Lishu county in Jilin province experimented with a method they called *haixuan*. Literally a "sea election," the method permitted individuals to receive a blank ballot and nominate whomever they wanted. The idea has spread. Two sections of the 1998 election law strengthen those who have been trying to connect the nomination process to the people: article 11 asserts that "no organization or individual is allowed to appoint" members of the village committee, and article 14 declares that "candidates should be nominated directly by villagers."

We have observed many methods of nominating candidates, and in those cases when many candidates are proposed, a second stage is necessary to reduce the number of candidates for each position to two or three. We identified six methods used in the first stage of nominations and four methods in the second stage. In the first stage, the methods include nomination by: Party branch; joint nomination by groups of five to ten villagers; village small groups (the old production brigades of about one-fifth of the village); village representative assembly (10–50 leaders of small village small groups, the Party branch and local NGOs); *haixuan* (individual nomination); and self-nomination.[14] In Fujian, provincial law provides for a single uniform method of candidate nomination: any group of five or more persons can nominate candidates by signing a form provided by the VEC.

The new methods that increase popular involvement in the nomination of candidates have the opposite problem as the old Party branch-dominated system. If the latter produced too few candidates, the other methods, particularly *haixuan*, generate too many, requiring a second stage. There are four methods used for the final selection: Party branch; village representative assembly; village assembly or direct primary by the entire village; and the highest numbers of votes received in the nomination process.[15] Determining the best method for selecting the final candidates for the ballot depends on one's criteria. The most democratic process would be a direct primary, and the least would be by the Party branch. The most efficient would be to use the highest numbers of votes

14. In other places, other nomination methods are used, such as household nomination or nomination by township governments. See Table 1.

15. There are other methods of selection that rely on informal consultations between village election committees and village groups, but it is difficult to assess precisely because the method is informal. See Table 1.

received in the nomination process, and an intermediate option would be to allow the village representative assembly to reduce the number by a secret ballot.

Not all villages have vice-chairs, and some villages have altered the ballot to permit losing candidates for the chair to be considered for the committee. This was done in Chengzi village in Jilin, for example, by having the candidates' names appear twice on the ballot. If the person lost the race for chair, those votes were added to ones that he or she received for the committee position. This cumulative method permitted losing candidates for the chair to win a spot on the committee, but it was very confusing to voters, and as we observed in another village in the province, Haitou, it produced a large number of invalid ballots because people checked the same person twice.[16]

Campaign. The final list of formal candidates is usually posted five days before the election, allowing very little time for campaigning. We have observed little or no campaigning, but the limited time is not the reason. In a small village, where everyone knows each other and where it is viewed as culturally inappropriate to promote oneself, most candidates have been reluctant to campaign. Moreover, there are no rules for election campaigns in the provisional or the new Organic Law, and few provinces stipulate any rules either. In a few instances, candidates have visited the homes of villagers or were permitted to use local cable or closed circuit radio systems. In Chongqing, candidates used posters, but only to describe their background, not to offer a programme.

The principal campaign opportunity comes in the short statement each of the candidates for chair is asked to make on the morning of the election. We observed this in Hebei and in Jilin provinces, and the statements, which averaged five to ten minutes, were instructive, concise and sometimes inspiring. The candidates described what they wanted to do for the community if elected; they were very specific, and the people listened intently. Candidates promised to build a new road; improve and expand the community enterprise in order to reduce taxes; invite outside, including foreign, investors or advisors to provide capital or high-yielding seeds; and so on. In one village in Chongqing, villagers asked the candidates some hard questions, but this laudable practice is not widespread. In both villages we observed in Chongqing, the campaign speeches were briefer and less substantive than the ones that we heard in Hebei and Jilin. In a few villages, the candidates also promised to contribute to the community even if they lost the election, a gesture of great importance in transitional elections.

It is hard to evaluate the effect of campaign speeches anywhere, but in Gujialingzi village, Jilin province, a very competitive election occurred

16. For an evaluation of the accumulative method, see Emerson Niou and Tianjian Shi, "An introduction and evaluation of the electoral system used in Chinese village elections," unpublished paper, Duke University.

after a spirited speech by the challenger against an incumbent, who was a Party member. The incumbent had a huge advantage over the challenger in the number of nominations he had received in the *haixuan* (1,104–184), but this margin was narrowed considerably in the final election (864–655), suggesting that the challenger might have swayed some voters as a result of his speech.

Voting. The casting of ballots is the most critical stage of the election. The legal methods do not vary quite as much as in the other stages of the electoral process, but the actual practice may deviate more from the mandated procedures. There are three voting styles: mass voting where all the voters go to a central voting place in the early morning, vote, and remain there until the end of the count; individual voting throughout the course of the day of the election; and proxy, absentee voting or "roving boxes."

The "mass voting" style was developed during the Maoist years when all the people in the village were brought to the square to vote unanimously in public for the Communist Party's proposals or list of candidates. For that reason, some of those who want China to be democratic prefer to encourage individual voting. But we saw an advantage to mass voting in early stages of the democratization process: it offers an opportunity for the entire village to be educated in the correct voting procedures at the same time. Moreover, villagers can hear the candidates present their programmes and watch the process from the beginning to the end. Some are concerned this is an inefficient use of farmers' time, but we were impressed at the speed and efficiency of the voting without compromising the secret ballot. In two villages in Hebei province in March 1997, we saw 786 people vote in 35 minutes (Fengyingzi) and 1,555 villagers vote in 50 minutes (Qiuwozi).

In Fujian, individual voters went to the polling station all day to cast votes while most of the other provincial sites (except for Dalian in Liaoning) used mass voting. The township election chair led the meeting in a very organized and precise way: the people brought chairs and sat in their village small groups; their leaders announced their attendance; monitors were approved; the candidates gave brief presentations; the process of voting was explained; ballot boxes were opened so that the voters could see that no one had yet voted; the citizens presented their voter identification cards at one of four to eight polling stations and then voted in one of 24 or 36 polling booths, which were desks joined together but also divided by cardboard so that the villagers could vote privately; then the votes were counted, and the results were announced.

The critical issue is not whether the voters should go to the square together or individually but whether the right to a secret and individual ballot is guaranteed. In the villages in Chongqing and in one in Hebei, the villagers voted in their seats where others could see them. In Chongqing, they were given the option to mark the ballot in a secret voting booth, but no one in one village and only a few in the other used that opportunity. Citizens must be required to use a secret voting booth; otherwise, people will be afraid that their leaders will interpret their decision to vote in secret as a vote against them. In a meeting with senior NPC officials after witnessing these elections, they initially defended the option to use secret booths, but after thorough discussion, several agreed that the language in the village election law should *require* secret ballots and voting booths. Nevertheless, the procedure in the province and the discussion in Beijing led us to conclude that the idea of a secret voting booth has not been fully grasped at either the local or the national levels, and it will require considerably more civic education.

A related issue concerns voting as an individual. The right to vote is an individual right that should not be transferred. Proxy ballots, which permit an individual to cast the votes for as many as three other people, are incompatible with that precept. However, only Fujian has prohibited their use; it is experimenting with absentee ballots as a way to permit voting by people who are sick, elderly or out of the area. The arguments in favour of proxy voting are that it is desirable to have high levels of voter participation, and the law requires that at least 50 per cent of eligible voters need to vote for an election to be valid. If there were no proxy voting, no roving boxes and no absentee ballots, the level of voter participation would decline and could render numerous elections invalid. Of course, the requirement that 50 per cent of the voters participate could be reduced or repealed.

The argument against proxy voting is that it trades the inalienable right to vote by oneself. It was clear in all of our observations that many proxies are used as a means of convenience or by the head of the household for the family. In some villages, the percentage of proxy votes was quite high. In Gujialingzi, Jilin, there were 374 proxy votes out of at total of 1,572 – more than 20 per cent. We suspect that the figures for other villages are much higher, but few villages keep a record of the proxies.

The other voting-related problem is the "roving ballot box," which is carried around the village to permit voting by people who cannot go to the polling station. In some villages, such as Jinzhou, Liaoning, more than 90 per cent of the votes were cast in roving boxes rather than at polling stations. These were villages with considerable activity in industry and fishing, and many villagers wanted to be able to vote very early in the morning before going to work. Although the boxes were accompanied by three polling officials and sealed with a lock that was opened in public view in the main voting station, there was no way to determine the integrity of the voting process in the houses that they visited. There are three problems with roving boxes: first, they diminish the sense of civic obligation that comes with going to the polling station; secondly, the secrecy of the vote can be easily violated; and thirdly, individuals voting as a family lose their individuality.

We also heard concerns about "vote buying." This illegal practice is facilitated by voting that occurs in the open, by proxy or by roving box. The cost-and-benefit calculation of "vote buying" is reversed if individuals can vote in secret. Then, citizens know that their vote is worth something, but they can still vote as they please. The procurer is less certain that his money has been well spent.

Vote count. In most transitional countries, the vote count is the most vulnerable moment in the election. As the count begins, the rumours fly – of stolen ballot boxes, of ballots being stuffed or discarded, of computers jammed or re-programmed. The fear of these deeds often provokes riots. The best weapon against them is an open and transparent vote count for the public to view in each polling site and a "quick count" (a random sample of polling sites to determine the winner of a national election). This is not a problem in village elections, nor is a "quick count" needed at that level, but it is important for the villagers to learn to do the count in public so that they can master the process before the electoral process extends to other levels.

In some sites, the count was done very quickly and efficiently with groups of officials dividing up the ballots, sometimes with the help of volunteers. Abacuses were sometimes used to record the votes. Invalid ballots were first identified. When there was a question about the validity of a ballot, the chairman of the village election committee rendered a judgement. (This is still another reason why the chair should be completely impartial). When conducted properly, the ballots were sorted by candidates in public view and then counted out loud so that the recorder could write the number on a blackboard. But we also saw the count done in classrooms or so quietly that the people could not see or hear what was happening or determine whether the ballots were read accurately. The results from the counting groups were added. The winners were publicly announced, certified and sometimes given an opportunity to speak. The 1998 law requires "open counting" and the immediate announcement of results. Additional training is needed on the proper procedures to do the count in a manner that involves the people and gives them confidence.

Assessing the Impact of the Village Election Law

How many village elections are conducted according to the election laws? Curiously, the Minister of Civil Affairs initially declined to answer this question at a luncheon that former President Carter hosted for him in July 1997. He admitted that he did not know. When pressed, he said: "Perhaps, 50 per cent of all the village elections, but frankly, we do not know."[17] The editor of the magazine *Xiangzhen luntan* (*Town and Township Tribune*), which has published many articles on village elections and conducted surveys around the country, estimated that "no more

17. Luncheon with Minister of Civil Affairs Duoji Cairang, Beijing, 25 July 1997. When the minister expressed a desire to know the answer to that question, Pastor proposed a national system for collecting election results and assessing the process, and that became the Carter Center project.

than 10 per cent" held democratic elections, but the criteria and the data on which he drew this conclusion are not clear.[18]

The Carter Center has observed about 55 elections in the country, and others have reported on perhaps another 200. That covers only 0.00027 per cent of China's 930,000 villages, and then only for a single round of elections. The sample is not only trivial, it is not random. This is sobering, but it should not obscure what we have learned. The observations have permitted us to identify the methods used in each of the six stages or elements of the electoral process and to calculate the discrepancy between the rules and the practice of conducting elections. We have also suggested a hypothesis to explain why some elections conform to the norms of free elections and others do not: leadership in the provincial civil affairs ministry.

To take the example of Fujian, the improvement in the electoral process is probably due to its director of the Division of Basic-Level Government in its provincial Department of Civil Affairs, Zhang Xiaogan. With a population of 31 million people, Fujian held its first village elections in 1984 – even before the NPC passed the law – and by 1997, it had completed six rounds of elections. The progress has been astonishing. In 1989, for example, Fujian did not use a secret ballot; by 1994, secret ballots and booths were employed in 37 per cent of the villages, and by 1997, 95 per cent of the villages used them. Of about 15,000 villages in the province, there were more than three times as many nominees for village office in 1997 as in 1989, and more than seven times as many primary elections. Zhang opened the nomination process so that any group of five or more citizens could nominate an individual. The province abolished proxy voting, experimented with absentee balloting, promoted the use of election monitors, encouraged campaigning, and expanded the time for voting from two to eight hours so that people could vote throughout the day. These experiments kept the province on the cutting edge of free elections in the country.[19]

What is missing is a national picture. We have not been able to test hypotheses about the causes or consequences of "good" elections on a national level, and we do not know the frequency and distribution of electoral methods around the country. There are many anecdotes and some good surveys, but the sad truth is that it is impossible to offer a definitive national assessment of how many village elections have been conducted in accordance with the Organic Law.

The picture, however, is not blank. We examined the local reports, which the MoCA uses to draw its estimates of elections, and we also read newsletters published by the Office of Rural Governance, including one published in August 1998. The data presented in Tables 1 and 2 were

18. Cited in Lianjiang Li and Kevin J. O'Brien, "The struggle over village elections," in Merle Goldman and Roderick MacFarquhar (eds.), *The Paradox of China's Post-Mao Reforms* (Cambridge, MA: Harvard University Press, 1999), p. 140.
19. Interviews with Zhang Xiaogan, Fujian province, China, 7–8 March 1997, and 24–25 June 1998.

compiled from these reports, documents and newsletters.[20] Two impor
conclusions lurk behind the tables. First, none of the data from any o
provinces are complete, and only six provinces and one municipality
filled in one-half of all the queries. The ministry first sent surveys to the
provinces in 1996. Those surveys sought demographic data on the village
leaders, information on the management of fiscal affairs and issues
related to governance. There were few questions related to the electoral
process. On the electoral procedures, the data reflect the provincial
regulations rather than the actual practice.

Secondly, the tables indicate the prevalence of many electoral methods;
there is no national or standardized approach on any of the six basic
elements and stages of the electoral process. On the critical issue of the
secret ballot, only eleven provinces and municipalities conducted or
partially conducted elections with secret ballots. In Ningxia, only one
county adopted secret ballots. Six other provinces reported open ballots,
and three used secret ballots only in parts of the province. Thirteen
provinces had no data or declined to send any on this procedure.
Nomination methods ranged from *haixuan* (individual nomination) to
township recommendation. While most provinces use a variety of methods for nomination, Ningxia and Qinghai permit nomination by township
governments and village election committees. The methods for selecting
candidates from the long list are also quite different. Table 2 shows that
almost all chairs are male, and a very high percentage are Party members.
In four of the five provinces with data, roughly 2–10 per cent of elected
chairs are also village Party secretaries. The exceptional case is Shanghai,
where about one-third of village chairs are Party secretaries. Incumbents
are returned to power often in urban areas like Shanghai and Tianjin.
Interestingly, competitive elections were rather common in Ningbo,
Zhejiang, where the private economy thrives.

The problem with the data is that they are incomplete. The Carter
Center's project had observed enough elections to learn about the range
of electoral methods but realized that more observations would not yield
a national picture. The only way to generalize about 930,000 village
elections would be to conduct a national survey. In March 1998, on
behalf of the Carter Center, we negotiated and signed an agreement with
the Ministry of Civil Affairs to establish such a system. The MoCA and
Carter Center then worked through hundreds of drafts of two survey
forms that would be filled out at the village level after the election to
collect election results (I) and assess the process (II).[21] These forms
would then be transmitted to the township, the counties and the
provinces. Software was developed to input the data from these forms to
computers at either the county or the provincial level, and the data would
be transmitted "rapidly and transparently" to the provinces, the National

20. We tried to select data that were comparable. The data were scarce and scattered in
various local reports. Table 2 only contains a few provinces with the comparable data.
21. For the agreement and the two forms, see Appendices 1 and 5 of the Carter Center's
Report on Village Elections, 2–15 March 1998.

Table 1: Village Election Data by Province

Province	Round	Date	Registered voters (E)	Votes cast		Village committees: no. and positions				Election lost by			Election procedures					
				Total	Proxy	Total	Chair	Vice-chair	Member	Chair	Vice-chair	Member	Election style	Nomination type	Candidate selection	Camp. (F)	Secret ballot (G)	VC
Beijing	4	1998	2,254,000			3,512	3,462	1,016	8,920				1	1,2,3,6	2,3	1	1,2	
Chongqing	1	1998																1
Shanghai	4	1998	1,761,892	1,528,475	129,548		2,133	6,903		39	181	647	1	1,2,3			2	
Tianjin	2	1994					3,743	2,162	9,180	272								1
Anhui	3	1995				30,646										2		
Fujian	6	1997												2	3	2	1	1
Gansu	2	1995		11,366,258		83,769						12,950(A)	1,2	3,5	2,3	1	1	1
Guangdong	1	1999																
Guangxi	1	1995																
Guizhou	3	1995				25,826	24,560	87,767										
Hainan	1	1995				2,529								1,2,3,6	2,3	1	2	1
Hebei	4	1996				50,201	49,069	148,016					1	1,2,3,5	2,3	1	2	1
Heilongjiang	4	1997											1,2	1,2,3,5,6		1		1
Henan	2	1994	26,937,774	24,133,154		48,124	45,242	48,867	88,757	5,723	9,740	16,796	2	2	3			
Hubei	4	1997	33,316,600	30,128,200	2,096,001	32,364	32,057	33,263		1,151			1	5	2			1
Hunan	3	1996	34,442,192	32,335,287	8,222,322		46,726	153,101	105,956		1,780	7,001			3	2		
Jiangsu	4	1996	19,653,909	17,371,951		32,655	31,204	76,857										
Jiangxi	3	1996				20,347	19,811						1,2	5		2	1,2	1
Jilin	4	1997												1,2,3			2	
Liaoning	6	1998				15,991	15,826	5,198	49,095			15,867	1,2	1,2,6	3		1,2	1
Inner Mongolia	3	1997												1,2,3	3		2	1
Ningxia (B)	3	1995	1,782,971	1,586,086		2,564	2,065	908					2,1	2,6	2,3	1	1,2	1
Qinghai (C)	3	1996	1,784,660	1,573,281	196,708	4,108	4,108	7,065		595	176	1,310		5	3		1	
Shandong	5	1996				88,332	70,433	15,606						3	2,3			
Shanxi1	4	1996				32,345	26,032						1	5	3	1	2	1
Shanxi2 (D)	3	1995												1,2,6	3		1	
Sichuan	3	1995				75,736												
Tibet	0																	
Xinjiang	3	1996																
Yunnan	2	1996															2	
Zhejiang	2	1995																

Notes:

Blanks appear in the table when no data were available at the Ministry. Two provinces, Guangdong and Tibet, did not have village elections by 1998.

(A) This number includes the loss of chairs and vice-chairs.

(B) Ningxia allows nomination by township party committees and candidate selection by township governments in consultation with villagers. Only Guyuan county adopted a secret ballot.

(C) Qinghai allows nomination by village elections committees in the southern and mountainous areas.

(D) Shanxi2 selected candidates through consultation with village groups and representative assemblies.

(E) Total registered voters in a given province.

(F) Campaign data were mentioned in provincial reports showing actual campaigns were conducted.

(G) Most provinces only began to implement a secret ballot in the last round of elections, and none of the provinces has 100% secret ballot.

Key to Election Procedures

Election Style
  1. Mass voting
  2. Individual voting

Nomination type – by:
  1. Village Party branch
  2. Villagers (freely associated)
  3. Village small groups
  4. Village representative assembly
  5. *Haixuan* (individual nomination)
  6. Self-nomination

Candidate selection – by:
  1. Village Party branch
  2. Village representative assembly
  3. Direct primary (village assembly)
  4. Number of votes received in nomination

Campaign
  1. Speech at mass voting meeting
  2. Speech at village representative assembly

Secret ballot
  1. Secret ballot and booth required
  2. No secret ballot

Vote count
  1. Open, public count
  2. No public count

Sources:

Data collected at the Ministry of Civil Affairs, Beijing, September 1998 from reports filed by provincial Civil Affairs Bureaus, MoCA documents and newsletters. Some provincial data are from *Minzheng bu jiceng zhengquan nongcunchu* (Division of Rural Governance at the Department of Basic-Level Governance, Ministry of Civil Affairs); and *Quanguo cunweihui huanjie xunjie xuanju ziliao huibian* (*Compilation of National Election Documents, 1995–96*), Beijing, 1996.

Table 2: **Data on Elections of Village Committee Chairs, Selected Provinces**

Province	Year	Chairs elected		Also Party secretary	Newly elected	Incumbent	% of Incumbents defeated	Party members	
		Total	Female					Number	%
Beijing	1995	4,350	n/a	n/a	n/a	n/a	n/a	3,385	78
Hebei	1996	49,069	n/a	n/a	n/a	34,155	30	40,010	82
Hunan	1996	46,726	n/a	n/a	n/a	34,904	25	n/a	n/a
Hubei	1997	31,692	803	3,399	6,226	25,466	20	28,167	89
Jiangsu	1996	31,230	1,066	2,277	9,579	21,628	31	26,358	84
Liaoning	1995	15,303	n/a	n/a	n/a	13,068	15	n/a	71[a]
Qinghai	1996	4,108	92	159	n/a	n/a	n/a	2,625	64
Shanghai	1996	2,133	132	775	n/a	2,094	2	1,959	92
Tianjin	1995	3,743	n/a	n/a	272	3,471	7	3,359	89
Zhejiang[b]	1996	4,668	181	374	2,260	n/a	48	2,954	62

Notes:
  (a) This is the percentage of all the village committee members.
  (b) Zhejiang only reported the data on Ningbo.
Source:
  Documents compiled by the Ministry of Civil Affairs, 1998; Minzheng bu jiceng zhengquan nongcunchu, *1995–96 Niandu quanguo cunweihui huanjie xunju ziliao huibian (Compilation of National Village Election Documents, 1995–96)*, Beijing, 1996.

Ministry of Civil Affairs and the public. These data would per minister to know which areas of the country had what kinds of pr and thus to devise and target specific educational programmes.] and July 1998, the Carter Center began implementing the project i pilot counties in three provinces – Fujian, Jilin and Hunan. Sub visits by ministry officials to the Carter Center in July and August 1990 and by Carter Center teams to the provinces in the autumn of 1998 assisted in the training of the officials. Data have already been generated in eight of the nine pilot counties from 2,906 villages. We shall refer to some of those data below.

In the long term, this project could permit a national picture of how well China is doing in conducting village elections but it is not clear whether the project will be completed or how long it will take. In the interim, we proposed a national sample based on provinces. Senior ministry officials did not oppose the idea but had reservations about its cost and utility. In January 1999, a national sample was approved, but further action is yet to be taken.

Evaluating Village Elections

The question at the centre of this volume is whether "limited democracy" can lead to genuine democracy. For our purposes, the issues are whether China's village elections constitute a form of "limited democracy" and what this means for the future of democratic reform in China. To determine the meaning of the elections, we must first define our terms and then establish the criteria for judging the elections.

There is considerable debate about the meaning of elections and democracy and their relationship. Some view the emphasis on elections as reflecting a Western bias and dismiss such a focus as ethnocentric or as "electoralism." Democracy, according to this view, needs to be built on independent institutions like a legislature and a court, and processes that include a free press and freedom of association. Most scholars agree that democracy can and should be more than just free elections, but it cannot be less. If the elections are free and fair, then most of the other elements of democracy – freedom of the press, association, independent institutions and so on – should be present. When elections are flawed, the regime cannot be considered democratic. "Electoral democracy," Larry Diamond reminds us, "is a system of government in which the principal positions of effective government power are filled, directly or indirectly, through democratic national elections."[22] Liberal democracy goes beyond "electoral democracy" to incorporate other conditions, such as accountability, rule of law and transparency in all of public life, not just elections.

How does one evaluate whether elections are democratic? The co-editors suggest three universal criteria: they must be free, fair and meaningful. "Free" means that the barriers to entry for parties and candidates are low; candidates are free to campaign; and the people vote

22. See the introduction to this volume.

in private. "Fair" means that the elections are administered by a neutral, impartial, independent, credible and competent institution. And "meaningful" means that the elected officials should have genuine authority. These three criteria could be amended to take into account the way in which many citizens approach an election. In practice, most people vote against a party or a candidate, usually an incumbent, rather than for someone. Instead of a "right to choose," another definition of democracy would be the people's "right to replace" their leaders at regular intervals. The "replacement factor" acts as the glue that keeps leaders accountable. If they do something wrong or do not measure up to their constituents' expectations, they will lose the next election. An election should not be judged on whether the people *do* replace their leaders, however; only by whether they *can*.

Translating those concepts into an operational definition of a free, fair and meaningful election is no easy matter, as international election observers have long recognized. Two scholars have developed an extensive "checklist" for identifying and assessing an election,[23] but some consolidated democracies might not pass the entire test. China certainly could not meet those standards. Political parties are not free to organize or contest village elections, although at the village level, where everyone knows each other, parties are not necessary. Because of the strong role played by village Party secretaries in the village election committee, some would question whether the administration of the elections is fair. There are also cases where newly elected leaders do not exercise as much authority over local decisions as the appointed Party secretaries. But just because the village elections are not fully free or fair, and some do not transfer complete authority, one should not conclude that they are unfree, unfair and meaningless. Elections should not be evaluated categorically but rather viewed as lying on a democratic continuum.

Besides the universal standards and the elaborate checklist for free, fair and meaningful elections, there are other criteria which could be used to judge China's village elections. One could judge an election within the context of a country's history. Using this criterion, a good election need only be better than the last or than what the country has had. The premise underlying this criterion is that democracy is nowhere perfect. It is a process of incremental improvement, and if an election helps a country move forward on a more civil, democratic path, then it is a satisfactory election. Within the context of 5,000 years of Chinese authoritarianism, there is no disputing that village elections represent a significant step toward a freer system, and many villages have seen improvement with each round of elections.

A third criterion would be whether the major candidates or parties that contested the elections viewed the process and the results as acceptable.[24]

23. See Jøgen Elklit and Palle Svensson, "What makes elections free and fair?" *Journal of Democracy*, Vol. 8, No. 7 (July 1997), pp. 17–61.

24. This definition is developed in Robert A. Pastor, "Mediating elections," *Journal of Democracy*, Vol. 9, No. 1 (January 1998), pp. 154–163.

They did so in national elections in 1990 in both Nicaragua and Haiti, although those elections had serious technical flaws. Why is this important? For a democracy to take root in a country, the key political actors must decide to work within the rules of the electoral game. Therefore, if all the parties accept the process and the result, they have taken an important step towards democracy. Although political parties are not contesting elections in China, competitive elections at the village level have winners and losers, and a question we have asked of the losers is whether they viewed the process as fair. This is a pivotal question, but not one that will be easy to answer until the overall political environment of the country is more liberal.

A fourth criterion would be to assess the most critical elements of the electoral process, and at the village level, there are two: choice (an open nomination process and more than one candidate for each position); and the right and requirement that the vote be secret and individual. Unless and until these two elements are mastered at the village level, then democracy has little chance to flower in China.

Choice. As long as voters have two genuine and independent candidates, they have a choice and the power to compel their leader to be responsive to their will. If the two candidates are not genuinely independent, however, then their choices are unduly constrained. It does not necessarily matter if the two candidates are both members of the Communist Party. As a way of illustration, consider three cases (all in Jilin and Liaoning provinces). In the first case, in Kaian village, the second candidate (a Party member) withdrew from the race at the last minute, claiming that he would prefer to be a committee member rather than the chair. The people were denied a choice. In the second case, in Hengdao, the two candidates ran a hard race. The incumbent defended his record and the challenger pledged that he could do better, and the challenger won. The fact that they were both members of the Party was not relevant; the language of the competition was between that of an incumbent and that of a challenger, and the people benefited. In the third case, in Chengzi, Dalian, the Party manipulated the process by preventing a non-Party challenger from competing against their preferred candidate.

For the nomination process to be genuine, there should be more candidates than positions and preferably two for each position. Although in most of the village elections we observed there were two candidates for chair, there was usually only one more candidate than the number of committee members being elected: four candidates for three positions, for example. The choice is therefore tightly constrained. Secondly, the process for nominating and selecting candidates should be as open as possible. The Organic Law of 1998 requires that there be more candidates than positions, and it provides for write-in votes. Both stipulations have widened the domain of choice for villagers. Among the various existing methods, voters have adequate means to nominate candidates in principle, but in practice, the Party branch or township officials sometimes exercise influence in ways that are difficult for outsiders to see.

Secret, individual ballot. There is perhaps no issue more important to the success of an election than the certainty that a voter will cast a secret ballot. This is a well-established principle in democracies. In China, however, this principle has not been firmly established, nor has it been regarded as essential by voters or election officials. Although most MoCA officials now realize the importance of secret balloting, and this principle is now incorporated into the new law, not all provincial officials follow it. Some provincial circulars like those in Inner Mongolia mention that secret booths may be used, but they are not required. Some secret booths in the Chengde area of Hebei were desks separated by cardboard or even newspapers. Other provinces, such as Liaoning, had screened booths. In Hengdao and Houshi, Jilin, villagers voted individually in a room and curtains precluded people from watching them vote. In Gujia-lingzi, Jilin, voters entered a room with five desks. Although asked to vote at separate desks, many would go to the middle one and look at each other's ballots as they marked their own. When asked to vote separately, they were bewildered, just as the children of an old man were when an official asked them to retrieve their ballots from their father and vote by themselves. In Chongqing, most villagers filled out their ballots in the courtyard where others could see them. Because of the widespread use of proxies and roving boxes, the rules do not assure individual voting, although they do assure a private ballot in principle. Without comprehensive and independent monitoring, however, no one knows the extent to which these rules are practised.

The Meaning of Village Elections

To assess the meaning of the village elections, one needs to ask, first, what is the prospect that elections in virtually all the villages will conform to the norms of free and fair elections, and secondly, will direct, democratic elections ascend from the villages to the township, counties, provinces and eventually the national government? One argument that is often used to postpone democracy in China is that people in rural areas lack the education necessary for free elections. As we have reported, there is some truth to this assertion, but it masks two more powerful truths. First, no matter how poor and uneducated, farmers know their interests and want to shape their own future. Secondly, farmers can be educated to master electoral procedures and translate that motive into democracy. We observed many more villages where farmers voted properly and according to the law than where they voted improperly.

China is right to start democracy at the village level where the members of the village know the candidates and where public decisions have the most direct effect on their lives. Each round of elections offers an opportunity for educating people in the proper techniques of free elections. Moreover, there is no evidence that national leaders are trying to control village elections. This may be because the Communist Party is not threatened by village elections and, indeed, there is evidence that it uses elections to identify and recruit new leaders and rejuvenate itself.

The Party's interest in free elections, however, might not be so impartial if the elections move up the ladder of government.

The village is the best level to start educating the rural population to the technical elements of a free election, but at the same time, it might be one of the most difficult places to introduce genuine political competition. Even in advanced democracies, small groups often control the politics and economics of small towns. In poor, authoritarian countries, one would expect the elite – defined by clan, new money or Party membership – to control local politics. Many officials already complain that the old clans or new entrepreneurs are manipulating elections for their own purposes, a charge that is also made by some against the Communist Party.

In thinking about the issue of who controls village elections, one needs to distinguish between the process and the outcome. The purpose of democracy is not to eliminate "factions" or groups, but rather to provide a framework within which these groups can convey their concerns and pursue their interests. Elections are the instrument by which the people select the leaders they want to follow. If entrepreneurs, clan leaders or Party members can win a free election by their personal skills, the process is working. If they manipulate the process then the process needs to be fixed. In small villages it is not always easy for an outsider – whether from Beijing or abroad – to tell if the process is being manipulated, but there are a few indicators or "warning signs" that should be monitored.

The most important indicator is a secret ballot. Some of the provinces have data on the percentage of villages that use a secret ballot, but reliable national data do not yet exist. The two more democratically advanced provinces of Fujian and Jilin had nearly 100 per cent secret ballots in their counties. The data for the counties in Fujian are roughly comparable to the data collected by the province.[25] A second indicator is competitiveness, and there are several dimensions to this. The election is not competitive if there is only one candidate. In a culture that is more accustomed to consensus and harmony than open disputes, close votes are quite meaningful indicators of political competitiveness. In the villages that we have directly observed, about 76 per cent conducted elections using secret ballots. In terms of election competitiveness, about half were competitive, as indicated by a winning margin of less than two-to-one.

Does incumbency affect competitiveness? Some people might interpret a low level of re-election for chairs as a sign that the electoral process is working, but a high level does not mean that the process is not working. People re-elect their leaders when satisfied with their performance or with their own lives, and they tend to replace them if they are dissatisfied. If people are dissatisfied and the leaders are returned to power, then one might want to look more closely at the electoral process. In our research at the MoCA, we found that few provinces sent data on incumbency and

25. The data received from the province were from a long interview with Zhang Xiaogan in March 1998.

turnover, but Table 2 has data on those that did. In Hunan, 25 per cent of incumbents lost their bid for re-election, and in Ningbo, Zhejiang province, 48.4 per cent of chairs in 1996 were newly elected. Overall, the re-election rate varied from a high of 98 per cent in Shanghai to a low of 52 per cent in Ningbo. Whether re-election is due to satisfaction or manipulation could be addressed in a future study that compared the rate of re-election with the growth of the economy and/or the perceptions of economic satisfaction.

The data from the provinces also showed that a high percentage of village chairs were Party members, around 80 per cent or higher, although a very low percentage of village chairs are Party secretaries (Table 2).[26] The issue of Party influence, however, is a complicated one. It was no surprise that a large number of elected officials were Party members given the continued influence of the Party in the countryside and the fact that it recruits the more enterprising villagers, including village chairs. But this continued influence does not mean they are manipulating the process. To reach such a conclusion, one needs to look at the nomination, voting and counting process.

So how meaningful are the village elections, and how do they relate to the broader issue of political reform in China? From the many debates that have occurred within the Chinese leadership on village elections, one could conclude that there is substantial support for them in principle. In September 1998, President Jiang Zemin reaffirmed his support: "Expanding basic-level democracy and guaranteeing the democratic rights of the peasants are not only the most extensive realization of socialist democracy in the countryside but also the utmost important policy that would return the initiative to the peasants [and] ensure long-term prosperity and security."[27] Li Peng praised the passage of the new electoral law and reaffirmed that "democracy starts with the grass-roots in China because for an ordinary villager, the person who is of direct concern to him is not the provincial governor or the county magistrate or even the head of the township but the chairman of the village committee."[28] Nevertheless, in their interviews both men made other points that are less encouraging. Jiang Zemin stressed the importance of strengthening the Party in the rural areas, and Li Peng declared that the government will not permit opposition parties.

Although the Chinese leadership supports grassroots democracy, there are numerous signs that village elections remain a low priority for them. To ensure that elections are being conducted properly in a country as vast as China would require leadership, a significant allocation of resources and a massive campaign on the national level. Although the MoCA upgraded the Basic-Level Government Division (*jiceng zhengquan jian-*

---

26. According to Ann Thurston's interview with a MoCA official, the percentage of non-Party members being elected seems to have grown from 20% in 1993 to 40% in 1995. See Thurston, *Muddling Toward Democracy* (Washington, D.C.: U.S. Institute for Peace, 1998), n. 81.

27. Cited in *Renmin ribao* (*People's Daily*), Beijing, 28 September 1998.

28. Li Peng's interview with Peter Seidlitz of *Handelsblatt* (Germany), 2 December 1998.

shechu) to a Department in 1988 to implement the provisional law, in Beijing, only six people were assigned to work full-time on village elections and 11 to work part-time. In 1998–99, the ministry, like the rest of the government, had to reduce its professional staff by half, and it did so – from 470 to 215. Although the group devoted to village elections remained at roughly the same level, they were assigned additional responsibilities (such as registering divorces). On a national level, of the ministry's 200,000 officials before the reduction of 1998, only 10,000 or 5 per cent were involved in basic-level government.[29] Such a small group cannot educate and supervise all 930,000 villages in the ways of democracy.

A central, albeit neglected question is how to build the technical capacity for permitting free elections. Not enough attention has been given to this question, but the success of the democratic experiment depends on it. Substantial progress has been made in introducing democratic ideas in the last decade, but the more difficult challenge is to make sure that they are implemented properly.

The Vice-Minister of Civil Affairs Li Baoku explained to us the importance of village elections by referring back to the economic reform. He said that the household responsibility system gave peasants economic freedom to achieve greater agricultural production, and village grassroot elections gave peasants political autonomy to manage their own affairs. In his judgement, both reforms have transformed the lives of the 800 million people living in the countryside.

And there is evidence that free elections can produce not only better leaders and policy, but also social stability. An instructive case is the contrasting behaviour of farmers towards a highway tax levy in Renshou and Pengshan counties in Sichuan. Peasants in Renshou, where there were no village elections, resisted the tax levy violently, whereas peasants in Pengshan, where village elections were implemented, approved the tax, and the highway was built.[30]

In assessing the direction and prospect for future political reforms, there are contradictory signs. On 19 March 1998, at his first press conference as prime minister, Zhu Rongji said: "Of course, I am in favour of democratic elections" for all positions including that of premier and president, but that he would need to study the subject before the government would consider "legal procedures." By the summer of 1998, the Chinese leadership began to request studies of political reforms and

29. The figures on the number of officials in Beijing before and after the reduction of 1998 and the number working directly and indirectly on village elections are from interviews in the ministry with the vice-minister and the director of the Office of Basic-Level Government. (Beijing, June–July 1998). The figures on the overall numbers of officials in the ministry on a nation-wide basis in 1996 are from Jude Howell, "Prospects for village self-governance in China," *Journal of Peasant Studies*, Vol. 25, No. 3 (April 1998), p. 106.

30. This example was cited by Wang Zhenyao in his speech at the training section of Hebei Fourth Round election officials, 24 June 1996, see Minzheng bu jiceng zhengquan nongcunchu (Division of Rural Governance of the Department of Basic-Level Governance, Ministry of Civil Affairs), *1995–96 Niandu quanguo cunweihui huanjie xunjiu ziliao huibian* (*Compilation of National Village Election Documents, 1995–96*), Beijing, 1996, p. 17.

suggest that they might be interested in experiments and pilot projects for township elections. A few months later, a group of individuals formed the Democratic Party and tried to register. The government hesitated but finally arrested the individuals. At the same time, reports of labour unrest as a result of lay-offs from state enterprises and government fears of instability related to the great anniversaries in 1999 – tenth for Tiananmen square and 50th for the revolution – might have led the government to postpone or, possibly, reject the idea of having direct democratic elections at levels above the village. We do not know whether this is temporary and linked to the year or more permanent and linked to a Party decision, but regardless, an idea of democracy is abroad in China, and townships and counties are already thinking about direct elections.

In December 1998, a small township called Buyun in Sichuan province held a direct election for township magistrate. The people proposed nominees, and they campaigned together with an official nominated by the Party. In the end, the Party representative won with 12 votes more than 50 per cent of the vote, and the election was declared valid. The people of the town were very proud of their initiative, and although the government's response was ambiguous at first, in the end, they allowed it to go forward. The new democratic movements are trying to test the system, but they are still watching very carefully for signs of approval or, at least, acquiescence from Beijing.

If China's economy continues to grow, the new economic forces and groups will demand outlets to defend their interests. But the need to open legitimate political channels for these successful entrepreneurs will not be nearly as important as the challenge of responding to popular dissatisfaction if there is a downturn in the economy. Then, the government will need an escape valve for the people to release their frustrations. Fortunately, the best mechanism for dealing with both economic success and economic failure is the same: a free, competitive election. If such a mechanism does not exist when there is a downturn, however, the pressures for change might be so compelling that the only alternatives would be repression or violent revolution.

The true meaning of village elections, therefore, is that all those living in rural areas are supposed to have access to the norms and procedures of free elections, according to a national law. Every three years, they should be able to exercise their rights to elect or replace their leaders peacefully and routinely. We do not know what percentage of this population is actually exercising these rights, but where peasants can choose their leaders freely and fairly, their leaders will need to be more responsive or they will be replaced. If the rural population demands these rights and masters these procedures, then elections could be extended to other levels and expanded to other groups. Some of the most profound changes and instructive lessons in China's history have come from the rural areas. The lesson this time is as fertile as the richest soil: that elections are the most effective instrument for assuring China's stability whether the economy does well or poorly.

Elections and Power: The Locus of Decision-Making in Chinese Villages*

Jean C. Oi and Scott Rozelle

While the election process is important, the significance of the Organic Law on Villagers' Committees rests with what happens after a village election. The existence of the law reveals little about the actual distribution of power and decision-making in China's villages. Even free and fair elections cannot be assumed to bring meaningful change to the contours of rural power where there is a dual authority structure – Party and government – in every village. The villagers' committee is now elected, but the Party secretary is still appointed by the higher levels of the CCP. Which is the locus of power?

Power, following a standard definition, can be measured as the extent of authority one party has over another. In Maoist China the basis of power was fairly straightforward. The source of power was appointment to political office by the CCP, buttressed by giving those in office economic control through a system of central planning and rationing.

Decollectivization radically changed the configuration of power in China's villages. Some rural cadres still have significant economic power, but others do not. Appointment to political office no longer automatically carries with it control over a significant array of scarce and valued economic goods and opportunities. Whether cadres have power depends not on their office but on their own ability to mobilize resources.[1] The institution of competitive elections further muddied the political water by introducing a new basis of power: that derived from the legitimacy of the election process.[2] In theory at least, this leaves open the possibility that the locus of power could be the CCP-appointed Party secretary,[3] the popularly elected villagers' committee chairman,[4] or the villagers' assembly or representative assembly. This article addresses the question of the likely locus of power in rural China's changing economic and political environment.

Unlike during the Maoist period, the answer to this question varies with the heterogeneity of China's villages. Our preliminary research suggests that, at least in the short run, the significance of village elections and emergence of local participatory bodies may depend on the economic

* The authors would like to thank Amelia Hughart, John Kennedy and Jennifer Solotaroff for assistance in the data work for this paper. The comments of Larry Diamond, Alex Inkeles, Guo Li, Thomas Metzger, Ramon Myers and Michel Oksenberg are greatly appreciated. We also gratefully acknowledge the financial support of the Ford Foundation, Beijing.

1. See Jean C. Oi, *Rural China Takes Off: Institutional Foundations of Economic Reform* (Berkeley: University of California Press, 1999).
2. There were elections during the Maoist period but they were not competitive and therefore failed to have legitimacy. See John Burns, "The election of production team cadres in rural China, 1958–74," *The China Quarterly*, No. 74 (June 1978), pp. 273–296.
3. Party secretaries may be popularly elected by Party members within the village.
4. There are also other bases of power, for example, those derived from family and kinship hierarchies such as clan ties.

context in which these political processes occur. The power of those elected hinges on concurrent economic power. Two key economic variables – the degree of village industrialization and the nature of villagers' ties to the economy outside their village's boundaries – are most likely to determine which decision-making body has power in the village and how that power is exercised.

The Research

Our findings are based on intensive fieldwork and a nation-wide survey to test the anecdotes and impressions gained from interviews. We conducted open-ended interviews on elections and local assemblies in eight provinces with a range of individuals. These included provincial, county and township officials, representatives to the local people's congresses, local Communist Party heads, directors of villagers' committees, representatives to the villagers' assemblies, farmers, out-commuting migrants, and local traders and entrepreneurs.

In 1996 we collected survey data on the election process, the emergence of assemblies and representative assemblies, and information on local leaders as part of a much larger effort to understand the political economy of China's local communities. The set of sample villages was relatively small, but nearly nationally representative (see below). The enumeration group was a team of social scientists from Beijing; the respondents were three leaders from each sampled village. The survey design chose prefectures, counties, townships and villages randomly, using a comprehensive sampling frame stratified on the basis of gross value of industrial output, a variable shown by Rozelle and others to account for large differences in regional development.[5] In each of the representative provinces (see tables for list of provinces), the enumeration team surveyed four villages in each of eight counties, yielding a total of 32 villages per province. In addition to information on village political institutions, we collected data on the structure of the village economy and the linkages that it had with the rest of China.

The Structure of Village Authority

According to the Organic Law, two bodies make up the formal decision-making structure of a village: the villagers' assembly or representative assembly and the villagers' committee.[6]

5. Scott Rozelle, "Stagnation without equity: patterns of income and inequality in China's rural economy," *The China Journal*, No. 35 (January 1996), pp. 63–92.

6. These two organizations are the successor to structures found in earlier periods of communist rule. The villagers' committee is the successor to the management committee of the agricultural producers' co-operative and to the management committee of the production brigade; the villagers' assembly is the successor to the general assembly of the agricultural producers' co-operative and the representative assembly of the commune members.

Villagers' assemblies. While most studies of the Organic Law have focused mainly on the fair and competitive election of the villagers' committee (*cunmin weiyuanhui*),[7] the villagers' assembly (*cunmin huiyi*), not the villagers' committee, in principle, is the highest decision-making body in villages. The Organic Law on the Villagers' Committees passed on 24 November 1987 states that "the villagers' assembly is the supreme decision-making body of village self-government, and all the major village affairs are to be decided by the villagers' assembly."[8] The villagers' committee is subordinate to the villagers' assembly and is elected by it.[9]

The crafters of the Organic Law conceived of the villagers' assemblies as a form of direct democracy that would supplement the indirect democracy of the people's congresses found at the higher levels.[10] The Law specifies that "all things which relate to the interests of the people shall be decided by people themselves."[11] Local regulations stipulate that villagers' assemblies "examine and approve the social and economic development plans of the village and the annual plans; electing and removing the members of the villagers' committee; discussing and deciding the division and adjustment of the contract responsibility land lots and land lots for one's own provisions; altering and annulling the inappropriate decisions of the villagers' committee; checking the financial accounts of the village; discussing the assignment plans for the distribution of household residence areas; deciding the other issues which relate to the interests of all the farmers of a village."[12] Some local measures specify that expenditures on non-production projects over 500 *yuan*, and on production projects over 3,000 *yuan*, are to be discussed by the villagers' assembly. Other items open to discussion by the assembly include birth control programmes, the administration and use of machines, power, water and other collective resources.

Villagers' representative assemblies. In practice, however, direct democracy, especially in large villages, proved unwieldy.[13] Many villages moved to a more manageable system of representative democracy, adopting "villagers' representative assemblies" (*cunmin daibiao huiyi*). The Ministry of Civil Affairs (MoCA) issued a circular on the establishment of villagers' representative assemblies in 1990. According to MoCA statistics, by 1994 about half of China's villages had estab-

7. Exceptions include Anne F. Thurston, *Muddling toward Democracy: Political Change in Grassroots China*, Peaceworks No. 23 (Washington, D.C.: United States Institute of Peace, 1998); and Susan Lawrence, "Democracy, Chinese style," *Australian Journal of Chinese Affairs*, No. 32 (July 1994), pp. 61–68.

8. *The Report on the Villagers Representative Assemblies in China* (Beijing Research Group on the System of Village Self-Government, December 1994), p. 1.

9. "There could not have been a villagers' committee, and hence true village self-government, without the villagers' assembly." *Ibid.* p. 5.

10. See Peng Zhen's speech at the 20th session of the Standing Committee of the Sixth NPC in March 1987, quoted in *ibid.* p. 4.

11. *Ibid.* p. 4.

12. *Ibid.* p. 116.

13. According to MoCA, the average villagers' assembly would be attended by 600 to 1,800 people, all members of the village 18 years and older. *Ibid.* p. 2.

lished this system. Our survey of rural China confirms the shift (Table 1). The number of villages with villagers' representative assemblies increased between 1988 and 1995, while the number of villagers' assemblies decreased. However, compliance varied by province. Shandong province had the best record in establishing villagers' representative assemblies (87 per cent in 1995); Shanxi had the worst (only 56 per cent).

The villagers' representative assembly became the "permanent organ when the villagers' assembly is not in session to handle important village affairs."[14] Although its authority is not exactly equal to the villagers' assembly,[15] the villagers' representative assembly "discusses and decides on all issues which fall within the sphere of the administrative village (*xingzheng cun*)."[16] The size of the representative assemblies varies according to the population and number of small groups in a village. A number of provinces stipulate a minimum number of members.[17] The lower levels within each province may also have their own regulations.[18] The MoCA puts the average somewhere around 30 representatives, with 50 in large and 20 in small villages.[19] Our survey found that of the villages that had representative assemblies, the average size was 34 per village in 1995 (Table 2, row 2, column 2); the smallest had 23 members; the largest had 44 members.

Limitations on villagers' assembly power. It is questionable whether practice mirrors the principle that the villagers' assemblies and representative assemblies should be the locus of decision-making. Fieldwork suggests that important issues such as expenditures are raised in villagers' representative assembly meetings.[20] For example, one villagers' representative assembly of 38 people was convened to discuss the establishment of a village enterprise. After the assembly came to agreement, it then called a village-wide discussion, initially organized within the village small groups and then in a villagers' assembly meeting. After the factory was up and running, the villagers' representative assembly met the board of directors of the factory to decide on the dividends from the factory.

14. *Ibid.* p. 114.
15. Regulations stipulate that representative assemblies are the only body with the power to elect and remove members of the villagers' committee and work out of the village conventions and village pledge. *Ibid.* p. 115.
16. Wang Zhenyao, "Village committees: the basis for China's democratization," in Eduard B. Vermeer, Frank N. Pieke and Woei Lien Chong (eds.), *Cooperative and Collective in China's Rural Development: Between State and Private Interests* (Armonk, NY: M. E. Sharpe, 1998), p. 253.
17. For example, Shandong requires no less than 30, as does Liaoning. Fujian states that it should be no less than 35 in villages with more than 1,000 households and no less than 25 in villages with less than 1,000. *The Report on the Villagers Representative Assemblies*, p. 100.
18. For example, some places in Hebei state that the number of members should be generally 2–3% of the villagers aged 18 and above, in others there should be 30–60 members. While in Shanxi, there should be 20–60 members, but in villages with less than 400 no representative assembly need be established, instead there should be a full villagers' assembly.
19. *The Report on the Villagers Representative Assemblies*, p. 100.
20. Oi observed villagers' representative meetings in Hunan and Henan in the summer of 1994. The ministry requires that villages keep detailed notes of the issues discussed and the decisions made during these meetings.

Table 1: The Proportion of Villages that have Villagers' and Representative Assemblies by Province in China, 1988 and 1995 (%, mean values)

	China		Zhejiang		Sichuan		Hubei		Shaanxi		Shandong	
	1988	1995	1988	1995	1988	1995	1988	1995	1988	1995	1988	1995
Villagers' assemblies	73	69	53	41	81	87	78	66	71	78	81	75
Representative assemblies	70	78	81	84	56	78	87	84	41	56	84	87

Source:
Authors' survey.

Table 2: **Attendance and Membership of Villagers' Committees, Representative Assemblies and Villagers' Assemblies by Province in China, 1988 and 1995 (mean values)**

	China		Zhejiang		Sichuan		Hubei		Shaanxi		Shandong	
	1988	1995	1988	1995	1988	1995	1988	1995	1988	1995	1988	1995
Number of members per village on villagers' committee	5.4	5.2	5.3	4.7	5.5	5.3	6.6	6.6	5.4	5.1	4.3	4.2
Number of members per village on representative assembly	35	34	43	44	42	39	42	38	20	23	25	26
Average % of members per village on representative assembly	3.6	3.7	3.7	4.4	3.8	3.2	4.2	4.0	2.6	2.6	3.4	3.9
Number of people attending villagers' assembly	437	451	538	451	596	619	457	461	323	342	295	290
Average % of people attending villagers' assembly	48	49	52	45	50	51	53	59	44	43	45	47

Source:
    Authors' survey.

The representative assembly and the board of directors also decided on the manager of the factory.[21]

It is not clear how typical the above example is. It is also unclear whether the decision to set up the factory was made elsewhere and the villagers' representative assembly was convened to discuss and approve – or rubber-stamp – the decision, or whether the meeting to decide on the dividends was simply a formality. Is the power of villagers' representative assemblies circumscribed much like that of the bodies that they are modelled on at the higher levels, the people's congresses? Are they merely forums where important issues are discussed, reviewed and approved, but decisions are made elsewhere? How much authority is there?

While research to date does not allow a full answer to these questions, the ability of a body to be a viable and influential political force can be gauged by examining the structural limitations on its operation. One measure is how often a body convenes. Both the villagers' assemblies and the representative assemblies meet infrequently (Table 3). The villagers' assembly may meet only once or twice a year (row 1). The representative assembly supposedly meets more often, but this is usually only three or four times a year (row 2). The survey data show that the average number of meetings of the villagers' assembly is less than twice a year for China as a whole. The highest average number in the provinces surveyed was 2.63 in Hebei in 1988, but this number declined to only 1.33 by 1995. The villagers' representative assemblies met somewhat more frequently, averaging 3.76 meetings across China in 1995.

A second measure is who has rights to attend the assemblies and who chairs the meetings. The make-up of the villagers' representative assembly varies by village. According to MoCA, the villagers' representative assembly consists of six kinds of individuals: villagers' representatives, members of the villagers' committee, chiefs of village small groups, deputies to the people's congresses at various levels, members of the CPPCC at various levels, the village Party branch secretary and members of the village Party branch.[22] Of these, some are elected while others are considered "natural representatives" who are simply given a place in the assembly.[23] The villagers' representatives are the elected members, primarily from the village small groups, and they constitute the largest number. Every ten to 15 households, organized according to residence, elect one representative for a three-year term. Special interest groups within a village, such as women, senior citizens, youth, teachers, private entrepreneurs or even factory managers, might also have a representative. The representatives are the spokespersons for their group. Before each session they are supposed to collect the opinions, suggestions and demands of their groups. After the meetings, the

21. China Interview (hereafter CI) 82494.
22. Some assemblies also allocate seats for retired village heads.
23. According to some accounts, these do not count in the total number of village representatives – but it is unclear what this actually means.

Table 3: Frequency of Meetings of Villagers' Assemblies and Villagers' Representative Assemblies by Province in China, 1988 and 1995 (mean values)

	China[a]		Zhejiang		Hebei		Liaoning		Shandong		H ubei		Sichuan		Shaanxi	
	1988	1995	1988	1995	1988	1995	1988	1995	1988	1995	1988	1995	1988	1995	1988	1995
							Mean values									
Villagers' assembly meetings (per year)	1.52	1.56	1.06	1.10	2.63	1.33	0.50	0.71	2.52	2.34	1.33	1.70	1.50	1.50	1.84	1.90
Representative assembly meetings (per year)	3.58	3.76	3.65	3.13	3.71	3.73	2.20	2.56	6.31	6.93	4.84	4.80	1.30	1.83	2.09	2.97

Note:
[a] Weighted average by rural population of seven sample provinces.
Source:
Authors' survey.

representatives communicate the essence of the decisions to their constituencies.

Rules of procedure state that any item that is advanced by one-third of the representatives should be put on the agenda for discussion. Some specify that a quorum of two-thirds of the members of the representative assembly must be present for the assembly to be convened. Decisions are by majority rule. Resolutions must be voted through by over 50 per cent of the villagers' representatives.

However, despite rules that suggest a democratic process, there appears to be a bias towards control of the representative assemblies by the non-elected members, particularly by those belonging to the CCP. All members of the villagers' committee – the body the assembly is supposed to oversee – are in the assembly. In addition, the Party branch members (usually two or three), the heads of the small village groups (who frequently, but not always, are Party members) and the village Party secretary are given seats in the assembly.[24] Even though MoCA reports indicate that these non-elected members are fewer in number than the elected representatives, they are a powerful minority.[25] There are also rank-and-file Party members who may be serving as elected members.

One MoCA publication states that Party members generally account for an average of 25 to 35 per cent of the total number of villagers' representatives.[26] However, based on Oujiakuang village in Zhaoyuan city, Shandong, which is given as a typical case, out of a rather large assembly of 112 members, 72 (64 per cent) were Party members.[27] Examples from our interviews also show a much higher Party presence than the reported average. For example, in a village in Henan, 21 of 32 villagers' representatives were Party members.[28]

The power of the cadre/official group is further enhanced by virtue of the fact that the head of the villagers' committee often chairs the assembly sessions, which puts him or her in an important position to set the agenda. In some cases, the village Party secretary directs the assembly. Moreover, some local regulations call for "a preparatory director meeting, which is attended by the director, deputy director and the main members of the villagers' committee" to decide the issues to be discussed at the forthcoming assembly meeting.[29] During the assembly the director or the deputy director then puts forward these issues for discussion along with a plan for solving the particular problems facing the village.

Poor attendance by some elected representatives may further allow the non-elected Party members to dominate the assembly. Interviews

24. In Oi's fieldwork, some villages said that the village Party secretary should not be there unless he is an elected villagers' representative. CI 81694.
25. The deputies to the People's Congress and members of the CPPCC within a village usually only number 2–3. *The Report on the Villagers Representative Assemblies*, p. 103.
26. *Ibid.* p. 79.
27. *Ibid.* pp. 80–85.
28. CI 82494.
29. *The Report on the Villagers Representative Assemblies*, p. 49.

suggest that members who are active and successful in commerce and enterprise are especially likely to miss meetings and have little or no chance to study the problems or sufficiently investigate the matters before the assembly. The underlying reason, as county officials openly noted, is that these individuals do not receive payment for their participation.

While more research is needed before any firm conclusions can be reached about the power of villagers' representative assemblies, the institutional structure of both them and the villagers' assemblies makes them ill-suited for quick, on-the-spot decisions. Representative assemblies may play a useful role as a formal legislative and oversight body, but the day-to-day decisions and agenda setting that are so important in determining village economic affairs are made elsewhere in most villages.

Villagers' committees. First established in the 1982 Constitution, the villagers' committee is designated the organ of self-government at the basic level.[30] By early 1985, according to MoCA reports, 948,628 villagers' committees had been established.[31] The 1987 Organic Law stipulates that they are elected directly by villagers.

Villagers' committees are supposed to implement policy, educate the masses and make decisions regarding all issues related to their villages. The 1994 Jiangxi regulations call for villagers' committees to prepare plans for village welfare, and for issues related to culture, education and public health. In addition, they should help develop collective, joint and household enterprises and organize support services for production to increase people's income and well-being.[32]

The villagers' committee is headed by a chairman or director, assisted by a vice-chairman. In our data, we found on average slightly more than five persons on villagers' committees, ranging from four in Shandong to nearly seven in Hubei (Table 2, row 1). As a small standing body, the villagers' committee is more suited to quick economic decision-making than the villagers' assembly or representative assembly. But that does not necessarily ensure that it is not subordinate to the village Party secretary.

There is no clear-cut, simple generalization about the power of the villagers' committee versus the Party secretary. The impact of village elections and the resulting power of the elected committee vary significantly across different types of villages. In some, the villagers' committee is the seat of decision-making; in others, the Party secretary keeps tight control of power in spite of elections. Variation seems to be tied to the nature of the village economy and the changing bases of power in China's countryside after decollectivization. The pattern, to the extent

30. In October 1983, the Central Committee of the CCP issued the "Circular on Separating Government from People's Communes and the Establishment of Township Governments," which stipulated detailed requirements for the establishment of these committees.

31. *Study on the Election of Villagers Committees in Rural China* (Beijing: Ministry of Civil Affairs, 1993), p. 1.

32. *Zhonghua renmin gongheguo cunmin weiyuanhui youguan fagui, wenjian ji guizhang zhidu huibian* (*Laws, Documents and Regulations of the PRC Concerning Villagers' Committees*) (Beijing: Minzhengbu, 1995), p. 40.

that one exists, seems to revolve around whether a village economy is based primarily in agriculture or in village-owned enterprises.

The Changing Bases of Village Power

Officials at the bottom of China's administrative hierarchy have always played a crucial role in determining the effectiveness of state policies and the well-being of the rural population. Even though the village is not considered an official level of government, village-level cadres remain key political as well as economic actors who shape the fate of China's rural inhabitants. What has changed is the context in which grassroots cadres carry out their tasks and the resources that they have at their disposal to exercise power. This difference in control over resources affects where the locus of village decision-making lies.

Leaders and power during the socialist era. After the Great Leap Forward, the production team was the legal owner of the land and the harvest and the unit to which individual households belonged and worked, and from which they received compensation.[33] In that system, the hierarchy of power was clear. The key decision maker was the production team leader, who almost always was a Communist Party member; there was no separate Party cell or officially designated leading Party cadre (or secretary).[34] There were elections, but there was no choice. The slate of one candidate per office was pre-selected by the brigade and commune officials. The team leader managed production, guided the work effort of team members, and carried out other productive and non-productive tasks assigned to him by the production brigade and commune. Most importantly for the purposes of this discussion, the team leader allocated work, grain and productive inputs, and distributed revenues. In other words, by virtue of holding office, all team leaders were in a position to be the gatekeepers of opportunities and resources for the team and all its members. Moreover, the power of the team leader, while underpinned by the Communist Party and the local commune government (its work teams, police force and other organizations), was amplified by Mao's development strategy that bound farmers to the land and the countryside.[35] Appointed officials could exercise power and get villagers to comply by offering to grant them access to goods and opportunities (such as income, inputs, leisure or social services), or by threatening to deprive them of these resources.[36]

While conflicts between state and local interests induced team leaders to take action to protect team resources and member interests, departing

33. See Jean Oi, *State and Peasant in Contemporary China: The Political Economy of Village Government* (Berkeley: University of California Press, 1989).

34. There usually were insufficient numbers of Party members in a team to form a Party branch.

35. For an elaboration and documentation of this system see Oi, *State and Peasant.*

36. For a discussion of team leaders as gatekeepers of their team members economic as well as political well-being see Oi, *State and Peasant.*

too far from the Party line would threaten one's own position of power. Leaders lacked the exit options either to channel local resources into the non-agricultural sector or to quit government service and pursue commercial interests. This prompted leaders to maintain at least the façade of compliance, if not to align themselves with commune officials to secure the one available source of power – appointment by a higher level official.

Function and power during the reform era. Much like production team leaders, cadres in the village are the linchpins of effective implementation of state policy. Adherence to production plans is now no longer a major issue, but at a minimum all village cadres still have overall responsibility for the economy, and implementation of state economic policies, including the collection of taxes, allocation and fulfilment of quotas on grain, and in some areas, on cotton or tobacco. In addition, they must oversee payment of fees and enforcement of corvée labour levies and social policies, such as family planning and cremation, and provide for schools and welfare. In many cases, a necessary (though not sufficient) condition for staying in office is the completion of these policy duties.[37]

Even though they are not considered state cadres, village leaders are expected to act as agents of the state, carrying out the bidding of the higher levels of government. They are paid a salary from village coffers, but they are still primarily dependent on their own labour for their income and grain. Rozelle's earlier description of the roles of a village leader remains apt: a) profit or income maximizer, who is an income-seeking and effort-minimizing individual; b) the lowest-level policy implementer of the state, who needs to finish administrative tasks imposed by higher-level government, and who, by virtue of his position, has access to privileged income-earning opportunities and other perks in the local community; and c) headman of the community who cares about the well-being of farmers and derives welfare from the satisfaction, status, and job security that comes when he/she can effectively address the concerns of villagers.[38]

While there is continuity, the particular role that village authorities play mirrors the variation that has developed in the nature of village economies in the post-Mao period. Some villages remain almost exclusively agricultural while others are primarily industrial. The tasks of village cadres in these different environments may vary widely. The variation and change in the work and resulting power of village cadres stem from three institutional reforms: decollectivization; the rise of

37. Scott Rozelle and R. N. Boisvert, "Quantifying Chinese village leaders' multiple objectives," *Journal of Comparative Economics*, Vol. 18, No. 1 (February 1994), pp. 25–45; Scott Rozelle and Li Guo, "Village leaders and land-rights formation in China," *American Economic Review* (May 1998), pp. 433–38.
38. Scott Rozelle, "The economics of village leaders in Reform China," Ph.D. dissertation, Cornell University, 1991.

markets and opportunities to move out of agriculture and beyond the village boundaries; and the emergence of elections and other village participatory bodies. Each of these has had an effect on the bases of power in China's villages.

Decollectivization. Most production teams became the village small groups (*xiaozu*), a subordinate organization under the village retaining little economic power. The village became the lowest level of administration. But like the production team, the village as a collective lost much of its direct control of agriculture and the ability of cadres to distribute collectively owned goods and resources decreased (see Table 4, row 1). In the early years, village officials still retained control over the allocation of some key inputs, such as fertilizer, farm services and land. But as input and service markets have gradually matured in China, this control has waned in importance. The major exception is land. Table 4 (row 2) shows that many village leaders still actively intervene in the distribution of land. That intervention has been theoretically and empirically shown to be tied to the struggle for power in the village.[39]

Equally if not more importantly, decollectivization eroded the ability of village leaders to rely on agriculture for collective revenue. With decollectivization the collective lost the right to the income from the sale of the harvest. The household became the unit of production and accounting. The in-kind and cash income derived from the consumption, marketing and other uses of harvested grain belong to households. This fiscal change has caused some villages to become "paralysed" because of impoverished coffers. Because they are not considered fiscal units of the state, villages receive no budget allocation from the upper levels. Village-level expenditures are tied completely to village revenues (Table 4, rows 4 and 8). Without rights to the income from the sale of the grain harvest, villages with only agricultural income are left dependent on *tiliu* and other fees paid by villagers to the village treasury (rows 5 to 7).[40]

New opportunities. While decollectivization had a negative impact on village agricultural income, on the other hand the reforms allowed the diversification of the rural economy and the re-opening of markets that afforded new opportunities for both local leaders and farm households. This greatly increased the scope for revenue generation and opened the door to a new channel to power – to the extent that power is derived from being able to provide (and deprive) goods and services that villagers demand. This occurred in villages with successful enterprises (Table 4, row 3).[41] Industrial firms and other village-operated economic activities

---

39. Rozelle and Guo Li, "Village leaders and land-rights formation."
40. The disbursement of such fees is often already earmarked, providing leaders with little, if any, discretionary control.
41. While all would have liked to shift into non-agricultural pursuits to generate revenue, physical, locational and human capital constraints have precluded all villages from benefiting equally from the reform opportunities. See Oi, *Rural China Takes Off* for details on how village enterprises developed.

Table 4: **Village Control over Agricultural and Industrial Activities, and Village Fiscal Accounts in Rural China, 1995**

	Unit	China (n = 215)	Zhejiang (n = 32)	Sichuan (n = 32)	Hubei (n = 32)	Shaanxi (n = 32)	Shandong (n = 32)	Hebei (n = 15)	Liaoning (n = 16)
Village management of agriculture and industry									
Villages with collectively run farming operations	%	1.4	0	0	6.3	0	0	0	0
Villages that have intervened in land distribution since initial allocation	%	69.8	65.6	21.9	90.6	93.8	84.4	80.0	100
Villages with collectively run enterprises	%	34.4	46.9	25	43.8	31.3	28.1	26.7	50.0
Village fiscal resources									
Village total revenues	yuan/person	456.6	463.7	778.0	536.2	22.7	149.8	213.1	350.8
Agricultural taxes	yuan/person	55.3	114.4	64.4	71.4	19.5	27.2	23.9	43.4
Village-level fees (tiliu)	yuan/person	22.5	12.9	14.9	18.9	9.2	35.2	27.3	68.4
Township-level fees (tongchou)	yuan/person	33.8	14.6	24.2	20.4	15.6	138.4	43.3	29.5
Village total expenditures	yuan/person	372.9	264.9	1069.7	227.0	14.9	90.3	199.5	242.1

Source:
Authors' survey.

have provided a potent new source of power for leaders, especially in places where and during periods in which villagers have no other opportunities to find jobs or purchase services besides those offered by local leaders. Profits from village enterprises have been used to build up community infrastructure, provide local farmers with jobs and other services, and reduce the tax and fee burdens of village households.[42]

Somewhat more gradually, households *on their own* also began to have access to more diversified opportunities to earn a livelihood, although, as in the case of leaders, villagers differ greatly in their chances in finding employment. The rise of labour markets and increases in wage-earning jobs, perhaps more than anything else, have created linkages between the village and the rest of the economy. Self-employment has experienced a larger absolute increase than any other sub-sector of the labour market. Migration has exploded. When farmers find jobs off the farm, the importance of agriculture in their portfolio of activities declines and the shadow value of access to the means of farm production also falls.

Village elections. Finally, the introduction of the Organic Law and village elections in 1987, at least in principle, created a new basis of power – popular election. As suggested above, this created the potential for three competing loci of power: the villagers' committee headed by the villagers' committee chairman, the villagers' assembly or representative assembly, and the village Party branch headed by the village Party secretary. In practice, however, it is clear that the likely locus of power is either the villagers' committee chairman or the Party secretary. Who wields actual power seems to hinge on the economic context in which elections take place.

Economic Variation and Locus of Village Power: Some Hypotheses

To examine the relationship between village economic structure and political power, imagine a two-dimensional continuum measuring two economic factors: the nature of ties to the outside economy and the level of village industrial development. In a box defined by two axes, specific types of villages can be identified.[43] The first axis differentiates villages by whether their members depend primarily on internal village resources or derive their income from sources outside the village. At one end of the second, agricultural–industrial, axis, is the heavily agricultural village, where villagers rely on farming for their income. At the opposite end is

42. In some villages, firms contribute fees and informal taxes to the village fiscal accounts. Most villages keep them separate; these revenues are used for many of the same pro-community purposes, such as investment in the community infrastructure and social services. Dong Xiao-yuan, "Public investment, social services, and productivity of Chinese household farms: a stochastic frontier analysis," paper presented at the Allied Social Science Associations Meeting, Chicago, 3–5 January 1998.
43. Although we treat villages as though they fit neatly into these four cells, in reality most fall somewhere in between.

the highly industrialized village, where members rely on industry for their income.

Focusing on the first axis, the nature of the ties of a village to the outside economy and society will influence local politics. When the interests of villagers are dependent primarily on what happens within the boundaries of their own village, they are likely to take a much greater interest in local assemblies and elections. A different dynamic arises when labour, commodity and other markets emerge and provide villagers with alternative employment and commercial opportunities. As linkages develop with outside markets, farmers will tend uniformly to reduce their interest in village politics, since their concerns lie outside of the village. Hence, we should expect villagers who run businesses in the village to be more interested in participating in local politics. In contrast, out-migrants will have neither the time nor interest to worry about local politics.

The internal–external orientation, however, reveals only part of the story. The locus of power will also vary because of differences in the degree of access that leaders and villagers have to earning streams from different types of income. In other words, interest in local politics of leaders and villagers will depend on the type of village resources on which villagers depend.

Location on the agricultural–industrial axis is the most obvious mani-festation of dependence.[44] In an agricultural village, the welfare of the household is closely tied to access to land. Since land issues – by law and in practice – are under the control of an office open to competitive election, villagers will have an incentive to participate in local assemblies and to contest elections. At the same time, leaders in agricultural villages have little incentive to resist pressures for political change that might arise from active assemblies or contested elections. The household re-sponsibility system circumscribed the access of leaders to the earnings from farming. Consequently, one would expect lively, uninhibited, villager-led political participation in villages where members of the community rely primarily on the output from the land for their income.

The situation in industrialized villages, although somewhat similar, is much more complex with a number of different outcomes possible. On the one hand, villagers primarily rely on village resources – in this case, village-owned industry. From this point of view, assuming the elected official or assembly chair can influence the distribution of earnings or access to employment, villagers may still want to contest elections and become involved in local assemblies. In fact, they should be expected to become actively involved, especially in villages in which they can

44. There is another important linkage between the structure of income in a village and the dynamics of local politics, namely the extent to which local political institutions are able to influence the distribution and use of the resources that generate different types of income (henceforth the "degree of political insulation"). This is discussed later in this section. The additional explanatory factor is assigned a secondary role in this article, not because it is any less important but mainly because our data set precludes us from offering any concrete empirical evidence on its importance. By omitting the degree of political insulation from our empirical work we are taking the risk of confounding our results, and as a result caution should be used in the interpretations that we derive from the data.

derive large benefits from a successful political change (such as those with highly profitable firms or where firms have traditionally contributed to local treasuries over which villagers may want to exercise control).

Unlike the case in the purely agricultural village, however, leaders in an industrial village may seek to limit the emergence of representative politics. They will try to establish tight control over the financial streams of industrial enterprises.[45] Local leaders in rural China use firm resources to increase their status, enhance their promotion possibilities, develop the economic and social foundations of their village, and increase their own personal wealth.[46] A leader of an industrialized village generally has more to lose than his counterpart in a purely agricultural village. As a result, these leaders should be expected to minimize the development of such political institutions.

Our general hypothesis is that local politics will be more active (that is, greater participation in local assemblies and contested elections) when the economic and social context of the village is such that villagers have an incentive to participate and leaders do not have an incentive to limit such activities. We propose two important sets of characteristics that define this context. First, as the economic ties of villagers become stronger with the world outside the village, interest in politics should be expected to diminish. In contrast, politics in more inward-oriented villages should be more active. Secondly, the more the economy is agriculture-dependent and reliant on its own resources, the higher will be the interest of farmers in local politics and the greater the likelihood that elected villagers' committees will have power. In industrialized villages, *ceteris paribus*, the leader should be expected to take action to dampen the political participation of villagers.

But there is an important caveat. To this point, it has been assumed that the key resources in each sector of the economy – for example, full managerial authority of firms in industrial villages – can be affected by those who come out on top in local political contests. In some villages this is clearly not the case. Some leaders retain managerial control over a firm, providing preferential employment, setting wages and distributing profits, regardless of the outcome of an assembly vote or contested election. More generally, there are villages where control and other rights regarding village resources are not affected by the outcome of an assembly vote or election.

There are many reasons why control of resources is subject to different degrees of political insulation. In some cases, physical factors may determine whether control of a resource can be a political issue. For example, Brandt, Li and Rozelle empirically demonstrate how land is almost never re-allocated in the mountainous villages in Sichuan and

---

45. Oi, *Rural China Takes Off*.
46. Rozelle, "Decision-making in China's rural economy: defining a framework for understanding the bahaviour of village leaders and farm households," *The China Quarterly*, No. 137 (March 1994), pp. 99–124.

Shaanxi provinces.[47] They argue that the nature of the cultivated land –
terraced and requiring a great deal of investment and care by the farmer
– nearly makes intervention an anathema, since the cost of tenure
uncertainty is so high (such as in terms of the damage caused to the land
from erosion). In such villages, since leaders have no degree of freedom
on their control over land, one should expect little interest in local
politics, even though villages in these areas are highly agricultural and
inward-looking.

In other cases, villagers' demands for elections wane if they believe
that the outcomes will have little impact on their lives. So villagers may
decide that the elections are unlikely to affect the operation and distribution of profits of village enterprises, or they may perceive that their
welfare could not be improved should they move away from the status
quo. Sometimes they set up a holding corporation (or some other
organization) that divorces enterprise management from the political and
social management tasks that are handled by the villagers' committee.[48]
For example, a village near Zhengzhou in Henan with an elected villagers' committee set up a separate industrial management office headed
by a board of directors (*dongshihui*).[49] While the name of the body may
vary, this arrangement is quite common in China's industrialized villages.
Whether the individuals making the decisions on industry are the same as
the villagers' committee bears directly on the locus of village power and
the impact of elections. Fieldwork and interviews suggest that there is not
always an overlap. Sometimes, the villagers' committee chairman will be
a member of the industrial management committee, as was the case in the
Zhengzhou village cited above. However, in other cases, this may be a
separate group entirely. Perhaps the most important feature of these
committees is that they often are headed by the one village leader not
subject to popular election – the Party secretary. Even in the Zhengzhou
village cited above, the committee head was only second in command to
the village Party secretary, who was chairman of the board of the
industrial management office.

In other situations, leaders distribute profits and make employment
decisions in such a way that villagers believe that they are receiving their
fair share from the enterprise and their lot would not be improved
whatever change in management occurred. In one village, each villager
had just received a new electrical service and an air conditioner unit.[50]
Not coincidentally, the "gift" occurred immediately before the election.
The leader candidly told us that before he installed the new services he
had reminded the villagers that these and any further improvements to

47. Loren Brandt, Guo Li and Scott Rozelle, "Land in China: a discussion of fact, fiction,
and the issues," Working Paper, Department of Agricultural and Resource Economics,
University of California, Davis, 1999.
48. The reasons why villagers allow this institutional arrangement to emerge, of course,
also need to be considered, but further in-depth examination of this institution is beyond the
scope of this article.
49. CI 82394.
50. Rozelle interview 079702.

the village were a result of his hard work and caretaking of the village. In short, despite having an incentive to become involved in politics (since their interests are affected by the economic management of the village), if villagers do not believe political action will improve the management of the resource that is providing their livelihood, their tendency to become involved in assemblies and elections will decline.

In such situations the villagers' committee may be given control of the civil and social welfare functions, and maybe control over agriculture, but the important revenue-generating activities remain in the hands of the Party secretary.[51] MoCA reports acknowledged that the functions of the Party and the government agencies are still combined. They recognize the core role that the Party leadership plays, but in doing so this highlights the fact that this sometimes overshadows other village organizations such as the village committee and the village assembly.[52]

The point is not that all Party secretaries are powerful and villagers' committees are not, but that real power is determined by control over income-generating enterprises, not elections. If the political reality of a village is such that important resources are not subject to influence by political change, there will be little incentive to participate in politics, and vice versa. Unfortunately, collecting data on such dynamics is difficult and our current data set allows few if any glimpses at such control. If we did have such information, we should describe the economic context of political participation by a three-axes continuum. Without such information, our focus remains on explaining elections primarily on the basis of the village's income structure and its degree of openness.

Patterns of village power and economic activity. This section examines how well our data accord with the hypotheses discussed above. The following results should be interpreted with care. First, the statistical confidence intervals around the means often make a mean from one category statistically difficult to distinguish from that of another. Secondly, many of the variables in our analysis move together, making it difficult to sort out which is actually more responsible for movements in the dependent variable. Partly to overcome these two problems, a later section uses multivariate regression to explain the determinants of assembly participation and contested elections.

Agricultural villages. Our theory suggests that the chances that villagers' committees are actually the loci of decision-making are highest in villages where farmers are primarily dependent on land and agriculture as their source of income, with little opportunity for migration and off-farm employment. Our survey shows that participation in villagers' assembly meetings and the likelihood of having competitive village elections are both higher where farmers are primarily dependent on the land for their income (Table 5, columns 1, 2, 6 and 7). Conforming to our hypotheses,

51. See Oi, *Rural China Takes Off.*
52. *The Report on the Villagers Representative Assemblies* and *Study on the Election of Villagers Committees.*

these are precisely the types of villages where villagers have the greatest stake in the outcome of elections.[53] In such villages some of the major roles for villagers' committees are "to manage the land and other assets belonging to the collective, to guide villagers to use natural resources properly, and to guide villagers to protect and improve the natural environment."[54]

At a minimum, we can also then say that democratic election of the villagers' committee will increase the accountability of real decision-makers to the village membership. It allows the village members the option of "throwing the rascals out" if they pursue policies that are not to their liking. With regard to land, this may then be translated into villagers' committees adopting policies that are least likely to stir dissatisfaction. This may explain our finding that villages with competitive elections are less likely to have land readjustments – a process that is often extremely contentious.

Industrialized villages. The situation is less clear-cut when a village has well-established industry in a relatively isolated regional economy (meaning villagers do not have many options outside the village). It is precisely in these types of villages where both leaders and villagers have an incentive to contest for control over the main income-earning activity. Our findings show that when a village has a collectively run enterprise, village assemblies meet less often and fewer people attend (Table 6, columns 3 and 4). Assemblies meet with even less frequency and there is a much lower percentage of contested elections in those villages in which the leader is also an enterprise manager (columns 7 and 8). It may be that in these villages leaders have been astute enough (or have enough power and control over resources) and have a great incentive (since their participation in the enterprise may depend on their political position) to resist efforts to promote institutions, such as active assemblies, that could undermine their power.

Interestingly, however, we find that there is a greater incidence of contested elections in villages with surplus revenue (columns 9 and 10). In one sense, this result appears to be contradictory, since larger treasuries are often connected with the existence of enterprises. But not all enterprises contribute to local fiscal revenues, and there are other sources of fiscal earnings (such as logging and mining). Without considering the openness of the economy, the data show either that a willingness on the part of whoever – whether it be the Party secretary or the villagers' committee chairman – to hold elections may simply be tied to the desire to maintain the image of an advanced unit; or that villagers are putting enough pressure on local leaders that political institutions have developed. On the one hand, cadres in these richer villages comply with upper-level directives to hold elections because it helps bolster their

53. See Jean C. Oi and Scott Rozelle, "Democracy and markets: the link between participatory decision-making and development in China's rural reforms," paper presented at the annual meeting of the Association for Asian Studies, Chicago, 13–16 March 1997.
54. Article 4, Organic Law.

Table 5: Farmer Interests, Village Assemblies and Contested Elections in China's Villages, 1995[a]

	Proportion of labour in long-term migration[b]		Proportion of labour in getihu (self-employed)[c]			Village land per capita[d]	
	Low	High	None	Between 0 and 10%	Over 10%	Relatively scarce	Relatively abundant
Frequency of villagers' assembly meetings (per year)	1.53	1.57	1.77	1.16	1.08	1.38	1.80
% of village population that attended villagers' assembly	48	39	42	54	49	42	48
% of villages in which most recent leader election was contested	65	58	52	67	83	54	69

Notes:
[a] All category divisions are made at approximately mean values.
[b] A village that has more than 13% (the national mean of labour in long-term migration in 1995) of its labour migrating has a "relatively high" level of migration.
[c] The mean value of self-employed labour, as a proportion of all village labour, was 2.0% in 1995.
[d] If a village has more than 1.25 *mu* per capita (the mean sample of land per capita in 1995) that village has "relatively abundant" land per capita.

Source:
    Authors' survey.

Table 6: Village Leader Interests, Village Assemblies and Contested Elections in China's Villages, 1995[a]

	Revenues from village activity[b]		Whether village has any village enterprise		Village labour in township and village enterprises[c]		Occupation of village leader[d]		Whether village has surplus or deficit[e]	
	Low	High	Has none	Has at least one	Below 5%	At least 5%	Farmer	Factory manager	Deficit or breaks even	Surplus
Frequency of villagers' assembly meetings (per year)	1.70	0.76	1.76	1.21	1.50	1.57	1.80	0.83	1.61	1.47
% of village population that attended villagers' assembly	45	65	47	41	41	46	44	67	45	45
% of villages in which most recent leader election was contested	58	74	62	60	59	62	59	33	50	72

Notes:
[a]All category divisions are made at approximately mean values.
[b]A village with annual revenues over 52,772 *yuan* (the mean sample of village activity income in 1995) derived from village activity alone has "high" revenues.
[c]Each value is calculated as the mean percentage of the left-hand-side variable and is based on the proportion of the village's total labour force that is employed in township and village enterprises.
[d]A value of 1 is given if the village leader works in agriculture, and 3 if the leader is a factory leader or manager; other job types (values 2 and 4–7) are excluded from the calculation.
[e]Villages retaining any income over zero after cost have a "surplus." The maximum for 1995 (measured in 10,000 *yuan*) was 73.107; the minimum was −70.1.
Source:
Authors' survey.

image. The reason why they risk doing this, while those in less wealthy villages do not, may be the perceived lower costs of holding an election. Unlike cadres in poor villages who control few resources and are often criticized and perhaps even resented by members, cadres in rich industrialized villages usually enjoy both power and respect. One might expect that such cadres who are able to generate surplus revenues are also powerful enough to block elections. However, they also have the resources to buy off the villagers by offering them jobs in the village-owned factories and to use profits from the village-owned enterprises to increase services and eliminate or reduce tax burdens. This may lead them to conclude that interest in contesting their existing leadership would be low.[55] Compliance with elections in such cases can be granted at little threat to their own power. Moreover, as suggested above, a powerful Party secretary can afford to hold elections and give a popularly elected villagers' committee head control over civil affairs and agriculture, while he or she retains control over the key economic decisions and resources that are the basis of village power.

Open economies. Interest in village elections and participation in assemblies are also clearly affected (but in a somewhat more complicated way) by the linkages of a village with the outside economy. We believe that individual entrepreneurs are interested in local politics because many still work out of their homes, while out-migrants have little interest in local economic issues. Interpreted this way, there is some evidence for our hypotheses. In villages with out-migrants, participation in village assemblies is lower and the percentage of contested elections falls (Table 5, columns 1 and 2). Without regard for the level of industrialization in a village, as farmers seek employment away from the village their ability and interest in participating in elections and assemblies fall.

In contrast, entrepreneurs show more interest in local politics, particularly in elections (Table 5, columns 2 to 4). Although in villages with the largest number of self-employed, village assemblies meet least frequently, the meetings are fairly well attended. Interestingly, the number of self-employed is highly correlated to the number of contested elections: the more self-employed, the more likely that the most recent election was contested. The greater interest in village elections may occur because private entrepreneurs, many of whom lack Party affiliation, see election to the villagers' committee as a viable way of countering the power of the Party – an organization that up until recently has shunned private entrepreneurs.[56]

---

55. Leaders in highly industrialized villages had two responses when asked in open-ended questioning about their views on elections. Some said they had insulated themselves from elections. Others said that the enterprises had already provided so much for villagers that they not only did not fear elections, they welcomed them as a sort of additional legitimization of their power.

56. We cannot rule out, however, the possibility that these villages may be the ones that the upper levels are targeting to implement elections in an effort to rebuild village government and resources. Such villages may have individual rich households, but the villages as a collective are often poor.

Multivariate analysis. To help overcome the problems of assigning statistical significance and disentangling the multivariate effects of the descriptive results reported in the previous section, we specify two regressions to explain the frequency of participation in villagers' assemblies and whether or not the most recent election was contested by more than one candidate. With all of the same caveats regarding the caution of interpretation and measurement discussed above, participation is explained as a function of income and market variables, the structure of the local economy (in terms of land and labour), and two variables that represent activities in which leaders should have high levels of interest.

The variables have been generated with data from our primary survey. Income per capita is from village records and is from 1988 to avoid endogeneity.[57] The study measures the general economic growth of villages using two variables developed by William Skinner. One measure, the City System variable, indexes the level of urbanization in the county to which the village belongs. The index ranges from 1 (very urban, as in the suburbs of Shanghai), to 6 (very rural, as in eastern Anhui and northern Jiangsu). The other variable (CPZ) locates the village in Skinner's Core-Periphery scheme, with 1 being in the core and 7 being in the periphery. A series of labour and land variables measure the orientation of the village's labour force, a way to judge the reliance of villagers on the village's own or outside resources. The land variable can also help situate villages on the agricultural–industrial axis on the continuum. Finally, the two variables are also included to measure the extent of interest that village leaders have in the village (and by extension, how much they would have an interest in discouraging participation).

The results from the regression analysis largely confirm, and make more precise, a number of the findings from the descriptive analysis, especially in the case of the determinants of contested elections (Table 7, columns 3 and 4). In villages with village enterprises and relatively large revenues from village activity, contested elections are less common. Such a finding is consistent with the original hypotheses. Industrialized villages may see less participation, since leaders, *ceteris paribus*, are less willing to encourage participatory politics and may take action to limit or dampen interest in contested elections. Although insignificant in the contested election equation, village assemblies meet more frequently (and significantly so in a statistical sense) in villages with high land holdings per capita (columns 1 and 2). The frequency of meetings rises when the

57. Endogeneity in this case means the concern that 1995 income and 1995 village elections may be simultaneously determined. That is, elections may be leading to greater incomes, as well as the reverse. If so, we may not be measuring the true causal relationship between income and elections. To avoid this problem we need to adopt an "instrumental variable" effect. This statistical method relies on finding a measure that is related to income in 1995, but is not "caused by" elections in 1995. One such measure that is both available and has this property is village income in 1988. To the extent that income in a village in 1995 and 1988 are correlated and to the extent that there is no way that village elections in 1995 could have affected income in 1988, this measure is an acceptable instrument that we can use in our analysis.

resources on which farmers depend are subject to influence by the village leadership.

Some of the findings also support the idea that as villages become more linked to the rest of the economy, participation falls. The most obvious case is observed in villages with large out-migration. Because the interests of these individuals lie outside the village, the incidence of contested elections declines significantly as the percentage of labour in long-term migration rises (columns 3 and 4). Additionally, with urbanization (City System) held constant, villages in more remote, less connected areas (CPZ) have higher participation in village assemblies (columns 1 and 2).

One of the most interesting findings is the complex effect of income on participation. In the case of contested elections, there is an inverse "U" relationship (columns 3 and 4, rows 1 and 2). As incomes rise, villages experience a rising likelihood of contested elections. The level of rise increases at a decreasing rate, however. In the richest villages in our sample, those in the 90th percentile, the incidence of contested elections begins to fall. In contrast, however, the frequency of villagers' assembly meetings does not fall with higher incomes.

In summary, then, there is fairly strong support for our hypotheses even though these results should be considered as preliminary. Our sample, though representative, is fairly small. And although the R-squares of both equations are both above 50 per cent, there still is considerable unexplained variance. Finally, despite many findings that are consistent with the hypotheses, a number of the variables that one would think should help explain participation (such as land holdings per capita in the contested election equation) have little explanatory power.

The Difference Elections Make for Village Politics

Regardless of whether ultimate power rests with the Party secretary or with the elected villagers' committee chairman, there is the separate issue of whether direct elections have affected village politics and the way that decisions are made. Is there any evidence that the direct election of villagers' committees or villagers' representative assemblies has had an impact on village affairs? Some preliminary findings include the following.

Based on interviews, we find that in some villages where there have been elections, there is more open accounting of village spending. Some villages have implemented the "ten opens" demand for publicly posted detailed accounting of village expenditures; in others, the *tiliu* amounts are now openly posted. We also find that even though a representative assembly and sometimes a villagers' committee may not be the best body to decide the economic affairs of the village, some may now, at least, have veto power on the general use of village resources – the right to guide, rather than directly manage.

There also is some evidence to suggest that elections have made some villages more compliant. Interviews in townships where villages have representative assemblies suggest that these representative bodies actually

Table 7: **Results Explaining Political Participation in Sample Communities: Frequency of Meetings of Villagers' Assemblies and Competitiveness of Most Recent Election**

Independent variables	Dependent variables			
	Frequency of villagers' assembly meetings		Most recent leader election was contested	
	Coefficients	T-ratios	Coefficients	T-ratios
Income and market environment				
Income per capita	0.001	(1.42)	0.002**	(2.12)
Income squared	$1.29e^{-08}$*	(1.62)	$-3.72e^{-07}$**	(1.98)
Remoteness (CPZ)	0.49**	(2.08)	0.06	(1.54)
Development level (City System)	−0.46*	(1.73)	0.09	–
Presence of village enterprises	−0.31	(1.32)	−0.62**	(2.45)
Labour				
% of village labour in TVEs	−2.23	(0.30)	−1.69	(0.17)
% of labour self-employed	−0.87	(0.14)	−0.45	(0.99)
% of labour in long-term migration	1.50	(1.53)	−1.85**	(2.33)
Land				
Population density (land per capita)	0.81**	(1.97)	−0.21	(0.05)
% of land adjusted	0.002	(0.86)	−0.03	(1.11)
Land has only been adjusted once or never	−0.36	(1.22)	0.70**	(1.89)
Leader interests				
Revenues from village activity	−0.005	(1.01)	−0.0003*	(1.72)
State of budget (surplus or deficit)	−0.01	(0.78)	0.003	(0.10)
R-Squared	0.51	–	0.63	–
Adjusted R-Squared	0.33	–	0.36	–

Note:
Each regression also includes provincial dummies which are not shown here for brevity.
** Indicates significance level below 5%; *indicates significance level below 10%.

facilitate the payment of certain fees. For example, a township in Xinye county, Henan, boasted that the number of villages that successfully paid their *tiliu* increased with the convening of the representative assemblies. Whereas in 1991, before the representative assemblies were established in this area, around seven or eight villages did not pay the full amount of their owed *tiliu*, by 1994 all paid their full amount.[58] This may seem counter-intuitive, but it is such a phenomenon that the central authorities was hoping for when they instituted village elections. Villagers may not listen to appointed officials, but they may listen to elected ones.[59]

While additional research is needed to draw definitive conclusions, our survey data demonstrate that a village's industrial structure and the nature of its linkages to the outside world affect local elections and the participation of villagers in assemblies and representative assemblies. Using these results, our study may suggest a more dynamic story. One can actually begin to speculate on the evolution of local political participation during the process of development and transition. In the case of China, at least, the reform era in the rural economy has been characterized by rapid industrialization in the early period (the 1980s) and then increasing liberalization that led to a wholesale emergence of markets in the more recent period. If these trends continue, our predictions will be fairly pessimistic in terms of progress towards increased electoral competitiveness and greater political participation in China in particular, and in other developing countries in general. In the early stage of industrial transformation, village leaders who are involved in running factories will try to resist calls for greater political participation. At the same time, while reform policy may lead to fewer barriers and greater market liberalization in many villages, at least in the short run, farmers' interest in promoting elections will wane.

If our micro-economic analysis is correct, and if in the early stages of development the shift to greater industrialization and liberalization contributes to higher incomes, in a dynamic sense, we may observe a negative relationship between incomes and contested elections, at least in the short term. Although our context is somewhat different, this result is at odds with the commonly held perception that political participation increases with rising wealth. But this does not mean that participation will necessarily fall in a monotonic, linear fashion. There are other factors that could lead to a turnaround in interest in local politics as incomes increase. For example, one set of results can be interpreted as suggesting that leaders might become confident in villages where they lead with little opposition and may encourage local political participation. It could also be that an inherent demand for true political voice increases once incomes exceed a certain level (one that China's villages have not reached yet). What this study suggests is that as income rises interest in political participation and popular control will increase only when people perceive it to matter to their interests.

58. CI 82494.
59. See Jean C. Oi, "Economic development, stability and democratic village self-gover-nance," in Maurice Brosseau, Suzanne Pepper and Shu-ki Tsang (eds.), *China Review 1996* (Hong Kong: Chinese University Press, 1996), pp. 125–144.

Cultural Values and Democracy in the People's Republic of China

Tianjian Shi

Are the values and attitudes of ordinary people in the People's Republic of China (PRC) compatible with behaviour necessary for a liberal democracy to evolve? Or are they likely to obstruct such evolution? Some surveys conducted in recent years within the PRC asked people of different backgrounds and residential areas if they were interested in politics and governance issues, if they conversed with others about their political interests, and if they believed they had some control over their political life. These and other related questions produced survey findings which are discussed and interpreted below to provide some conjectures about the questions posed above.

Political Culture and Democratization

Some classic research works about political culture and the evolution of Western democracies offer insights for understanding how non-democratic countries have developed.[1] Almond and Verba, for example, tried to explain why some democratic societies avoided severe crises but others did not.[2] Their study found that for democracy to be vital, citizens obeyed their leaders and the law even as they questioned and challenged political authority in their everyday life.[3] They concluded that if democracy was to survive a severe crisis, citizens had to be involved in politics and seek relevant information and knowledge to improve their government's efficiency.[4]

1. Max Weber, *The Protestant Ethic and the Spirit of Capitalism* (New York: Scriber's, 1958); Gabriel A. Almond and Sidney Verba, *The Civic Culture: Political Attitudes and Democracy in Five Nations* (Princeton: Princeton University Press, 1963); Robert A. Dahl, *Polyarchy, Participation and Opposition* (New Haven, CT: Yale University Press, 1971); Robert Dahl, *Democracy and Its Critics* (New Haven, CT: Yale University Press, 1989); Ronald Inglehart, *Cultural Shift in Advanced Industrial Society* (Princeton: Princeton University Press, 1990); Ronald Inglehart, *Modernization and Postmodernization: Cultural, Economic, and Political Change in Forty-three Societies* (Princeton: Princeton University Press, 1997); Alex Inkeles, "Making men modern: on the causes and consequences of individual change in six developing countries," *American Journal of Sociology*, Vol. 75, No. 2 (1969), pp. 209–255; Alex Inkeles and David H. Smith, *Becoming Modern* (Cambridge, MA: Harvard University Press, 1974); Larry Diamond (ed.), *Political Culture and Democracy in Developing Countries* (Boulder: Lynne Rienner, 1994).
2. Almond and Verba, *The Civic Culture*, p. 19
3. See Gabriel A. Almond and Sidney Verba, *The Civic Culture Revisited* (Boston: Little, Brown & Co., 1980); Among the features of a "participant citizenship" as identified by Inkeles, that might be considered especially important for democracy are an active interest in public affairs, as validated by keeping informed and expressed through participants in civic actions, and an orientation towards modern forms of authority and objective rules rather than towards traditional and/or arbitrary forms of authority. See Inkeles, "Making men modern," pp. 208–255.
4. Lucian W. Pye and Sidney Verba, *Political Culture and Political Development* (Princeton: Princeton University Press, 1965); Leonard Binder *et al.*, *Crises and Sequences in Political Development* (Princeton: Princeton University Press, 1971); Lucian W. Pye, *The*

Other studies found that as democracies evolved in the West, their leaders and elites learned they needed citizenry support because at election time other politicians could replace them. But to exercise their voting power, citizens had to evaluate their leaders intelligently, participate in direct elections and work continually to improve the government's performance.[5]

The relationship between political culture and authoritarian regimes was different. Some studies argued that political culture was nothing more than the popular faith and trust of the people in their powerful leaders.[6] In the case of imperial China, citizens only connected to the state in a hierarchical relationship, different from the reciprocal relationship of people and their governments in Western democracies.[7] In China the people were expected to be obedient and respectful to their rulers, who in turn were expected by the people to use state power to protect and nourish them. In fact, imperial subjects had the moral right to use violence to replace their leaders if they failed in their duties to provide for the people. But they were never to question and challenge imperial authority. In ordinary life, they peacefully resolved their everyday difficulties and conferred maximum loyalty on authority figures such as parents, local officials and the emperor.[8] This behaviour was the opposite of citizens in a liberal democracy, who obeyed the law while asserting their rights and standing up for democratic institutions.[9] According to Lucian Pye, a very different political culture from that of Western democracies propped up authoritarian rule in East Asia over the centuries.

Citizens in a liberal democracy also believed in the benefits of a

---

footnote continued

Dynamics of Chinese Politics (Cambridge, MA: Oelgeschlager, Gunn and Hain, 1981); Lucian W. Pye, *Asian Power and Politics: The Cultural Dimensions of Authority* (Cambridge, MA: Harvard University Press, 1985); Tai-chun Kuo and Ramon H. Myers, "The great transition: political change and the prospects for democracy in the Republic of China on Taiwan," *Asian Affairs*, Vol. 15, No. 3 (1988), pp. 115–133; Lucian W. Pye, *The Mandarin and the Cadre: China's Political Cultures*, Michigan Monographs in Chinese Studies, No. 59 (Ann Arbor: Center for Chinese Studies, University of Michigan, 1988); David Myers and John Martz, "Political culture theory and the role of professionals: data from Venezuela," *Comparative Political Studies*, Vol. 30, No. 3 (June 1997), pp. 331–355.

5. Sidney Hook, *Reason, Social Myth, and Democracy* (New York: Humanities Press, 1950) as cited in Kyong-Dong Kim, "The mixed role of intellectuals and higher education in building democratic political culture in the Republic of Korea," in Diamond, *Political Culture and Democracy in Developing Countries*, p. 12.

6. Alex Inkeles, "National character and modern political system," in Francis L.K. Hsu (ed.), *Psychological Anthropology: Approaches to Culture and Personality* (Homewood, IL: Dorsey Press, 1961).

7. Lucian W. Pye, *The Spirit of Chinese Politics*, New Edition (Cambridge, MA: Harvard University Press, 1992), 93.

8. In Western culture consensus is supposed to be achieved through competition of different interests according to certain procedures. Almond argues that one of the most important cultural values conducive to democratic development is the belief in the possibility and desirability of political co-operation mixed with a belief in the legitimacy of conflict. However, consensus in traditional Chinese political culture is supposed to be achieved by individuals giving up their private interests for collective ones. Those who dare to give voice to particular interests are usually regarded as selfish. Pye, *The Mandarin and the Cadre*, pp. 58–59.

9. Dahl, *Democracy and Its Critics*, p. 262.

capitalist market economy, which efficiently generated enormous wealth. Moreover, democratic governance was also compatible with the development of the capitalist market economy. Democracy made possible continuous political reform, so that capitalist economic development and the evolution of democracy naturally became intertwined.[10]

Understanding Chinese Political Culture

If a society's political culture comprises different values, norms, attitudes and beliefs that influence political behaviour,[11] then the following four attitudes are judged to be compatible with those held by citizens in liberal democracies: popular attitudes towards politics, political efficacy, attitudes towards power and authority, and attitudes towards reform.

Popular attitudes towards political and governmental affairs. In a democracy, citizens must be interested in their government's decision-making process and monitor the performance of their leaders and representatives.[12] Citizenry interest in politics can be measured by examining how many people rely on newspapers, television and radio to acquire their political information. Another approach is to judge how well people understand political and governmental issues. These two approaches were used to survey a sample of ordinary Chinese people and determine if they cared about democracy and its practices.

Table 1 shows that many people in mainland China in 1993 were interested in political and governmental affairs. Note that around one-quarter of the Chinese interviewed reported reading newspapers at least once a week, a figure higher than that found in Italy in the 1960s. Because of the limited number of Chinese newspapers available (virtually all are controlled by the government), most news has a political content. But when people's access to the electronic media is considered, this reveals that a higher percentage of people acquire information about political and

10. Juan J. Linz and Alfred Stepan. *The Breakdown of Democratic Regimes* (Baltimore: Johns Hopkins University Press, 1978), p. 16. Seymour M. Lipset, *Political Man* (Baltimore: Johns Hopkins University Press, 1981), p. 64 and Diamond, *Political Culture and Democracy in Developing Countries*, p. 71.

11. Recent research using this approach to Chinese political culture include Qi Min, *Zhongguo zhengzhi wenhua: minzhu zhengzhi nanchan de shehui xinli yinsu (Chinese Political Culture: Elements of Social-Psychological Difficulties in Democratic Politics)* (Yunan: Yunan People's Publishing House, 1989); Andrew J. Nathan and Tianjian Shi, "Cultural requisites for democracy in China: findings from a survey," *Daedalus*, Vol. 122, No. 2 (Spring 1993), pp. 95–124; Andrew J. Nathan and Tianjian Shi, "Left and right with Chinese characteristics: issues and alignments in Deng Xiaoping's China," *World Politics*, Vol. 48, No. 4 (July 1996), pp. 522–550; Siu-Kai Lau and Hsin-Chi Kuan, The *ETHOS of the Hong Kong Chinese* (1988); Tianjian Shi, "Cultural impacts on political trust: a comparision of mainland China and Taiwan," *Comparative Politics* (forthcoming)

12. Sidney Verba and Norman H. Nie, *Participation in America: Political Democracy and Social Equality* (New York: Harpers & Row, 1972), Sidney Verba, Norman H. Nie and Jae-on Kim, *Participation and Political Equality: A Seven Nation Comparison* (New York: Cambridge University Press, 1978), Samuel H. Barnes *et al.*, *Political Action: Mass Participation in Five Western Democracies* (Beverley Hill: Sage, 1979).

governmental affairs than in nearly every other society: more than 65 per cent of people reported that they followed accounts of politics and governmental affairs on radio and television at least once a week. In the 1990s, the PRC experienced extensive technological innovation, especially the spread of television.

Although media access is widely used by students of political culture to measure people's political interest, there are two problems about this information. First, the media function differently in democratic and communist societies. While mass media in the former provide people with independent information on politics and governmental affairs, in the latter the Communist Party controls all information to indoctrinate people in the official ideology.[13] Thus, the high level of media access in China may actually indicate the success of the regime in mobilizing its citizens rather than a high level of political interest in the society.

But while the government tries to monopolize political information, some citizens try to break out and gather independent information from unofficial channels.[14] To check the validity of these indicators, we asked our respondents to report whether they had tried to gather information through "grapevine rumours" about economic, social and political affairs. If a person sought information from independent sources, we know that the person is deeply interested in politics. Among all respondents, 27.6 per cent reported they tried to seek information from unofficial channels. This figure, nearly identical to the percentage of respondents who reported they read newspapers and listened to radios, suggest that one out of four is seriously committed to trying to obtain reliable information.

A second problem is that when people access the mass media, they do not necessarily ponder its content and meaning. Those not interested in politics and public affairs will surely not engage in public discussions. A better way to measure political interest is to show how frequently people talk to each other about political matters. Talking with others about politics is an active form of political participation, whereas accessing the media is relatively passive. Moreover, talking about politics implies a degree of self-assurance in order to speak out. Almond and Verba have pointed out, "talking politics means taking a chance; in totalitarian countries, a big chance."[15] Finally, political discourse is a necessary step before considering political action.[16] To examine these issues, we asked respondents whether they had engaged in political discussion with others, and Table 2 presents the findings.

13. Donald Munro, *The Concept of Man in Contemporary China* (1977), Alex Inkeles, C. Montgomery Broaded and Zhongde Cao, "Causes and consequences of individual modernity in China," *China Journal*, No. 37 (January 1997), pp. 31–59.

14. Shi, *Political Participation in Beijing*.

15. Almond and Verba, *The Civic Culture*, p. 79.

16. Lester Milbrath and M. L. Goel, *Political Participation: How and Why Do People Get Involved in Politics?* (Chicago: Rand McNally, 1977). Verba and Nie, *Participation in America*, Verba, Nie and Kim, *Participation and Political Equality*; Sidney Verba, Kay Lehman Schlozman and Henry E. Brady, *Voice and Equality: Civic Voluntarism in American Politics* (Cambridge, MA: Harvard University Press, 1995).

Table 1: Following Reports of Public Affairs in the Various Media by Nation

Percentage who follow accounts	U.S.	U.K.	Germany	China	Italy	Mexico
In newspapers at least weekly	49	43	53	24	16	31
On radio or television at least weekly	58	36	52	65.4	20	28
Radio	–	–	–	26.3	–	–
TV	–	–	–	60	–	–
In magazines (ever)	57	21	45	–	26	25
Through the grapevine (last month)	–	–	–	26.7	–	–
Total number	970	963	955	3,296	995	1,007

Note:

Actual text of the questions in China are "Did you read the news in a newspaper last week?" "Did you have a chance to listen to news broadcast on a domestic radio station last week?" "Did you have a chance to listen to news broadcasts on foreign radio stations last week?" "Did you have a chance to watch TV news last week?" "Last month, did you hear anything through the 'grapevine' (*xiaodao xiaoxi*) concerning economics, politics, or society?"

Sources:

Data from China come from 1993 nation-wide survey on political culture and political participation. Data from other countries come from Table II.5 in Gabriel A. Almond and Sidney Verba, *Civic Culture: Political Attitudes and Democracy in Five Nations* (Princeton: Princeton University Press, 1963).

Table 2: Frequency of Talking Politics with Other People, by Nation

Percentage who report they	U.S.	U.K.	Germany	China	Italy	Mexico
Never talk politics	24	29	39	55.3	66	61
Sometimes talk politics	76	70	60	44.4	32	38
Others and don't know	0	–	1	0.3	2	–
Total percentage	100	99	100	99.9	100	99
Total number	970	963	955	3,296	995	1,007

Note:

Actual text of the questions in China are "Do you often, occasionally, sometimes or never talk about political issues and national affairs with other people?"

Sources:

Data from China come from 1993 nation-wide survey on political culture and political participation. Data from other countries come from Table II.5 in Gabriel A. Almond and Sidney Verba, *Civic Culture: Political Attitudes and Democracy in Five Nations* (Princeton: Princeton University Press, 1963).

Again, the percentage of people in mainland China who talk about politics with others falls between the high level of Germany and the low levels registered for Italy and Mexico. Although open criticism of the government in the mass media is still not allowed in mainland China, this finding suggests that among people concerned with politics and governmental affairs, there exists considerable self-assurance that one can discuss political issues with family, friends, neighbours, work groups and colleagues. If one-quarter of the population in China is now deeply interested in political and governmental affairs, the proportion of people psychologically involved in discussing political matters is even higher than in Italy, a democratic society.

Political efficacy. Political efficacy refers to a feeling that one has some control over one's political environment. Without any political efficacy, there exists political apathy and withdrawal from political life, and strong feelings of efficacy tend to make people interested in political activities. Such feelings are necessary for a democracy to work. Political efficacy can be divided into internal and external efficacy. The former refers to one's competence to understand politics and to participate effectively in political life; the latter refers to beliefs regarding how responsive governmental authorities and organizations are to the demands of citizens.[17]

We asked eight questions to measure political efficacy and present their responses in Table 3. The distribution pattern suggests that the measure of external efficacy among ordinary Chinese exceeds that for internal efficacy. Except for one indicator measuring efficacious feelings regarding work-unit affairs, the percentage of respondents who gave positive responses to measures of internal efficacy ranged from 19.2 to 28.3. At the same time, the percentage of people who gave positive answers to measures of external efficacy ranged from 25.1 to 43.4. The right side of the table reports the exploratory factor analysis of these eight variables: four internal efficacy questions have rather high loadings on a single factor and the four external efficacy questions have reasonably high loadings on another factor.

Without comparable data, we do not know whether the efficacious feeling in China is low or high. Almond and Verba measured civic competence by asking respondents to imagine themselves in a government office and having a problem requiring official action. How did they think they would be treated? Those believing the government would treat

17. Robert A. Lane, *Political Life: Why People Get Involved in Politics* (New York: Free Press, 1959); George I. Balch, "Multiple indicators in survey research: the concept 'sense of political efficacy'," *Political Methodology*, No. 1 (Spring 1974), pp. 1–43; Kenneth M. Coleman and Charles L. David, "The structural context of politics and dimensions of regime performance: their importance for the comparative study of political efficacy," *Comparative Political Studies*, No. 9 (1976), pp. 189–206; Stephen C. Craig, Richard G. Niemi and Glenn E. Silver, "Political efficacy and trust: a report on the NES pilot study items," *Political Behavior*, Vol. 12, No. 3 (1990), pp. 289–314; Richard G. Niemi, Stephen C. Craig and Franco Mattei, "Measuring internal political efficacy in the 1988 national election study," *American Political Science Review*, Vol. 85, No. 4 (1991), pp. 1407–13

Table 3: **Internal and External Efficacy in Percentages of Chinese Population**

Percentage who are	Efficacious	Not efficacious	Don't know	Factor 1 loading	Factor 2 loading
Understand politics/governmental affairs like others	28.2	56.1	16	0.77	—
Understand political issues facing the country	27.3	57.3	5.4	0.73	—
Understand village/work unit affairs	50.3	41.8	7.8	0.72	—
I am qualified to participate in politics	19.2	70.2	10.6	0.73	—
People like me have no say in the work unit/village	27.0	68.6	4.4	—	0.67
People like me have no say in politics	43.4	47.4	9.2	—	0.58
Work unit/village leaders don't care about people like me	34.9	56.3	8.9	—	0.75
Government officials don't care about people like me	25.1	60.4	14.4	—	0.63
N = 3,296					
Eigenvalues				2.30	1.44
% of variance explained				28.77	18.02

Note:

Actual text of the questions: "Do you strongly agree, somewhat agree, somewhat disagree, or strongly disagree with the following statements?" "I feel that I have a pretty good understanding of the important political issues facing our country." "I think that I am better informed about politics and government than most people." "I feel that I have a pretty good understanding issues concerning my work unit/village as most people." "I consider myself to be well qualified to participate in politics." "In our unit/village, people like me have no say in public affairs." "People like me have no say in politics and governmental affairs." "Leaders in my work unit/village don't care what people like me think." "Government officials don't care too much about what people like me think."

The answers to these questions are first recorded. Strongly agree and agree answers are combined to form one category and strongly disagree and disagree answers are combined to form another. In most cases, agreement with the statement is the more "efficacious" answer except for three questions in which the disagreement with the statement is the efficacious answer.

Source:

Data from 1993 nation-wide survey on political culture and political participation.

them equally are supposed to have civic competence. We asked our respondents how they thought they would be treated by their government, and their answers are compared in Table 4 with data from Almond and Verba's study.

The pattern that emerges seems similar to that reported in Table 3. The distinction between the United States, Britain and Germany, and China, Italy and Mexico compares well for political efficacy. The level of civic competence in mainland China is higher than that in Italy and Mexico. Because Italy is a democratic society, China again passes the threshold for the minimal level of democratic behaviour to take place.[18]

Attitudes toward power and authority. In democratic societies, citizens elect their officials to make public policy. If the government fails to provide people with good policy and accountability, or if government officials are not "good men or women," citizens will replace them. For that to occur, citizens must view their relationship with the state as a reciprocal one, and they are willing to enter into conflict with others to advance their interests.

How do people in mainland China perceive their relationship with authority? Are they willing to enter into conflict with others to advance their interests? We designed six questions to measure people's attitudes, which are presented in Table 5. A majority of people perceive the relationship between the individual and the state to be hierarchical, and less than 15 per cent perceive their relationship with authority to be reciprocal.[19] At the same time, we found substantially more people willing to enter into conflict with others to promote their own interests.

Are the attitudes of Chinese people towards power and authority an impediment to democratization? Without comparative data, no concrete answer can be given. Because such a low percentage of the population sees its relationship with the authorities as reciprocal, few people want to replace their government even if it did not deliver what they want. This is not to say that a transition to democracy cannot occur in China. However, the finding suggests that such a transition, if it indeed happens, is more likely to be the product of endogenous change within the system.

Attitudes towards political and economic reform. Since the seminal work of Barrington Moore, political scientists have realized that democracy is associated with private property, capitalism and a bourgeoisie.[20] The ruling elites in communist societies always believed they must control the society, mobilize resources and suppress any opposition. Communist ideology dictated that the state control property, the means of

18. The finding that the level of external efficacy in mainland China is higher than that of the internal efficacy indicates some political stability. This is because those who are capable of participating in politics usually believe those in authority are responsive to their demands.

19. More people tell our interviewers that they believe children need not obey their parents unconditionally.

20. Barrington Moore, Jr, *Social Origins of Dictatorship and Democracy: Lord and Peasant in the Making of Modern World* (Boston: Beacon Press, 1966).

Table 4: Expectation of Treatment by Governmental Bureaucracy, by Nation

Percentage who say	U.S.	U.K.	Germany	China	Italy	Mexico
They expect equal treatment	83	85	65	51.7	53	42
They don't expect equal treatment	9	7	9	38.3	13	50
Depends	4	6	19	–	17	5
Other	–	–	–	1.1	6	–
Don't know	4	2	7	8.9	11	3
Total percentage	100	98	100	99.9	100	100
Total number	970	963	955	3,296	995	1,007

Note:

Actual text of the questions in China: "If there was a certain problem which you needed the help of a government official to resolve, do you think you would be given equal treatment? That is, do you think the government would treat you the same as others?"

Sources:

Data from China come from 1993 nation-wide survey on political culture and political participation. Data from other countries come from Table II.5 in Gabriel A. Almond and Sidney Verba, *Civic Culture: Political Attitudes and Democracy in Five Nations* (Princeton: Princeton University Press, 1963).

Table 5: Orientation Towards Power and Authority, in Percentages of Chinese Population

Percentage who are	Disagree	Agree	Don't know	Factor 1 loading	Factor 2 loading
Individual is cog in machine	14.9	71.1	15.0	0.77	–
Government officials like family heads	18.2	73.3	8.5	0.74	–
Senior people resolve conflict	16.6	81.6	1.8	0.57	–
Children should obey parents	63.6	35.7	0.7	–	0.78
Wife should obey mother-in-law	41.8	66.6	1.6	–	0.74
Accommodate other people	34.0	61.6	4.4	–	0.61
	N = 3,296				
Eigenvalues				2.02	1.11
% of variance explained				33.74	18.57

Note:
Actual text of the questions: "Do you strongly agree, somewhat agree, somewhat disagree, or strongly disagree with the following statements?"
"Top government officials are like the head of a big family. Their decisions on national issues should be followed by everyone." "The state is like a big machine and the individual is but a small cog, with no independent status." "Even if parents' demands are unreasonable, children still should do what they ask." "If conflict occurs, one should ask senior people to uphold justice." "When a mother-in-law and a daughter-in-law come into conflict, even if the mother-in-law is in the wrong, the husband should still persuade his wife to obey his mother." "When one has a disagreement with someone, the best way to deal with it is to accommodate the other person."
The answers to these questions are first recoded. Strongly agree and agree answers are combined to form one category and strongly disagree and disagree answers are combined to form another.
Source:
Data from 1993 nation-wide survey on political culture and political participation.

Table 6: Attitudes Towards Political and Economic Reform

Percentage who say	Traditional reform position	Just right	Against (too fast)	DK & NA	Factor 1 loading	Factor 2 loading
Government restrictions on individual incomes	27.6	–	62.9	9.5	0.82	–
Government restriction on private enterprises	22.7	–	61.5	15.8	0.82	–
The country needs political reform	57.5	–	10.4	32.1	–	0.74
Pace of political reform	11.5	43.2	24.1	21.2	–	0.74
N = 3,296						
Eigenvalues					1.35	1.09
Percent of variance explained					33.12	26.72

Note:
Actual text of the questions are: "Some people think that an individual's legal income should not be restricted no matter how much it is. Others believe that a certain limit needs to be set for a minority whose income is especially high. What is your opinion?" "Some people think private enterprise in our country has developed to the point where it has shaken the economic foundations of the public ownership system, and it should be restricted. There are also some who think that the development of private enterprise is good for the national economy, and should not be restricted. What is your opinion?" "Some people believe that the pace of political reform in our country in recent years has been too fast, others think it has been too slow, and still others think it has been just right. What is your opinion?" "Some people believe that our country not only needs to conduct economic reform, but also needs to speed up political reform. Others think that political reform will cause instability and should not be carried out now. What is your opinion?"
Source:
Data from 1993 nation-wide survey on political culture and political participation.

production and production itself. Although in the last two centuries democratization was often accompanied by an enlarged role for the state to protect individual liberties and economic well-being, in the former socialist countries the state's role has diminished.[21] What are the attitudes of ordinary Chinese towards their economic and political system? What do they perceive to be the proper role of government in economic life? How many people want to reform their political system?

We asked respondents four questions, two of which examined attitudes about the state limiting individual income and private ownership, and two of which examined attitudes toward the pace of political reform. Table 6 shows that a majority of Chinese support reform of both the political and the economic systems. While more than 60 per cent of respondents support private ownership and oppose government restrictions on income inequality, a majority of respondents (57.5 per cent) also believe that China needs political reform. Less than 10 per cent believed the current reforms were moving too slowly and wanted more political change. At the same time, about 25 per cent believe the current pace of political reforms are moving too quickly and want them slowed down.

The Relationship of Social Cleavages, Elections and Political Culture in Mainland China

How are citizen attitudes and preferences distributed throughout China's social strata? If we had some idea about this distribution pattern, we could offer some conjectures about the relationship between political culture and political development. Moreover, as the three marketplaces develop, different social groups will become wealthy, have access to power, gain education and acquire social status. These complex developments can strengthen or weaken those attitudes and value preferences favourable for promoting democracy. This section briefly examines how some recent changes in education, income, gender, political power, age, rural elections and influence correlate with popular attitudes and value preferences.

Considerable research suggests that improved education can change people's orientation towards political activity, make them become deeply involved in politics[22] and strengthen their convictions to participate in politics.[23] Our findings indicated that citizen education is only weakly

21. Ada W. Finifter and Ellen Mickiewicz, "Redefining the political system of the USSR: mass support for political change," *American Political Science Review*, Vol. 86, No. 4 (December 1992), pp. 857–874; Arthur H. Miller, Vicki L. Hesli and William M. Reisinger, "Reassessing mass support for political and economic change in the former USSR," *American Political Science Review*, Vol. 88, No. 2 (June 1994), pp. 399–411; Ada W. Finifter, "Attitudes toward individual responsibility and political reform in the former Soviet Union," *American Political Science Review*, Vol. 90, No. 1 (March 1996), pp. 138–152.

22. Seymour Martin Lipset, "Some social requisites of democracy: economic development and political legitimacy," *American Political Science Review*, Vol. 53, No. 1 (1959), pp. 69–105; Karl W. Deutsch, "Social mobilization and political development," *American Political Science Review*, Vol. 55, No. 3 (1961), pp. 493–514; Almond and Verba, *The Civic Culture*.

23. Neil Wollman and Robin Stouder, "Believed efficacy and political activity: a test of the specificity hypothesis," *Journal of Social Psychology*, Vol. 131, No. 4, pp. 557–566, Norman H. Nie, Bingham G. Powell Jr. and Kenneth Prewitt, "Social structure and political

correlated with political efficacy, weakly supports political change, and negatively influences support for economic reform based on privatization and reducing government management of the economy. Other findings also indicated that more economic wealth in China does not necessarily make people become more politically efficacious. Income is only weakly associated with internal efficacy and has no effect on external efficacy. Income negatively influences attitudes towards economic reform that emphasizes privatization and does not influence attitudes towards political reform.

Why do our findings show that increasing economic wealth in China has no influence on popular attitudes to support economic reform?[24] One reason is that the lower strata are poor and want government policies that help them to alleviate their poverty. But unlike the urban people, the rural poor of China benefited from economic reform and *de facto* privatization. Their experiences primed them to expect that more privatization and less government intervention would bring them an even better life. Their attitudes differ from those of the lower strata in other societies, who prefer more government intervention in the economy.

The wealthy in China worry about preserving social stability so they can continue enjoying the benefits of economic reform. They also realize that economic reforms require a "safety net" for the needy population. Because the current reforms fail to provide any specific safety net, they favour state intervention in the economy to create one. This finding is consistent with conditions in the Soviet Union before it collapsed.[25] Most people in China are still peasants, so there exists solid popular support for economic reform.

In mainland China the regime tried very hard to mobilize women, but, as hard as the regime tried to transform political culture, Chinese women played only a small role in political life and feel more neglected than

---

footnote continued

participation: developmental relationships, part I," *American Political Science Review*, No. 63, No. 2 (1969), pp. 361–378; Norman H. Nie, Bingham G. Powell Jr. and Kenneth Prewitt, "Social structure and political participation: developmental relationships, part II," *American Political Science Review*, No. 63, No. 3 (1969), pp. 808–832; Balch, "Multiple indicators in survey research"; Albert Bandura, "Self-efficacy: toward a unifying theory of behavioral change," *Psychological Review*, Vol. 84, No. 2 (1977), pp. 191–215; Albert Bandura, "Self-efficacy mechanism in human agency," *American Psychologist*, Vol. 37, No. 2 (February 1982), pp. 122–147; Philip H. Pollock III, "The participatory consequences of internal and external political efficacy: a research note," 36 (1983), pp. 400–409.

24. Among Soviet emigrés, the more highly educated are more likely to favour private/individual rights and solutions to problems over collective/state rights and solutions. See James R. Millar, *Politics, Work, and Daily Life in the USSR* (Cambridge: Cambridge University Press, 1987). More recently, Duch found that the correlation between education and endorsement of free-market culture variables is negative. See Duch, "Tolerating economic reform." The Iowa survey of the former Soviet Union found the correlation between education and the four-item locus of responsibility index is positive and significant (Pearson $r = 0.19$ and 0.15 in 1991 and 1992 respectively). See Miller, Hesli and Reisinger, "Reassessing mass support for political and economic change in the former USSR," table 2.

25. See among others Finifter and Mickiewicz, "Redefining the political system of the USSR," Ada W. Finifter, "Attitudes toward individual responsibility and political reform in the former Soviet Union," *American Political Science Review*, Vol. 90, No. 1 (March 1996), pp. 138–152.

men. Men are more likely than women to be interested in politics and governmental affairs, they are more likely to perceive themselves as capable of understanding and participating in politics, and they are more confident of their ability to influence the decisions of government officials. Women were supposed to take care of domestic affairs and let men be responsible for activities outside the family. They usually bore the burden of handling domestic matters, so that men had more leisure time than women. Thus, women are less concerned about politics and participating in politics.

There is no gender gap in people's orientation towards power and authority, although Chinese men seem to pursue their interests more aggressively. Men and women equally support economic reform, but men are slightly more likely to support political reform than women. These findings are consistent with those in both the former Soviet Union and the West, which show that women usually have less political interest and less efficacy but are politically conservative and tend to support the status quo more than men.[26]

Because the Chinese Communist Party (CCP) dominates the political centre, its control over society affects the attitudes of Party members towards reform and has a significant influence on the future of China's political change.[27] If Party members favour reform more than non-Party members, future reform in Chinese society is a more likely prospect. But whether CCP membership will promote democratic values is unclear.[28]

26. M. Kent Jennings, Klaus R. Allerbeck and Leopold Rosenmayr, "Generation and families: general orientations," in Barnes *et al.*, *Political Action: Mass Participation in Five Western Democracies*, pp. 449–486; M. Kent Jennings and Richard G. Niemi, *Generations and Politics: A Panel Study of Young Adults and Their Parents* (Princeton: Princeton University Press, 1981); M. Kent Jennings, "Gender roles and inequalities in political participation: results from an eight-nation study," *Western Political Quarterly*, No. 36 (1983), pp. 364–385; Robert Y. Shapiro and Harpreet Mahajan, "Gender differences in policy preferences: a summary of trends from the 1960s to the 1980s," *Public Opinion Quarterly*, No. 50 (1986), pp. 43–61; M. Kent Jennings *et al.*, *Continuities in Political Action: A Longitudinal Study of Political Orientations in Three Western Democracies* (Berlin: Walter de Gruyter, 1990); Ellen Carnagham and Donna Bahry, "Political attitudes and the gender gap in the USSR," *Comparative Politics*, July 1990, pp. 379–399; M. Kent Jennings, "Political participation in the Chinese countryside," *American Political Science Review*, Vol. 91, No. 2 (June 1997), pp. 361–372.

27. See Minxin Pei, " 'Creeping democratization' in China," *Journal of Democracy*, Vol. 6, No. 4 (October 1995), pp. 65–79; Minxin Pei, "The fall and rise of democracy in East Asia," in Larry Diamond and Marc F. Platter, *Democracy in East Asia* (Baltimore: Johns Hopkins University Press, 1998), pp. 57–78; Tianjian Shi, "Village committee elections in China: institutionalist tactics for democracy," *World Politics*, No. 3 (April 1999), pp. 385–412. In fact, the introduction of semicompetitive elections in rural China has been characterized as endogenous by several students of Chinese politics. They argue that the success of the electoral reform depends on the efforts of local and incumbent party and officials. See Kevin J. O'Brien, "Implementing political reform in China's villages," *Australian Journal of Chinese Affairs*, No. 32 (July 1994), pp. 35–59; Daniel Kelliher, "The Chinese debate over village self-government," *China Journal*, No. 37 (January 1997), pp. 63–86; Kevin J. O'Brien and Lianjiang Li article in this volume.

28. Barrett L. McCormick, *Political Reform in Post-Mao China: Democracy and Bureaucracy in a Leninist State* (Berkeley: University of California Press, 1990); Barrett L. McCormick, "Democracy or dictatorship? A response to Gordon White," *Australian Journal of Chinese Affairs*, No. 31 (January 1994), pp. 95–110; Barrett L. McCormick, "China's Leninist parliament and public sphere: a comparative analysis," in Barrett L. McCormick and Jonathan Unger, *China After Socialism* (Armonk, NY: M.E. Sharpe, 1996), pp. 29–53.

Our findings about the relationship between CCP membership and democratic orientations show that CCP members are interested in and knowledgeable about politics; they are more confident in their ability to understand and participate in politics; and they are more likely than other groups to perceive government officials as being responsive to people's demands. Members of the CCP are also more willing than non-members to engage in conflict with others to protect their own interests. However, we found no statistically significant difference between Party members and non-members in terms of their attitudes towards power and authority. Finally, Party members were not strongly supportive of privatization, but they aggressively supported political reform.

As for attitudes and preferences for different age groups, our empirical results show that age has only a moderate influence on political interests and on people's attitudes towards power and authority. The relationships between age and internal efficacy and between age and economic reform are very weak, and no significant relationship exists between age and external efficacy and support for political reform.

Turning to rural elections, have grassroots elections had any impact on people's value orientations? Do they produce a traumatic social change that can alter the political culture? Our analyses of grassroots elections and various aspects of political culture show that elections can hardly change political culture. Except for any psychological involvement in politics, grassroots elections are in no way associated with any of the other cultural attitudes and values examined above. They have had little impact so far on democratic sentiment – either because the rules of the political game at the grassroots level cannot induce cultural change in Chinese society, or because grassroots elections do not constitute a traumatic political event that can induce cultural change among the Chinese population.[29] Indeed, we can find no evidence of traumatic cultural discontinuity caused by grassroots elections.

In Table 7 there are six multiple regression equations (ordinary least squares) correlating different variables with five types of attitudes and orientations. These correlations indicate that the relationship between economic development and political culture is much more complicated than described by modernization theorists, who believe that increasing society's resources will change social attitudes and values.

Table 7 indicates that socio-economic resources can foster popular interest in politics and governmental affairs. For example, such things as education, income, gender, Party membership and grassroots elections explain 38 per cent of the variance of popular attitudes reflected in political life. Among those variables, education plays the most important role, followed by income and Party membership. The occurrence of grassroots elections also elevates people's interest in politics. In our bivariate analyses, age is negatively associated with psychological involvement in politics: the relationship between age and political interests disappeared. This finding should not be interpreted as indicating that age

29. Jun Liu and Lin Li, *Neoauthoritarianism – the Debates on the Principle of Reform* (Beijing Economic Institute Press, date unknown), p. 32.

Table 7: Regression Equations for Democratic Values

Independent variables	Psychological involvement		Internal efficacy		External efficacy		Hierarchical orientation		Conflict avoidance	
	B	Beta	B	Beta	B	Beta	B	Beta	B	Beta
(Constant)	-0.88*** (0.10)		-0.77*** (0.16)		0.48** (0.16)		-0.08 (0.14)		0.51*** (0.14)	
Education by years	0.11*** (0.01)	0.42	0.04*** (0.01)	0.14	0.03*** (0.01)	0.1	0.06*** (0.01)	0.23	0.06*** (0.01)	0.22
Income	0*** (0)	0.2	0 (0)	0	0 (0)	-0.03	0 (0)	0.13	0*** (0)	0.12
Gender	0.17*** (0.03)	0.09	0.24*** (0.04)	0.12	0.15*** (0.04)	0.07	-0.02 (0.04)	-0.01	0.01 (0.04)	0.01
Party membership	0.55*** (0.06)	0.14	0.34*** (0.08)	0.09	0.63*** (0.08)	0.17	0.1 (0.07)	0.03	0.25*** (0.07)	0.07
Age	0 (0.01)	-0.03	0.02 (0.01)	0.22	-0.04*** (0.01)	-0.62	-0.02** (0.01)	-0.29	-0.04*** (0.01)	-0.68
Age squares	0 (0)	0.02	0 (0)	-0.15	0*** (0)	0.60	0* (0)	0.26	0*** (0)	0.55
Elections	0.14** (0.03)	0.04	0.02 (0.04)	0.01	0.11* (0.04)	0.05	0.04 (0.04)	0.02	0.07* (0.04)	0.04
R^2	0.38		0.06		0.06		0.11		0.14	
Adjusted R^2	0.38		0.05		0.06		0.10		0.14	

Source:
   Data from 1993 nation-wide survey on political culture and political participation.

has no effect on political interests. It does. But younger people in China are more concerned about political and governmental affairs than older people because they are better educated and/or have higher incomes.[30]

While Table 7 shows that grassroots elections are significantly associated with political interests, it reveals little about the causal relationship between them. An alternative, competing explanation is to reverse the causal relationship between political interests and grassroots elections: rather than elections making people more interested in politics, those interested in politics are more likely to vote.[31] To determine the direction of causality in the relationship between grassroots elections and political interest, we replaced the variable "voting in elections" with the variable of "semicompetitive grassroots elections." This new variable measures whether a village holds elections without regard to whether a particular respondent voted or not. People who fail to vote in grassroots elections can also report that semicompetitive elections are held at their residence. If the causal sign goes the other way – that is, greater psychological involvement in politics will cause people to vote in elections rather than elections making people become psychologically involved in politics – the new variable should have no independent (or a much weaker) effect on people's psychological orientations, as compared with the variable used in the previous model. This analysis generated a similar result (not shown in the table). Thus, we conclude that grassroots elections can elevate people's concern about politics and public affairs.

Socio-economic resources and elections are less successful in predicting people's attitudes towards reform (the adjusted R-squares are 0.02 and 0.01). Education, age and grassroots elections also do not influence people's attitudes towards reform. In fact, income is the only variable that has a significant impact on people's attitudes towards economic reform. After one controls for effects of other variables, economic wealth is still negatively associated with support for economic reform. Finally, all the variance in support for political reform is derived from education. The higher the respondents' education, the more likely they are to support political reform.

Higher levels of education and income play a significant role in making people transcend their traditional culture. People with higher education and income not only tend to perceive their relationship with authority as reciprocal but are also more willing to enter into conflict with others to assert their interests. The more traditional segments in Chinese society –

30. An alternative explanation is that the phenomenon is due to life-cycle effects. Without panel data, we could not rule out this important competing explanation; that is, young people are more concerned about politics because they are more energetic, but when they grow old, they leave public life and behave the same way as their predecessors. However, our findings suggest that this explanation is unlikely to be the case. Instead, generational effects better explain the relationship between age and political interests. Because the younger generation is better educated, they are more likely to be interested in politics.

31. In an analysis of 1990 survey data, the author found that political interests are closely associated with participation in semicompetitive grassroots elections, Tianjian Shi, "Voting and nonvoting in China: voting behavior in plebiscitary and limited choice elections," *Journal of Politics*, Vol. 61, No. 4 (1999).

that is, people with less education and lower income – tend to perceive their relationship with authority as hierarchical and are more willing to forfeit pursuing their private interests for establishing social harmony. The relationship between age and any Confucian orientation appears to be a convex curve – the ageing process increases the likelihood for a respondent to hold Confucian orientations. The older the respondent, the more likely he will hold a traditional orientation towards power and authority. Grassroots elections cannot alter people's disposition towards power and authority, but they make people more assertive to articulate their interests.

Finally, our multivariate analyses show that education, gender and Party membership have positive effects on both internal and external efficacy. Education makes people see complexity, so the educated are more informed about their political system. Because they are more sophisticated, they know how to persuade or coerce local officials to comply with their demands. Age has no effect on internal efficacy. The relationship between age and external efficacy is again a convex curve. While middle-aged people tend to believe that government officials do respond to their demands, both younger and older people tend to think differently. Similarly, grassroots elections have no effects on internal efficacy, but they make people perceive government officials and village leaders as responding to their demands, even after we control for the effects of socio-economic status. The significant relationship between elections and external efficacy suggests that elections in China do make government officials at the grassroots level more responsive to people's demands than they would otherwise be.

Conclusion

By comparing the distribution of certain attitudes and values in Chinese society with those of other societies that are compatible with democracy, it seems that some similarities exist. True, only 20 to 30 per cent of the population in China have attitudes favourable for democratic behaviour, but their share of the population exceeds that in some democratic societies.

Grassroots elections do not produce great change in people's orientations. People living where semicompetitive elections are held tend to be more interested in politics than people living in places without such elections. They also are more likely to believe government officials will respond to their demands, and they are more willing to enter into conflict with others to protect their interests. At the same time, grassroots elections have not yet changed people's attitudes towards power and authority nor made them support reform. These findings suggest that elections do have some influence on people's values but they are limited to specific popular values and preferences.

But it is China's elites who will play a crucial role in whether political change takes place in the near future. Whether they will initiate any political breakthrough like that in Taiwan when Chiang Kai-shek promoted local elections and Chiang Ching-kuo initiated a democratic breakthrough remains to be seen. For such a breakthrough to occur on the Chinese mainland, remarkable elite mobilization will have to take place.

Index

anti-communism in Hong Kong 54, 58
Asia, social change in 11
Association for Democracy and People's
  Livelihood (Hong Kong) 64, 66–7,
  90
authoritarian pluralism 8 n. 13
authoritarianism 4

Bai Gang 127
Basic Law of the Hong Kong SAR 47
  implementation of 64–5, 69–70
  provisions of 58–63, 67, 72, 76–9, 96, 99
Basic-Level Governance, Department of
  (PRC) 127, 146–7
Basic-Level Governance, Research Society
  of (PRC) 119–20
Bendix, Richard 12, 34
Bo Yibo 113
bureaucracy, PRC:
  attitudes toward 110–11, 184–8, 193–4
  and local elections 114–19, 155, 157,
    159–68, 171, 175

candidate selection in China 131–2, 137,
  138–9, 143
Carter Center 128, 129, 136, 137, 141
censorship in Taiwan 30, 34, 36, 42
Central Organization Department (PRC)
  113, 116
Chan, Anson 95
Chek Lap Kok Airport 94–5
Chen Kewen 25
Cheung Bing-leung 97
Chiang Ching-kuo 23, 40, 44
Chiang Kai-shek 23, 44
China:
  candidate selection in 131–2, 137, 138–9,
    143
  democratization in 59
  direct elections in 72
  economic power in 161, 163–7, 184,
    187–8, 193
  electoral abuses in 115–16, 117–19,
    134–5
  Hong Kong fronts of 54, 63
  legislature of 18 n. 32
  local government in 102–7, 123, 138–40,
    151–2, 158–63
  mass media in 178–80
  political campaigning in 132–3
  political opposition in 146, 148
  political participation in 138–9, 151,
    153–6, 158, 164–71, 173–5, 178–84,
    188–94
  political parties in 142, 148
  political thought in traditional 11 n 23,
    177
  rural elections in 104–5, 112–15, 126–41,
    144–5, 191, 193–4; demand for fairness
    in 117–18; and economic structure
    163–75; extent of 120–2, 147–8
  voter registration in 130–1, 138–9
  voting styles in 133–4, 137, 138–9, 144
  see also bureaucracy, PRC; Ministry of
    Civil Affairs (PRC); and National
    People's Congress
China Social-Democratic Party (ROC) 32
China Youth party (ROC) 30, 32
Chinese Communist Party:
  foster local elections 103, 105, 127,
    144–5
  informal power of 159–61, 167, 171
  primacy of 124, 130, 131, 137, 146, 157,
    158, 190–1
Chinese People's Political Consultative
  Conference 66, 68, 69, 71, 72
Citizen's Party (Hong Kong) 84
colonies, governance of British 48–9
Confederation of Trade Unions (Hong
  Kong) 91, 97
corruption and PRC elections 117, 119
Cui Naifu 113

Dahl, Robert 5
Dahrendorf, Ralf 24
dangwai 27–8, 35, 36–40, 44
Daxue zazhi 35–6
democracy 2–3
  requisites for Chinese 105–6, 109, 115,
    124
  social requisites for 11, 44, 176–8
  transitions to 2, 8, 10–13, 43, 44
democracy, electoral 2–3, 75
  breakthroughs to 11
  non-liberal 3–4
  prerequisites for 12–13, 141–4
democracy, liberal 3, 4, 5, 141
democracy, limited 8
Democratic Alliance for the Betterment of
  Hong Kong 63, 87
  differs with administration 95–6, 97–8
  wins offices 67, 83, 90, 92
Democratic Party (Hong Kong) 60–1, 97
  political alliances of 66, 70, 83–4
  wins offices 64, 66, 90–1
Democratic Party (PRC) 147
democratic states, prevalence of 1, 4
democratization 1, 4
  in China 59
  in Hong Kong 58–62, 64, 66, 72–3
  in Taiwan 43, 44
Deng Xiaoping 55, 75, 103, 126
Discipline Inspection Commission (PRC)
  117
"District Administration in Hong Kong"
  56